FIFE IN HISTORY
AND LEGEND

Raymond Lamont-Brown

JOHN DONALD

First published in 2002 by
John Donald Publishers,
an imprint of
Birlinn Limited
West Newington House
10 Newington Road
Edinburgh
EH9 1QS

www.birlinn.co.uk

ISBN 0 85976 567 9

British Library Cataloguing -in -Publication Data
A catalogue record for this book is available from the British Library

Typeset by Textype, Cambridge
Printed and bound by Antony Rowe Ltd, Chippenham

CONTENTS

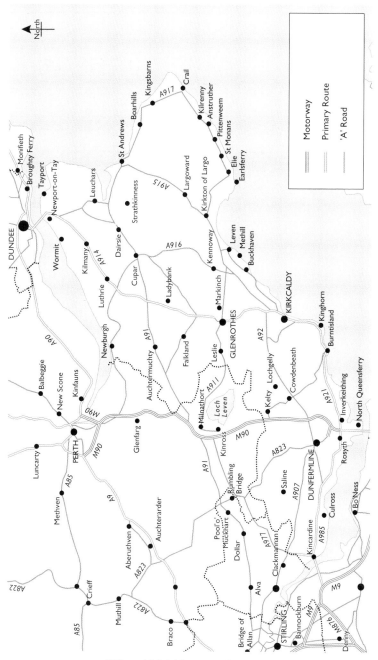

Fife and Neighbouring Counties

INTRODUCTION: KEYS TO THE KINGDOM

With the birth of a new Scots parliament, it is time to look afresh at the history and legends of Fife. Who are the Fifers? How did Fife come about? Each Fifer has a chain of ancestors linking together clues to the county's history and legend; no Fifer died without contributing something to the wide picture. What are the keys to telling their story?

From Fife Ness to the extreme south-west, Fife measures 41½ miles, and its breadth from Burntisland to Newburgh is 21 miles. Fife's coastline takes in some 115 miles and its landward boundary is around 61 miles, all enclosing an area of 505 square miles.

Fife's regional boundary begins in the centre of the River Forth just west of Kincardine Bridge; it heads north-east for Kilbagie and meanders on to turn right at Cult Hill to make a dash around the north edge of Loch Glow and plough through Blairadam Forest to cross the M90 at Keltybridge. It then turns north again at Benarty Hill and east to Auchmuirbridge; then north-west to Butterwell and Burnside to turn east along the Carmore Burn just south of Newton of Balcanquhal. Turning north for Pitmedden Forest, the boundary skirts to the west of Newburgh and meets the Tay at the South Deep, west of Mugdrum Island.

Fife has a diversified countryside of rolling hills; to the west and north lie the Ochils which enter Fife from Perthshire and run on to Newburgh and Tayport. To the east rise the Lomonds which roughly divide Fife into west and east. There are no lofty mountains in Fife and the principal hills include: Kellie Law (557 ft), Largo Law (965 ft), Norman's Law (850 ft), East Lomond (1,471 ft), West Lomond (1,713 ft), Knock Hill (1,189 ft), Saline Hill (1,178 ft) and Benarty Hill (1,167 ft). Once these hills gave rise to weather lore:

When Largo Law the mist doth bear,
Let Kellie Law for storms prepare.

And:

> When Falkland Hill puts on his cap
> The Howe of Fife will get a drap.

The old kingdom's two main rivers are the Leven, which enters the Firth of Forth at Largo Bay, and the Eden which runs through the Howe of Fife to enter the North Sea at St Andrews Bay.

In terms of geology, the northlands of Fife, stretching some 15 miles inland along the Firth of Tay to Newburgh, are mostly basalt and andesite of the Carboniferous and Lower Old Red Sandstone Age; with a volcanic conglomerate around Auchtermuchty. Along the valley of the Eden to its source just outside Fife is sedimentary rock of the Old Red Sandstone Age. Around the coast from St Andrews to Elie it is calciniferous sandstone of the late Carboniferous period. South of the Eden valley to the sea, and east to west from Ceres to Kincardine is a parallelogram of carboniferous rock, ranging from the barren red coal measures around Kirkcaldy to the calciniferous sandstone inland of Inverkeithing. All of these factors, terrain, climate and geology have contributed to Fife's history and legend.

Why call Fife a kingdom at all? For a thousand years Fife had been a favoured place of royalty. The Stewarts in particular made Fife a place of hunting and feasting, but neither the Stewarts nor any other named dynasty gave the region its pretensions to a kingdom. Its seeds of regality are, though, a part of Fife legend.

The medieval kingdom of Scotland developed with Malcolm III (reigned 1016–34), preceded by the Pictish Confederation. In the days of St Columba (c.521–97), the most famous of Scotland's saints, it was written that Cruithne, the ancestor of the Picts, had seven sons each given a parcel of land, as the old Fife doggerel has it:

> Seven children of Cruithne
> Divided Alba[1] into seven divisions
> Cat, Ce, Cirech[2]
> Fibh, Flota, Fortriu, and Moireath.[3]

1 Scotland
2 Caithness, Mar and Buchan; Angus and Mearns
3 Fife; Atholl and Gowrie; Streathearn and Menteith; Moray

From the name Fibh we get Fife; it was the medieval historians who identified the parcel of land of Fibh as a sovereignty. One such was Andrew of Wyntoun (*c.*1355–1422), the historian and Augustinian canon regular of St Andrews, and erstwhile prior of the house of St Serf, Lochleven. He wrote his *Orygynale Cronikel of Scotland* at the request of Sir John Wemyss of Rires and Kincaldrun, Fife; herein Wyntoun described Fife as 'ane Kynrick' (kingdom).

The story of Fife begins long before the Maeatae tribesmen's revolts drew Emperor Septimus Severus's legions into the region in 208–11. Some 10,000 years ago, the glaciers of the last Ice Age melted and plants began to colonise the land, followed by grazing animals and meat-eating predators including early humans. People first came to the area we know as Fife around 8000 BC; they came from the south and from across the North Sea, travelling by sea coast and river to penetrate the Tay, the Kinness Burn, the Forth and the Eden estuary. These people were hunter-gatherers who existed mainly on deer, wild cattle, birds, fish and shellfish, nuts, berries, roots and leaves. They formed two distinct folklores. Those who dwelt by the coast, like those at Morton – once an island but now on the Tentsmuir peninsula – invested the sea and its creatures with their totems and superstitions, while those at such places as Balfarg, Glenrothes, created their domestic gods around nearby flora and fauna. Their henges and circles, settled areas and burials, all over Fife, speak of their ceremonial ways, their communion with the dead and the beginnings of Fife's long history. Whoever they were and wherever they came from, these Fife ancestors cleared forests, attempted to control nature, worked in gold and bronze and by intermarriage and trade began a genealogy of Fife inhabitants. Every so often a cataclysmic change occurred: for 600 years, for instance, the Picts lived in Fife – suddenly they disappeared, and like the rest of Scotland, Fife became a crucible of different peoples; new social structures appeared and fresh epochs began.

History and legend in Fife

History and legend are closely linked in Fife. Forged between the anvils of the Highlands and what was for a long time the English-dominated south-east of Scotland, Fife struggled with a poor return from its territorial wherewithal. Yet the people were rich in their devotion to their faiths, strong in pride for their region and courageous in the face of adversity. Fife's history is touched by the feuds, abductions, blackmail, cruelty, betrayals and murders of Scotland's story, but out of these dastardly deeds Fife's history absorbed an individualistic strain of themes, lore and annals which were inspiration for the chroniclers and the makars, those fifteenth- and sixteenth-century Scots poets. Fife's history and legend has been influenced by being in the cockpit of learning, politics and religious prejudice and fervour. All interlarded with the comings and goings of heroes (Robert I, the Bruce), champions (the Marquis of Montrose), gallants (the Earl of Moray), benefactors (the earls of Fife), immortal women (Margaret, Queen and Saint), and turbulent priests (John Knox): each of these characters was flavoured with the supernatural skills credited to the famous by a peasant society.

Thanage in Fife

Historically the designation 'Thane' depicted a minor noble who acted as an official of the crown with certain fiscal or judicial duties; they ranked as barons under the feudal system and had certain authority over specific tracts of land. The word thane is Saxon, and it is unlikely that it was ever used in a title such as 'Thane of Fife'. When the Saxon princess Margaret became queen of Malcolm III (Canmore), there was an influx of Saxon followers, one of whom, acting as chronicler, may have translated the Gaelic *Mormaer* (great steward) into its Saxon equivalent of thane.

We have Shakespeare to thank for giving a high profile to Macduff, 'Thane of Fife', as murderer of Macbeth. Shakespeare was following historians such as John of Fordun, who conjured up Macduff in 1384, and Andrew Wyntoun, who in 1428 credited Macduff with killing Macbeth (Macbeth was probably killed in battle against Malcolm III at Lumphanan on 15 August 1057). Just as Macduff is an early medieval historian's figure of myth, so is the title Thane of Fife.

The earldom of Fife

Many early charters relating to Fife bear the title *Comes de Fyf* (Earl of Fife) after certain names. As a title it appears to be twelfth century in origin and was a peerage in the reign of Alexander I. The earldom (cf. mormaership) of Fife, within Forthreve, constitutes one of the seven original earldoms of Scotland. With it went certain privileges. Ceremonially, the Earl of Fife was given the court prerogative of handing (that is leading by the hand) the monarch to the coronation chair at crownings; the earl also was placed in the vanguard of the Royal Army in battle formation. In terms of the law, the earl was not subjected to a capital charge if he were to commit murder; if found guilty he would receive a fine. The medieval earls of Fife had certain identifiable castles, churches and lands in their remit, many of which they could dispone to others; some came to them by forfeit as crown gifts. Here are some of the known properties of the earl of Fife: the lands of Fernie; the barony of Burnturk; the estates of Ramornie, Auchtermuchty, Montrave and Aithernie, Cluny, Mountquhanie, Myrecairnie, Rathillet, Parkhill, Denmiln, Inchary and parcels of land within the barony of Creich.

The earl's castles included Fernie and Markinch, while churches included Kilconquhar and Markinch. It is known too that the earls of Fife founded monasteries – Malcolm, the sixth earl, founded the Cistercian house at Culross, *c.*1217; Duncan, the tenth earl, founded the Dominican Friary at Cupar in 1348, and Duncan, fifth earl, founded the convent hospital at Ardross, *c.*1154.

Early records of the sequence of earls of Fife are vague but with a reasonable amount of certainty the following may be identified:

1115   Beth.
1120   Constantine of Kirkcaldy, also dubbed Earl of Forthreve.
1129   Gillemichel Macduff. By this time the title had become hereditary.
1135   Duncan, said to have been Regent of Scotland in 1153, during the early minority of Malcolm IV, 'The Maiden'. Malcolm ascended the throne at the age of eleven on the death of his grandfather, David I. Duncan accompanied

       Malcolm on a tour of Scotland to win the boy's acceptance as king.

1154   Duncan, Justiciar of Scotland. Negotiated the Treaty of Falaise, 1174. Married Ada, neice of Malcolm IV, c.1159. Through this marriage he received title to the royal estate of Falkland, which remained a portion of the earls of Fife until 1371, whence it reverted to the crown.

1203   Malcolm. Married Matilda, daughter of Gilbert, Earl of Strathearn. Buried in the abbey he founded at Culross, 1228.

1228   Malcolm. Pro-English. Guardian of the Realm. Married Helen, daughter of Llewellyn, Prince of Wales.

1266   Colbran. Married Ann, daughter of Sir Alan Durward.

1270   Duncan. One of the six regents of the Kingdom on the death of Alexander III in 1286. Married Joan, daughter of Gilbert de Clare, Earl of Gloucester. He was murdered by Sir Patrick Abernethy and others at Petpolloch.

1288   Duncan. A signatory of the letter to Pope John XXII of 6 April 1320 (The Declaration of Arbroath). Present at the court of English-puppet king John Balliol. Prisoner with King David II after the Battle of Neville's Cross, 1346. Released on ransom. Married Mary, daughter of Ralph, Lord Monthermer.

1353   Isabella now *suo jure*, Countess of Fife. Married (1) William Ramsay of Coluthie; (2) Walter Stewart (she resigned the earldom to her husband's brother, Robert, Duke of Albany); (3) Sir Thomas Byset of Upsettlington; (4) John de Dunbar.

1371   Robert Stewart, Earl of Mentieth, third but second surviving son of Robert II. Duke of Albany, 1398. Regent of Scotland 1406–20, during the English incarceration of James I.

1420   Murdoch Stewart, Duke of Albany. Prisoner in England after the Battle of Homildon Hill, 1402. Regent of Scotland 1420–24, the year of James I's release from captivity. Executed 1424. The title of Earl of Fife now merged with the crown.

On 12 May 1567, three days before his marriage to Mary, Queen of Scots, a marquisate of Fife was conferred on James Hepburn, fourth earl of Bothwell (c.1535–78). The title was never conferred again. The earldom of Fife, however, was revived in 1759, by George II, within the Peerage of Ireland, to add to the titles of William Duff of Grange and Dipple (Banff), Viscount Macduff (d.1763). The title was assumed by James Duff (d.1809), Baron of Fife; then Alexander Duff (d.1811), and James Duff, Viscount Macduff, Baron of Fife (d.1857), at whose death the Barony of Fife became extinct. Heir James Duff (d.1879), married the daughter of Elizabeth Fitzclarence, Lady Erroll, the sixth illegitimate child of King William IV and Mrs Dorothy Jordan.

The great-grandson of King William IV, through his relationship with Mrs Jordan, Alexander William George Duff (1849–1912), Viscount Macduff, Baron Braco of Kelbryde, married Princess Louise Victoria Alexandra Dagmar (1867–1931), third child of King Edward VII and Queen Alexandra, in 1889. In 1900 he was created Duke of Fife and Earl of Macduff. The dukedom survives.

The Sheriffdom of Fife

During the period 1115–1425, responsibility for the government of Fife rested upon the earls of Fife, but local administration of justice was devolved to resident barons, titled and non-titled landowners. These men were given the designation of sheriff and the office evolved as a hereditary one. When the earldom of Fife became extinct the monarch conferred the title of sheriff for the county on suitable resident noblemen. For some 300 years the office was held by the Earls of Rothes, but in 1748 heritable jurisdiction was abolished. The first recorded Sheriff of Fife is David de Wemyss (1200), while the last under the old hereditary system was John, eighth Earl of Rothes. Thereafter a system of sheriffs-depute came into being. Today sheriffs are full-time salaried lawyers acting as judges

Lords Lieutenant of Fife

Just as the civil administration of Fife by the ancient earls of Fife was devolved to sheriffs and sheriffs-depute, the military duties were given in charge to the lords lieutenant of Fife. The office of lord lieutenant dates from 1557 in the reign of Mary I, but the title originated in the reign of Henry VIII. The need for such persons as lieutenants of counties grew out of Tudor experiments with decentralisation and the establishment of regional councils. Elizabeth I made such lieutenants a more permanent fixture in her attempts to impose an efficient control over law and order.

Commissions as lieutenant were rare after the Union of the Crowns in 1603, except in times of national emergency, or the actual difficulties following the accession of King James VII and II. The lieutenancies were revised by royal warrant of George III in 1794 and were set out on a shire basis. From 1797 to around 1854 the principal concern of the lord lieutenant was the fulfilling of the Militia Acts. After this their duties diminished and the modern structure of local government reduced the lieutenants' functions, yet they are still known as 'the monarch's first representatives'. Today the office of lord lieutanant is still an appointment of the crown through letters patent under the country's Great Seal. After the revision of 1794 the families of the earls of Crawford, Morton, Kellie, Rosslyn and Elgin and Kincardine predominated in the choice of lieutenants, with George, twenty-second Earl of Crawford, serving between 1794–1808. Deputy lieutenants began after 1794 with two early appointments of David Monypenny of Pitmilly and George Cheape of Pusk in 1803.

Religious dignitaries for Fife

Early churchmen played a great role in the history and legend of Fife, as the mention of individual ecclesiastical houses in the county will show. Fife was represented in ecclesiastical politics by the bishops of St Andrews, with Celtic bishops sited at Kilrymont (St Andrews) from the episcopacy of St Adrian around 870. From the ascendancy of the Anglo-Normans in Scotland, Fife was represented by an unbroken line of Bishops of St Andrews from Turgot (served 1107–15) to the last full incumbency of James Kennedy (served 1440–66).

In 1466 Patrick Graham, Bishop of Brechin, was promoted to the See of St Andrews, and in 1472 the See was elevated to an archbishopric by the Bull of Pope Sixtus IV. The last of the medieval archbishops of St Andrews was John Hamilton from 1546 until his execution at Stirling castle on 6 April 1571 for supporting Mary, Queen of Scots.

From 1572–1688 there were seven tulchan (titular) Protestant archbishops of St Andrews from John Douglas (served 1572–74), Principal of St Mary's College, to the last holder, Arthur Ross, who served from 1684 to the abolition of episcopacy in 1688. After the Revolution of 1688 bishops of Fife existed without the diocese, and in 1720 the bishoprics were revived. Fife does not appear today in the diocesan appellations of the Scottish Episcopal Church or in the Roman Catholic hierarchy. Moderators of the General Assembly of the Church of Scotland were appointed annually from 1562, and many prominent holders of the position had Fife connections, including George Buchanan, Principal of St Leonard's College, in 1567, and Andrew Melville, Principal of St Mary's College, serving in 1582–87 and 1594.

Fife and the Scots parliament to 1707

Prior to the fourteenth century the administration of Fife fell within the autocratic and despotic power of the contemporary ruler, aided by local prelates and nobility. As learning was almost entirely confined to the clergy, senior priests played a large, early role in governance of Scotland, and as their governance developed into the Three Estates of the Realm, the clergy were strongly represented in the trio of Sovereign, Lords Spiritual (the clergy) and Lords Temporal (the nobility). Thus many Fife medieval clergy were involved in government business, and it was not unusual for the medieval Scots parliament to meet on church property; in 1304 the conquering Edward I held a parliament at St Andrews cathedral. The 'common folk' (that is, burgesses and freeholders) had no role in the governance of Scotland up to the fourteenth century, witness their appearance at the parliament held by Robert I, the Bruce, at the Augustinian abbey of Cambuskenneth on 15 July 1326. In the sixteenth century it was usual for the Scottish Parliament to meet at Edinburgh or Stirling, but with the completion of Parliament House in 1639 it always met at the capital. Incidentally, Parliament Hall (St Mary's College, St Andrews) takes its name from the fact that the Scottish parliament sat here from 26 November 1645 to 4 February 1646 as the plague raged in Edinburgh.

During the period from the mid-fourteenth century to the Union of the Parliaments, which came into force on 1 May 1707, Fife was represented in the Scottish parliament at varying times by a county MP for Fifeshire, and representatives from fourteen burghs, namely:

Fifeshire:	First mention in official returns, 1593: Sir John Leirmonth of Balcomie.
Anstruther Easter:	1593. Robert Clephane; David Wade.
Anstruther Wester:	1645. Andrew Richardson.
Burntisland:	1586. John Clephane.
Crail:	1357. Roger Hendchyld; Richard Scroger.
Culross:	1648. James Aitken.
Cupar:	1357. David Cumming; Nicholas Cupar.
Dunfermline:	1594. William Pratenis.
Dysart:	1594. Robert Mewo.
Inverkeithing:	1357. Thomas Johnson; Roger Phipill.
Kinghorn:	1579. John Boswell.
Kirkcaldy:	1585. Robert Hay.
Kilrenny:	1612. Alexander Bethune.
Pittenweem:	1579. Thomas Beniston.
St Andrews:	1357 Adam of Kirkyntolach.

Burgh status

The word burgh appears in Fife place-names from around the twelfth century, and has various spellings from bourgh to bourow. The term means a town with special privileges conferred by charter and, particularly from the late fourteenth century, a municipal corporation. The word burgh was added to nouns to describe burgh possessions, or officers, as in burgh-acres/land – territory belonging to the burgh, or, burgh-clerk – a town clerk. Old Fife documents also preserve such old usages as burgh-greff – a magistrate, or burgh-rudis – cultivated land belonging to the

burgh. Terms that will be used in this book may be defined as
follows:

Royal burghs: the town belonged to the monarch.
Burgh of regality: the town superior (a person who, in law,
                        granted land to a vassal or tenant) was clerk in
                        holy orders, with royal favour, or in some cases
                        a peer of the realm.
Burgh of barony: The superior was a member of the influential
                        laity; usually a baron.

1
SHORELANDS OF THE TAY

Come into Fife by the old north-western pilgrimage route and you are plunged at once into the old kingdom's history and legend. In medieval times the pilgrims en route from Perth, and the Augustinian abbey of the Holy Trinity and St Michael at Scone, crossed the River Tay by ferry at its confluence with the River Earn and entered the western boundary of the lands of the earls of Fife.

Today the A913 from Abernethy leads the visitor to a car park at the edge of Newburgh and a panoramic view of the Fife shores of Tay. To right and left lie two locales of Fife's early history: the Roman fort at Carpow House (the second Carpow House hereabouts was destroyed by fire in 1961; the later dwelling and policies are not open to the public) and the prehistoric sites at Clatchard Craig. It is as well to reflect on these two sites, for out of their associations Fife received its name and early boundaries.

Classical historical sources show us that modern Fife was occupied in the early centuries by a Celtic tribe called the *Venicones*, who with the *Vacomagi* formed a confederation mentioned by the Roman historian Cassius Dio Cocceianus as the *Maeatae*. They constituted a people known as Proto-Picts who were recognised for their metalwork. The lack of permanent Roman installations in Fife, following the conquest of Scotland by Gnaeus Julius Agricola during AD 78–84, would suggest that the *Venicones* were philo-Roman.

The Romans first moved into Fife in AD 82, and after the commencement of the governorship of Antoninus Pius, *c.* AD 138, a necklet of forts were constructed from the Forth to the Tay, effectively protecting the peninsula of Fife. By AD 170 the Romans abandoned the area. In AD 209 the imperial task force of Emperor Septimus Severus moved into Scotland, and the Romans began construction of the half-legionary fortress at Carpow, to be used by the II Augusta and VI Victrix legions.

The site of Roman Carpow – which they called *Horrea Classis* – was once in the possession of the nearby Abbey of Lindores, and was excavated during 1964–79. In passing it may be noted that these excavations revealed remains of the *praetorium* (commander's residence), the *principia* (headquarters building), and a *horrea* (granary), along with the *via principalis* (the main street running across the camp), and the *porta praetorium* (the east gate). From Carpow the activities of the *Maeatae* were monitored as well as the camp acting as a base for the Roman fleet's activities in the *Tava Fluvius* (River Tay) area.

The term *Picti* (Latin meaning 'painted') only appears in classical writing from the end of the third century, but by the time that the tribesmen were ravaging the territory north of Hadrian's Wall in the great raid of AD 367, the Picts were a fully developed entity. Legend tells us that the first king of the Picts was Cruithne and that his seven sons gave their names to the regions of Pictland. From one such regional kingdom, Fibh, comes today's Fife. In the mid-ninth century the area we know as Fife was divided into two with a line roughly from Leven to Auchtermuchty – to the west was Forthrif and to the east was Fibh. In Pictish times, Fife's area included Perthshire as far as the Ochils and had its capital at Kilrymont, whose site developed as modern St Andrews, and until the fourteenth century it included Kinross. Fife is mentioned for the first time, it seems, by St Columba (521–97) as a province of Pictavia. Today the Picts are remembered in Fife through dozens of place-names and their homes and fortresses are everywhere, for instance at Clatchard Craig.

The multivaleate defences of the Dark Age hillfort at Clatchard Craig occupy the eastern elevation of Ormiston Hill, above Newburgh. Excavations in 1953–4 and 1959–60, provided evidence of Neolithic, Iron Age and Dark Age activity. Here Fife's early inhabitants pursued employment as metalworkers, corn grinders, glassmakers, potters and makers of artefacts for hunting and war. They even had a flourishing trade in penannular brooches. Atop the hill lies 'The Bluidy Well' which local folklore avers was a sacrificial hollow in the rock. In his *Lindores Abbey and its Burgh of Newburgh*, written in 1876, Alexander Lang averred that the Bluidy Well was the place where combatants washed their swords after battle. In peace and war then, Clatchard Craig witnessed the birth of today's Fife.

In time the throne of Pictland was annexed by Kenneth McAlpine, the Scottish king, and by 850 the Picts had ceased to be independent power. The new kingdom of Alba, of which the area of modern Fife was a part, had its capital at Scone. From here the web of political and ecclesiastical power spread and Fife was colonised in a religious sense at such sites as St Andrews. By the twelfth century there was a royal reform of the kingdom and burghs were founded; settlements at such places as Pittenweem, Dunfermline and St Monans were to assure Fife's continued importance down the centuries.

From medieval times Fife enjoyed a high standard of living, from the well-watered howes (vales) of Eden, Leven and Ore, the low-lying margins of the Forth and Tay, and the moors burned to submission for the grazing of sheep and stock cattle. As the historian George Buchanan (1506–82) recorded, Fife was 'a district provided within its own bounds with all things necessary for the use of life', to which subsequent visitors and commentators added remarks on the lush farms, doocots, fisheries and rural society.

Newburgh

In the centre of such an area lies Newburgh, bisected today by the A913 Perth–Cupar road. The settlement owes its foundation to the Abbey of Lindores, whose chapter and abbot were granted a charter *novus burgus juxta Monasterium de Lindoris* by Alexander III on 4 March 1266. In 1593 James VI confirmed the rights of the burgesses of Newburgh and on 29 January 1631, Charles I confirmed the 1457 charter erecting Newburgh into a royal burgh. Newburgh is likely to have developed from a hamlet of fishermen's bothies and cottar-houses.

A good starting point to absorb something of the history of Newburgh is to visit the Laing Museum in the High Street. It was first opened in 1896 as a gift of Dr Alexander Laing (1808–92), a banker and historian, to form the basis of the modern collection. Laing made a special study of the hillfort at Clatchard Craig, producing early plans of it, and promoted various local 'self-help' schemes so dear to the Victorian philanthropist.

Newburgh is the only clearly developed town between Newport-on-Tay and Perth, and its buildings are mostly eighteenth and nineteenth century. A wander through its streets and wynds affords architectural specimens from its manse (c.1790) and George Hotel (1811) to St Katherine's Church (1833) and the Town House (1808). A living was formerly earned from fishing, agriculture, horticulture and weaving, and within more modern times at the Tayside Floorcloth Company (1896) which closed in 1978. In living memory Newburgh's piers were busy exporting whinstone, boiled salmon, grilse and potatoes, and importing ochre, sprats and whiting; excess fish was used as agricultural fertiliser. Writing in his *The Fringes of Fife* (1894), The *Scotsman*'s feature writer John Geddie recalled the legend of how 'Newburgh supplied the navy of Great Britain with steady, well-behaved and gallant mariners'. In the heyday of the paddle-steamers on the Tay – the largest being the 1800-passenger *Slieve Bearnagh* – hundreds of excursionists called at Taylor's and Rennie's town piers, and in 1846 the Edinburgh and Northern Railway opened a station; the Newburgh and North of Fife railway opened in 1909.

To the north-west of Newburgh the estate of Mugdrum came into the possession of the Orme family in the sixteenth century, having been a part of Abernethy church lands, and from them it passed to the Leslies, the Lords of Lindores. At one time it was the home of the Jacobite Lord George Murray, Prince Charles Edward Stewart's erstwhile lieutenant-general during the 1745 rebellion; Murray died in exile in Holland in 1760. In 1794 the superiors of Mugdrum were the Hays, who held title until the twentieth century. Georgian Mugdrum House burned down in 1916. One of Newburgh's earliest relics is the Cross of Mugdrum; it depicts Celtic symbols suggesting an antiquity in excess of 1,200 years. It remains the subject of contested legends. Another cross stood above Newburgh, known as Macduff's Cross; it was regarded locally as a place of sanctuary for members of the Macduff clan, retainers of the Celtic earls of Fife. A large part of the cross was destroyed by Reformers in 1559, yet from its base Sir Walter Scott assessed the vista as 'one of the finest and noblest in the world'.

Newburgh was once known for its fair on the Feast of St Katherine the Virgin and Martyr whose feast day was 25 November; this became known as the 'Haggis Fair' when its religious overtones were debunked. The fair survived into modern times. Up to 1900, too, the members of the Masonic Lodge held a torchlight procession in full regalia to mark the Festival of St John the Divine, the Apostle and Evangelist, whose mass was said at the abbey of Lindores on 27 December.

Hill Road rises steeply from Newburgh High Street, where the thoroughfare makes its junction in front of the Laing Museum at the County Buildings, under the railway to the eminence above the burgh. Here the visitor can enjoy a panoramic perspective of the Tay, the neighbouring island of Mugdrum and the Carse of Gowrie on the opposite shore. Here on Mount Pleasant is the site of Bethune's Cottage (1837). Although extended and improved it was the home, built with their own labours, of two largely self-educated brothers, Alexander and John Bethune, who broke stones for the Newburgh road and are a part of Fife legend. Although Alexander became a cripple following a quarry explosion and John died in 1839 from privation and overwork, they are remembered as competent local poets. Indeed the Revd Charles Kingsley, of *Water Babies* fame (1863), declared that their cottage should rival that of Robert Burns at Alloway, Ayrshire, as a literary shrine.

Alexander Bethune published their joint works as *Tales and Sketches of the Scottish Peasantry* (1838), and after his brother's death endeavoured to sell the title as a two-volume edition to pay for a tombstone for his brother. Because of ill-health Alexander was unable to take up the proffered editorship of the *Dumfries Standard*; he died in 1843 aged thirty-nine. The two brothers are buried in Abdie churchyard. The Rev. Thomas Thompson selected their names to be immortalised with the good and the great 'Eminent Scotsmen' who appeared in his edition of Robert Chambers' *Biographical Dictionary* (1870).

Alexander penned these verses in memory of his brother:

> Looking across the roofs of our Newburgh
> I remember boyhood days . . .
> When evening's lengthened shadows fall
> On cottage roof and princely hall,
> Then brothers with their brothers meet,

And kindred hearts each other greet,
And children wildly, gladly press,
To share a father's fond caress:
But home to me no more can bring
Those scenes which are life's sweetening.

No friendly heart remains for me,
Like star to gild life's stormy sea;
No brother, whose affection warm,
The gloomy passing hours might charm;
Bereft of all who once were dear,
Whose words or looks were wont to cheer; –
Parent, and friend, and brother gone,
I stand upon the earth alone.

Lindores Abbey

On the edge of modern Newburgh lie the sorry remains of Lindores
Abbey, set now within the ambience of Abbey House, built in 1872
on the site of an earlier building. Although now much neglected,
the site recalls a history which was central to that of Scotland in
general and Fife in particular.

Lindores Abbey was a tiny piece of France set by the River Tay. It

Carved oak panels from Lindores Abbey. (Author's collection)

The seal of the Chapter of Lindores Abbey,
showing abbot and monks in adoration of the
Madonna and Child. (Author's collection)

was founded by David, Earl of Huntingdon, born about 1144,
grandson of King David I, possibly first as a priory in 1178 to be
elevated to abbey status in 1191. Dedicated to the Virgin Mary, St
Andrew the Apostle and Martyr and All Saints, the abbey was given
to the grey-robed monks of the French Benedictine Order of Tiron.
The story of the monks of Lindores began in France in 1109, when
the abbot, the Blessed Bernard of Abbeville, became dissatisfied
with the state of his abbey of St Cyprian in Poitiers and left to
found the monastery of La Sainte-Trinité de Tiron in the woods of
Tiron (Thiron-Gardais, Eure et Loire), where the life of the monks
would be more austere and disciplined. King David I had a special
devotion for the Tironesians, a devotion mantained by his son Earl
Henry and grandson Earl David.

According to the legend recorded by Dundee-born chronicler

Lindores Abbey from the south-west, as it may have appeared in the
fifteenth century. (Author's sketch)

Hector Boetius, Earl David was travelling home from the Third
Crusade with Richard I of England when he was caught in a storm
in the North Sea. Should he be saved, vowed Earl David, he would
found a monastic house dedicated to the Blessed Virgin Mary.
Boetius wrote that David was saved and landed in his rudderless,
sail-less ship at Allectum (today's Dundee), where he founded the
church of St Mary-in-the-field-called-Triticium (wheatfield) as an
immediate gesture.

Lindores Abbey was located within the old Fife forest of Earnside
on lands gifted to Earl David by his brother King William the Lion.
The original foundation lands measured some four miles by two,
with easy access to the sea via the Tay, and included the *magnus
lacus* (loch of Lindores) and the island of *Redeinche* (now
Mugdrum).

The fare on the dining table of the twenty known abbots of
Lindores was rich and plentiful from the farms and fishing rights
the abbey owned. The abbey gardens were famous for their sweet-
smelling flowers, herbs, the mellow pears and celebrated plums.
The orchard trees long survived. The physician and naturalist Sir
Robert Sibbald attested during his visit in the early 1700s that
'vastly big old pear trees still flourish'.

During the period 1316–30 records show that the woods around

The common abbatical seal of
Lindores Abbey. (Author's collection)

Lindores Abbey were infested with snakes, identified in the old
texts as *natrix torquata* (the collared snake). An abbey neighbour,
Sir James Balfour of Denmylne, noted that the 'plague' lasted
fourteen years and was only eradicated by the miraculous
intervention of the Blessed Virgin.

The fifteenth century was the golden age of Lindores Abbey. By
this time its abbots appeared regularly in the councils of the
Scottish monarchs, and acted as arbiters in disputes amongst the
laity; on 19 September 1395 the Abbot of Lindores became a mitred
abbot, ranking him second only to the diocesan bishop. We know

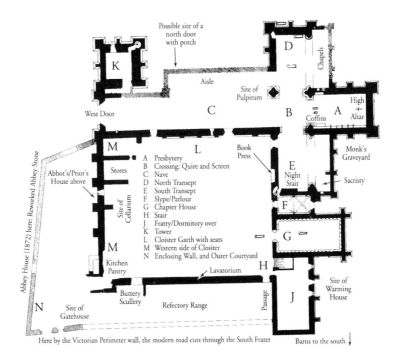

Ground plan of Lindores Abbey.

too that Abbot Guido was a papal judge-delegate able to resolve cases concerning church lands, rents and so on without recourse to Rome; Lindores clerics were therefore well known in Christendom and two became important figures in Fife and Scottish history, namely Laurence of Lindores and John Leslie.

Born around 1372, Laurence of Lindores was a native of the old hamlet of Lindores and (possibly) a novice at the abbey. He is likely to have continued his education at St Andrews and became a capable organiser and administrator of the early university there. Intellectually influential, he comes down to us as a rather sinister figure: as Inquisitor of Heretical Pravity, he was responsible for lighting fires under Scotland's first religious martyrs. He died a man both feared and honoured in 1437.

John Leslie was a lawyer, musician, spy and mapmaker. Born illegitimate *circa* 1527 he rose to high office in the church as Bishop

John Leslie, Bishop of Ross, last titular
Abbot of Lindores. He acted as
Mary, Queen of Scots' ambassador in England
after her imprisonment. (Author's collection)

John Leslie produced his map of Scotland for his history of
the country in 1578. (Author's collection)

of Ross. A devotee of Mary, Queen of Scots, Leslie risked his life in intrigues for his royal mistress in such conspiracies as the Ridolfi Plot of 1571. He died in exile in Brussels in 1596, still bearing the honour and style of the titular Abbot of Lindores. By then the abbey had long been defunct.

At the Reformation Lindores Abbey was one of the first to be attacked by the Protestant mob. The abbey had already been attacked by dissidents in 1543, probably as a consequence of a running battle between the provost and baillies of Dundee over Lindores lands and property in the city. Throughout Fife in the 1540s religious agitation brewed, yet it was more to do with objection to the 'worship of images', the belief in 'pretended miracles', the 'abuse of excommunications', and the financial rapacity and supposed immoral lives of the clergy than with theological argument. Yet the politico-religious pot was to boil over when the ex-Roman Catholic priest John Knox preached his defamatory sermon on 11 June 1559 on Christ's ejection of the buyers and sellers from the temple, and thus inaugurated the Reformation acts, vandalisms, robbery and proceedings in Scotland. As a consequence the 'reforming' mob marched on Lindores.

Writing a few days after the events at Lindores in June 1559, Knox was to record: 'The abbey of Lindores . . . we reformed their altars, overthrewn their idols, vestments of idolaterie, and mass-books we burned in their presence, and commanded them to cast away their monkish habits'. On 17 August 1560 John Philp assented to the new Church of Scotland and the long line of incumbent abbots ceased. Deposed Lindores clerics went on to be ministers of the reformed church, from Abdie to Strathmiglo and beyond, while a few used the despoiled abbey as their home into the 1600s. The revenues of Lindores were finally granted to Sir Patrick Leslie of Pitcairlie. The abbey and its lands remained in that family until 1741, and by 1841 they were owned by the Hays of Leys. The abbey buildings were freely plundered for ashlar well into the nineteenth century.

From the ruins of Lindores Abbey the road climbs steeply past Parkhill Farm. Below, the Firth of Tay spreads out with its curiously named sandbanks of Eppie's Taes and Peesweep. Since the days of the Romans these waters have carried a volume of traffic from Dutch coasters laden with stone from Newburgh to an international trade of sloops and freighters from Perth. The first habitation of note encountered as the road follows the south Tay shore is Ballinbreich and its eponymous castle (pronounced 'Balmbreich').

Ballinbreich

The red-stone castle lies neglected in a difficult to access location down the farm track. It is known that the Leslies acquired these lands around 1330 through marriage with an heiress of the de Abernetheys, and their castle dates from this time, with sixteenth-century enlargements and reconstructions to an L-plan. Relics of a huge kitchen chimney breast, gateway, gun-looped round tower, staircase and chapel are still to be seen. The lush gardens, orchards and fishponds of Ballinbreich have now vanished. The Leslie earls of – and one duke of – Rothes used the castle as their chief seat while hereditary sheriffs of Fife; thereafter the estate passed to the Dundases of Zetland. Mary, Queen of Scots, visited in 1565 and dined on 'partriches' at 'a crown apiece'. The Leslies were strongly implicated in the murders both of the Queen's Secretary David Rizzio in 1566 and her husband Henry Stewart, Lord Darnley, in 1567. Used as a quarry over the centuries, the castle gave its name to the last sailing ship to be launched at Perth in 1879.

Along the road from Ballinbreich, Flisk Wood runs down to the Tay with the redundant chapel of Flisk at its southern edge. The chapel is now a roofless shell with a small surrounding graveyard where lie decades of locals alongside former ministers of the parish and the bones of Andrew Leslie, fifth Earl of Rothes and his kin. The shell is of the kirk raised in 1790 and renovated in 1888 and is on or near the foundations of a pre-Reformation church rededicated to St Adrian in 1242. Many of the medieval rectors of Flisk achieved high office; one such was Sir James Balfour of Pittendreich, dubbed 'the most corrupt man of the age'. He mixed practice of the law, as President of the Court of Session, with skulduggery: Balfour was suspected of a leading role in the murder of David Rizzio and Henry Darnley. Balfour's brother's house at

The common seal of the abbey of Balmerino, showing the Madonna and the Arms of Scotland. (Author's collection)

The seal of Abbot Alan [?] of Balmerino. (Author's collection)

Edinburgh was adjacent to that of Kirk o'Field where Darnley met his pyrotechnic death.

Balmerino

From Flisk the road skirts the hills which retain relics of prehistoric settlements, and at Hazleton Walls crossroads the Tay shore road veers left via Coultra farm to Balmerino and its abbey. Because of their habit of white cloth with a black apron, or scapular, over it, the Cistercians of Balmerino were called the White Monks by locals. Their abbey, dedicated to 'Our Lady and St Edmund the Confessor, King and Martyr' was founded by Alexander II, King of

Scots, and his mother Queen Ermengard de Bellomonte (Beaumont), widow of William the Lion, on the feast of St Lucy the Virgin and Martyr of Syracuse, 13 December 1229.

Tradition has it that Ermengarde came to the Tay shores at Balmerino 'for the benefit of her health' long before the founding of the abbey, from her dowager residence at Forfar. She probably stayed at the manor of one Adam de Stawel, proprietor of Balmerino, Cultrach (Coultra) and Ardint (Ardie). Certainly she bought the land for the abbey from de Stawel for 1,000 merks in 1225. Ermengarde died very soon after the foundation of the abbey and was buried in front of the high altar. Her grave was rediscovered in the early 1830s and the queen's bones dispersed; soft stone from her white sarcophagus was used by a doughty Calvinist farmer's wife to sand her kitchen floor.

Although the Cistercians – whose order originated at Cistercium (Citeaux), near Dijon in Burgundy – followed an interpretation of the Rule of St Benedict of Nursia, renouncing personal wealth and luxury, the abbey at Balmerino was liberally endowed by Scotland's royal family. Their possessions included lands and properties in Angus and in Fife as far as Anstruther.

By the abbacy of Ralph the Cellarer, 1236–51, there were some fourteen monks at Balmerino, with a large number of employees to run the abbey granges and fishing rights. Abbot Thomas, *c.*1282, rose to be a 'lord of parliament' and many of the Balmerino abbots witnessed many important state papers. The last abbot of Balmerino was Robert Forester, *c.*1507, who was dead by 1559. He took a part in the proceedings at St Andrews Cathedral which resulted in the heresy trial of octogenarian Walter Myln, who was burned at the stake in 1558. Mary, Queen of Scots, visited the abbey during 27–28 January 1565 to stay with John Hay the Commendator, who held the court role of Principal Master of Requests and was later to be Mary's ambassador to the court of Queen Elizabeth I of England. Certainly Balmerino was to be a centre of academic excellence, having a 'perpetual student' admitted and funded to the chapter at St Andrews Cathedral. Several important books, too, were deemed to have been written at Balmerino Abbey, including Abbot Alan's *De Perfectione Religiosa* ('Concerning religious perfection').

St Ayles House, Anstruther, the sixteenth-century town
house of Balmerino Abbey, as it looked around 1850.

Today the abbey church of Balmerino has all but vanished. Once
it ran to 206 ft in length, but only a part of the north nave wall
remains. Only the east range of the conventual buildings survives,
set to the north of the abbey around a cloister. The chapter house
still displays its vaulting. To the east of this site lies a building
thought to be the abbot's house, of which only the vaulted cellars
remain. The abbey barn has now been set within modern farm
buildings. The stone from Balmerino Abbey came mostly from
Nidie Quarry.

As a casualty of the assault on Scotland by the Duke of Somerset,
Protector of England, Balmerino Abbey was attacked on the night
of Christmas 1547 by Admiral Thomas Wyndham. His force landed
at the monks' pier on the Tay and set fire to the abbey as well as the
tenants' properties. No real damage seems to have been done to the
stonework and life went on at the monastery.

During the third week of June 1559, Balmerino was attacked

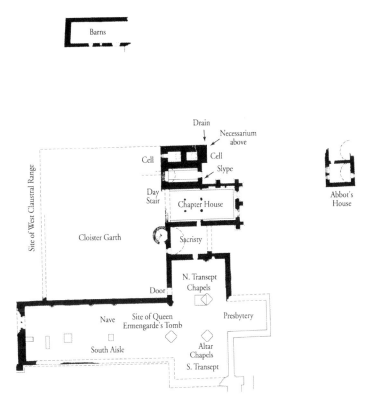

Ground plan of Balmerino Abbey, showing surviving stonework.

again, this time by the reforming rabble led by James Stewart, Earl of Moray and Commendator of St Andrews Priory, and Archibald Campbell, Earl of Argyll. How much damage they did is uncertain. Without a doubt 'the monuments of idolatry' would be destroyed, the tombs broken into and robbed and all useful moveables purloined. Thus 330 years of conventual life ceased at Balmerino. Monks who remained and were willing to embrace the new faith were promised pensions, the rest were expelled. By 1586 only two monks, Thomas Stevenson and John Yester, were still living at the despoiled abbey.

As time went by stone from the abbey was used for other purposes. Wood from the abbey church, for instance, was used for a new transept of the parish church of Dundee in 1588 and again in

1788–9. Ashlar was also carted away to be re-used for a church at Monifieth and house-building at St Andrews.

By 1603 the lands of the Abbey of Balmerino were erected into a temporal lordship for Sir James Elphinstone (1557–1612), Secretary of State to James VI, and his heirs. After 1606 Elphinstone sat in parliament as Lord Balmerino (using the hamlet's old name of Balmerinoch), until his attainder. His heirs had the title restored until the Jacobite Arthur Elphinstone, Lord Balmerino and fifth Lord Coupar (b.1688) was captured by the Grants at Culloden (16 April 1746). He was tried for high treason and beheaded at Tower Hill, London, and buried at St Peter ad Vincula chapel at the Tower. The Balmerino peerage was forfeit and attainted in 1746, but the title would have died with Elphinstone in any case.

The property known as the estate of Balmerino, including the abbey site, was bought in 1755 by John, eighth Earl of Moray, and the property remained in the Moray family to be disposed by way of the Moray Estates Development Company to the Scrymgeour-Wedderburns of Birkhill House in 1931. In 1936 Henry James Scrymgeour-Wedderburn, who in 1953 was to successfully claim the title of fifth Earl of Dundee, disponed Balmerino Abbey to the National Trust for Scotland, who remain its owners.

During 1980 excavations were undertaken near the site of the west door of the abbey where steps were being built to facilitate access to the nave. Skeletons were found at a shallow depth and were thought to have been cadavers of the casualties of Admiral Wyndham's attack of 1547. On this occasion it is known that members of the abbey's lay retainers, probably foresters and the like, endeavoured to repulse the marauders and were killed.

In the policies of the abbey are three chestnut trees worthy of note. The massive Spanish chestnut at the east end of the grounds was scientifically examined at the time of the abbey's 750th anniversary in 1979, and cores taken to assess its age. Results showed that the tree had been planted somewhere between 1554 and 1589, possibly around the time of the abbey's despoiling. The old local tale that the tree was planted by Mary, Queen of Scots, need not therefore be purely romantic. Two other trees were planted at the time of the 750th anniversary. Access to the abbey site is somewhat restricted due to the dilapidation of the fabric.

The rich agricultural land of Balmerino lies mainly within the two old estates of Birkhill, with its 1857–9 baronial mansion incorporating one of 1780, and Naughton with its fine country mansion of 1793 built by James Morrison. Behind the house, on private land, is the site of Naughton Castle, reputed to have been first built in the twelfth century by Robert de Lundin, the natural son of William the Lion. In the sixteenth century it was a stronghold of the Hay family and local legend has it that the family caused a lamp to be placed at the top of its tower to guide Tay shipping. The hamlet of Balmerino proper owes its foundation to the abbey. A relic of the monk's pier is still to be seen and was used by paddle-steamers up to 1915. The old ferry was on the pilgrimage route to the Tironesian abbey of St Thomas the Martyr of Canterbury at Arbroath and St Andrews Cathedral. On the right as visitors enter Balmerino lies the 1948 David Scrymgeour-Wedderburn Memorial Square recalling the death of a family member during the Anzio campaign in the Second World War. Across the road was the abbey 'plumyard' whose trees were finally felled in 1863.

Across the hill from Balmerino lies the hamlet of The Gauldry, once a weaving centre and now a dormitory of Dundee, St Andrews

Second Tay railway bridge under construction. Opened 1887.
(St Andrews Research and Lecture Projects)

and elsewhere. The road system hereabouts leads on to Wormit, another rural hamlet until the Tay rail bridge of 1878 made it a dormitory for Dundee. It is said that Wormit was the first village in Scotland to have electric light, introduced by one Alexander Stewart who built one of the many Victorian houses here. Power was generated by a windmill on Wormit Hill, supplemented by a steam engine which gave way to a coal-gas engine which chugged away until the grid of 1930.

Woodhaven

From Wormit the B946 travels west to Woodhaven which was the northern starting point for the coach across Fife to Pettycur on the Forth. Recognised in 1669 as a public ferry, Woodhaven pier was until the mid-nineteenth century the most important of the south Tay ferries. Here in 1715 Rob Roy MacGregor crossed the Tay with his marauding horde. During his tour of Scotland in 1773 with James Boswell, Dr Samuel Johnson crossed the Tay from Woodhaven and complained: 'Though the water was not wide we paid four shillings [20 p]'. Here too during the Second World World War the Catalina and Sunderland flying boats of 333 Squadron Royal Norwegian Airforce were serviced; a memorial by the Wormit Boating Club marks the visit by King Haakon VII of Norway to the flying boats in 1944. Still today the Wormit Boating Club flies the Norwegian flag on the birthday of King Harald of Norway (the present monarch) and other notable anniversaries.

From 1869 until 1929 the training ship the *Mars* was a familiar sight moored off Woodhaven. TTS *Mars* was built as an 80-gun warship of the Royal Navy in 1848. After service in the Crimean War 1854–56, the vessel was refitted as an industrial training ship. *Mars* was brought to the Tay in 1869 and became the home for 400 boys between the ages of twelve and sixteen. On board they were given a basic education and training in seamanship, woodwork and tailoring, with emphasis too on rowing, boxing, swimming and gymnastics. Many of the boys came to the *Mars* on a naval scholarship to learn the basics of a sea career, while others were there because they were orphaned, homeless or guilty of civil misdemeanours or persistent truancy.

In all some 7,000 boys were trained aboard the *Mars*, but by 1929 numbers had decreased. *Mars* was then towed to Inverkeithing for breaking. The *Mars* was known for its band and choir and the boys served aboard a rescue vessel for the Tay. Woodhaven's old granary by the shore served as a hospital for the boys. Woodhaven pier is now the home of the Wormit Boating Club, and by the old boathouse (1799) is the Celtic cross memorial to the 'old boys' of the *Mars* who died in the First World War.

Newport

By the time the Tay reaches Newport-on-Tay, as the longest river in Scotland, it has travelled nearly 120 miles from its source on the northern slopes of Ben Lui under the names of the Fillan and Dochart until it joins Loch Tay and flows on as the Tay to form a two-mile-wide firth at Dundee. Salmon fishing on the Tay was always a major industry and Newport folk had the right to fish the river. Newport initially earned its living from a ferry on the site from at least the twelfth century and once called Seamylnes, with its protective chapel dedicated to St Thomas the Martyr of Canterbury. Possibly first administered by the monks of Arbroath Abbey, the ferry passed to one Alan Kynnaird of Naughton. By 1639 it was in municipal control, and for about 200 years pinnaces, yawls and row-boats plied the waters. In the early 1820s a new pier was constructed at Newport from the designs of Scottish engineer and stonemason Thomas Telford (1757–1834) and the ferry service continued into the present century. The greater portion of Newport was built on Tayfield estate, which formed part of the old barony of Inverdovat. The area has been associated with the Berry family ever since the present mansion was built in 1788 and remodelled 1829–30.

Tayport

The northernmost habitation in Fife, Ferry-Port-on-Craig, was erected into a burgh of barony by the 1598 charter of James VI in favour of Robert Durie of that Ilk as superior. Since 1846 the little burgh has been known as Tayport. A ferry site was used here by

Macduff, spurious 'Thane of Fife', during his mythical flight into English exile from Macbeth's castle of Dunsinane. There is a delightful local legend that when Macduff arrived at the ferry he found that he had no money, so he paid the boatman with bread, thus giving ferry the soubriquet 'Ferry of the Loaf'. By the twelfth century a hospice and chapel for travellers had been built here and were run by the monks of Arbroath Abbey. A popular ferry for merchants and cattle drovers, it cost 'one penny Scots' for each person and horse to cross in 1474. By the fifteenth century, too, the crossing to Angus was considered of such strategic importance as to warrant a castle for protection. In 1855 only fragments of the Z-plan castle remained and they were demolished to make way for the rapidly expanding burgh; the site of the castle is now Castle Cottage, Castle Road.

The old parish church in Castle Street was built in 1607 and restored in 1794 and 1825, and its spire still leans towards the church because of a weakness in the Scotscraig vault below. The graveyard epitaphs shows how the parish developed as one of handloom weavers and jute spinners, with salmon fishing and shipbuilding as lucrative additions. Here too are recorded many tragedies at sea: among the graves near the kirk lie crew and passengers who perished when the steamer *Dalhousie* went down on Abertay Sands in the winter of 1864.

Tayport expanded from an early foundation in Dalgleish Street and Tay Street; the site of the old market cross is now preserved in the wall in Dalgleish Street opposite Market Place. In 1846 the Edinburgh and Northern Railway Company bought the ferry rights and built Tayport harbour to accommodate the huge iron paddle-steamers which were fitted with rails for the carrying of loaded coal trucks across the Tay. A new harbour was constructed in 1851 and Tayport developed as a busy port for the handling of china clay, timber and esparto grass. Here too was a fleet of 'puffers' used to dredge mussels from the Tay. Out to sea still stands the old Pile Lighthouse, a distinctive superstructure on stilts dating from 1848. The ferry-boat service ceased to run in 1939 and the railway closed to passengers in 1966. At the beginning of Tay Street, on the site of Tayport railway station, is a plaque commemorating the visit to Tayport in 1877 by US President Ulysses S. Grant who came here to view the ill-fated Tay Bridge.

Rising above Tayport, Craig Law and Hare Law take in the Scotscraig estate which dates back to the twelfth century, and was once owned by the murdered Archbishop James Sharp; a sundial of his day remains and his initials and arms are to be seen on a gateway. Various familes have owned the estate from the de Quincys to Sir Michael Scot of Balwearie, father of 'The Wizard' whose legend and history are described elsewhere. From the Duries to the Dalgleishes, who built the present mansion house in 1807, the estate was purchased by Vice-Admiral W.H. Maitland-Dougall in 1845. Hare Law is also known as Tower Hill after the watchtower rebuilt in 1815 to commemorate the victory over Napoleon at Waterloo.

Over the hill from Tayport lies Forgan, one crest sporting the Leng family memorial chapel of 1897 which stands above Vicarsford cemetery like a miniature French cathedral. Built by Sir John Leng (1828–1906), proprietor of the *Dundee Advertiser*, the chapel has at its foot the ruins of St Fillan's Church. A ruin since the 1890s, following its redundancy in 1841, the site was probably first founded around 1188–1202 when one Alan de Lasceles of Naughton granted the church to the Prior of St Andrews along with local tithes and revenues for its upkeep. Dedicated to the eighth-century Irish missionary monk St Fillan MacFeardach – made popular by Robert I, The Bruce, who thanked the saint for intercession at his victory at Bannockburn in 1314 – the T-shaped church incorporates stonework of the late twelfth to late medieval periods. Its graveyard contains lairds of the old prominent families of the area from the Stewarts of St Fort to the Gillespies of Kirkton. In the policies of the nearby ruined Old Kirkton House was a cruciform stand of yew trees, said by local legend to have magical powers. A sprig of this tree under the pillow would stimulate dreams to show where lost property was to be found.

Forgan Church, which replaced St Fillans, lies by the A92 St Andrews–Dundee road and dates from 1841. It is no longer used for religious services and the whole area, which once saw skirmishes with Viking invaders at such nearby sites as Inverdovat, is now dominated by the golf and residential complex at Drumoig. Across the way from this is the curiously named Pickletillem, probably corrupted from *pette-talamh*, 'small portion of enclosed land'.

Villages of the shorelands

From Forgan or Tayport, the visitor can make a circular tour back to Newburgh by taking the A914 at Wester Frairton crossroads to its junction with the A913 Cupar–Perth road and thence to Newburgh. This offers a glimpse of more interesting villages which have contributed to the history and legend of the shorelands of Tay.

The first to be encountered is Kilmany with its parish church of 1768, originally a rectory granted to St Salvator's College, St Andrews University, by Bishop James Kennedy. One of the most famous ministers of Kilmany was the Revd Dr Thomas Chalmers who served here from 1803 to 1815. Buried in the churchyard is the Earl of Melville, one of the Scottish noblemen who supported William of Orange when he became joint ruler with Mary II in 1689.

The next hamlet encountered is Rathillet, an ancient property of the earls of Fife. Rathillet House dates from *circa* 1790 and in its steading is the house associated locally with a famous assassin. For here lived David Hackston, one of the Covenanting murderers of Archbishop James Sharp in 1679; Hackston heirs held the property until the nineteenth century. To the north-west of Rathillet is Mountquhanie estate, with its ruined sixteenth-century castle and mansion of 1820. Once belonging to the earls of Fife, Mountquhanie became another Balfour property and was acquired by the Lumsdens; one famous scion of Mountquhanie was General Robert Lumsden who defended Dundee against General George Monck and Cromwell's army in 1651. When Dundee fell Lumsden's head was fixed on a spike on the Old Steeple and there it remained until the eighteenth century.

Just off the A914 is the medieval estate of Colluthie with its eighteenth-century mansion complete with baronial façade of 1883. This leads into the parish of Moonzie. The first encounter with medieval history hereabouts is the ruin of the late fifteenth-century four-storey rectangular keep of Lordscairnie Castle with the remains of its courtyard defences. Built by Sir Alexander Lindsay of Auchtermoonzie the castle is in the process of being restored. The castle was used as a church in 1688.

Moonzie old church was immortalised in an old rhyme:

Gae ye east, or gae ye west,
Or gae ye ony way ye will,
Ye winna get tae Moonzie Kirk
Unless ye gae up Moonzie hill.

The doggerel referred to the random rubble church being visible from the Tay; sailors heading for St Andrews Bay, or mariners of the Dundee whaling fleet making for the Tay used it as a landmark.

Dedicated to the Holy Trinity in 1245, Moonzie Church's extant fabric dates from *circa* 1625; it was renovated in the eighteenth century and in 1882 and is in the care of a preservation trust that mounts displays of the parish muniments at set times. Moonzie House dates from 1804–06 and was renovated in 1848; it was once the manse, and its appurtenances show how country clergy could live in some comfort.

A trio of hamlets lie in the North Fife Hills abutting the Tay in Luthrie, Brunton and Creich. At one time Luthrie station was the most important stop on the North British Railway's now-vanished North Fife line. Closed to passengers in 1951, the station won its fame as a loading point for 4,000 tons of potatoes annually. Up to the sixteenth century Luthrie belonged to the crown, and thereafter properties here were owned by John Murray, barber-surgeon to James V. Both Luthrie and Parbroath mansions have disappeared, the latter once belonging to the Hopetoun estates. There are still eighteenth-century houses standing at Colluthie and Carphin.

Brunton is a very scattered hamlet of narrow roads and cottages of mixed age and state of preservation, and at one time had one of Scotland's tiniest farms, the result of feuing of tenants in the eighteenth century. Many of Brunton's old cottages had looms for the production of osnaburgs and dowlas, the coarse linen made from the locally grown blue-flowered flax. Stacked like corn, the flax piles were a common sight hereabouts, and up to the end of the First World War it was harvested by women and children.

The main feature of Creich is its hilltop woods with magnificent views, once the hunting grounds of the earls of Fife. Its fourteenth-century church, with a sixteenth-century aisle, lies in ruin. Creich Castle remains within a farmstead and may be viewed from the approach road. There has been a castle here from at least the thirteenth century, but the sixteenth century L-plan ruin is remembered particularly today for its occupancy by the Beatons of Balfour, hereditary Stewarts of Fife.

Mary Beaton of Creich is remembered in Fife and Scottish romantic legend. In July 1548 Mary, Queen of Scots, left Scotland for France and in her suite was a group of young aristocratic men and women of Mary's age. Amongst them were her four 'Maries' – a corruption of the Icelandic word *maer* (maiden) and a pun on their Christian name – as maids-of-honour in Mary Beaton, Mary Seaton, Mary Fleming and Mary Livingstone. Mary Beaton was the daughter of Robert Beaton of Creich, and granddaughter of Sir John Beaton, the queen's Hereditary Keeper of Falkland Palace; her mother had been a French lady-in-waiting. Educated at the French court and by the Dominican nuns at Poissy, along with the other 'Maries', Mary Beaton and the 'Maries' were in the queen's entourage when she returned to Scotland in 1561. The pranks and escapades of the four 'Maries' and the queen brought scorn from such as John Knox – a death's head at any feast.

The A913 leads towards Newburgh via the parish of Dunbog. This sparsely populated area comprises the two estates of Aytounhill and Zetland, of which the latter's mansion was built in 1660. Dunbog House was established around 1580, but is much altered; the ruined sixteenth-century square keep of Collairnie Tower, home of the Barclays, lies towards the south-east. Mary, Queen of Scots visited in 1564. The tiny hamlet of Glenduckie lies to the north of Dunbog and was within the hunting grounds of the Earls of Fife. Ayton's seventeenth-century chapel of Dundermore lies in ruins; Dunbog Church of 1803 was altered in 1837 when a tower was added.

Lindores is the only village in Abdie parish and the Priest's Burn from nearby Lindores Loch to the Tay once supplied power for nine mills. Once too there were three lochs between Abdie Church and Dunbog, but Lindores is the only remaining one, although the 'bottomless' Black Loch and Red Myre on Weddersbie Hill are still close historic neighbours. Within sight of the loch is the site of the now-demolished Inchrye Abbey, a mansion of 1827, and Lindores House of 1820.

On the far shore of Lindores Loch lies Abdie Church (1827),

abutting the now-ruined church of St Magridin, dedicated in 1242 and in use until 1827. Within the churchyard is the memorial to Sir Frederick Lewis Maitland (1777–1839), captain of the British warship HMS *Bellerophon* which took the defeated Napoleon on board in 1815, transferring him to the Northumberland which carried him to exile on St Helena. Rear-Admiral Maitland of Lindores House died in his ship off India. The Denmylne Aisle of 1661 is worthy of note, as is the Pictish stone which now stands in a stone shelter by the churchyard gate. The stone shows a mirror symbol – long the token of aristocracy amongst the Picts – on one side, and a cauldron device, a V-rod design and a carved crescent on the other. At one time a thrifty Fifer carved a sundial on the stone which was once part of a nearby dyke. Among other tombstones is part of a defaced tomb effigy. Abdie House is a former manse and dates from 1840.

At Den of Lindores, the A983 links with Auchtermuchty and bypasses the old monastic farm sites of Grange of Lindores, Ormiston, Berryhill and Hilton.

From Lindores village the A913 leads back to Newburgh. On the left, opposite the quarry which gave Newburgh employment, stand the ruins of the fifteenth–sixteenth century Denmylne Castle; an early fortress of the earls of Fife stood here, after which the present castle was built by Alexander Balfour, to be abandoned when the policies were sold in 1772. A famous owner was Sir James Balfour of Kinnaird, Lord Lyon King of Arms, who, as a noted antiquarian, amassed a huge collection of historical manuscripts upon which many Scottish historic and legendary records are based. He was also involved in the survey of the sheriffdom of Fife used by the cartographer Timothy Pont.

Mary, Queen of Scots

Mary Stewart's name has already occurred in connection with several places in Fife, and it will continue to do so. The panel below summarises the queen's main Fife connections.

MARY, QUEEN OF SCOTS: FIFE ITINERARIES

[Born at Linlithgow Palace, 8 December 1842. Crowned at Stirling Castle, 9 September 1543. As Dowager Queen Consort of France, lands at Leith, 19 August 1561, to begin the second part of her Scottish reign to 1567.]

21 September 1561	Mary at St Andrews; lodges at Priory House hosted by half-brother James Stewart, Earl of Moray, Commendator of St Andrews Priory. On visits thereafter she lodged at 'Queen Mary's House' South Street. Gives audience to Sir Thomas Randolph, Queen Elizabeth I's ambassador to the Scottish court. Describes herself as 'a bourgeois wife' living 'with my little troop'. Spent time in gardening and archery. Is tutored by George Buchanan, Principal of St Leonard's College. Visits Earlshall Castle for the hunt; host Sir William Bruce.
10–23 March 1562	St Andrews. Has coach repaired.
24 March–1 April 1562	Falkland. In transit visits Dunfermline Abbey; host Commendator Robert Pitcairn. Other Dunfermline visits on Fife sojourns.
2 April–11 May 1562	St Andrews.
14 February 1563	Burntisland castle; host Sir Robert Melville of Murdocairney. An infatuated Pierre de Boscose de Châtelard discovered secreted in her bedroom. Repeats this serious *lesé majesté*; condemned to death 23 February, executed, St Andrews.
20 February 1563	St Andrews.
11 March 1563	Pitlethie for the hunt; host Sir

	William Bruce.
14 March 1563	St Andrews.
18–20 March 1563	Falkland.
25 March 1563	Pitlethie.
26 March–2 April 1563	St Andrews.
6 April 1563	Falkland.
18 April–16 May 1563	St Andrews.
12–13 March 1564	St Andrews.
23–26 March 1564	Falkland. Sometime around this time visits Strathendry House, hosted by the Forresters.
1 April 1564	Falkland.
4–7 April 1564	St Andrews.
11–18 April 1564	Falkland.
22–23 January 1565	Falkland.
24–25 January 1565	Visits Tower of Collairnie; host David Barclay, Bailie of Lindores.
26–27 January 1565	Visits Ballinbreich Castle; host Andrew Leslie, 4th Earl of Rothes. Around this time visits Creich home of her maid-of-honour Mary Beaton.
28 January 1565	Visits Balmerino Abbey; host John Hay, Principal Master of Requests at court and Commendator of Balmerino.
28 January–9 February 1565	St Andrews.
9–16 February 1565	In transit, visits Anstruther Castle, St Monans, Newark Castle; hosts Sandilands family.
17 February 1565	Visits Wemyss Castle; host John Wemyss; meets Henry Stewart, Lord Darnley. (Married Darnley, 29 July 1565.)
12–13 September 1565	St Andrews.
13 May 1568	Mary's army defeated at Langside. On 16 May she crossed the Solway into English exile. Executed at Fotheringay Castle, 8 February 1587.

2
FALKLAND AND THE HOWE OF FIFE

The whole of central and north-west Fife is dominated by the twin plugs of old volcanoes. These form the Lomond Hills which rise to almost 1,750 ft at West Lomond and 1,500 ft at East Lomond; these remain a part of 'a working landscape' and a portion of the 1986 designated Fife Regional Park. The Lomond Hills began to form in the Carboniferous Age, some 350 million years ago, and today the heather moorland is managed for red grouse, which share the hill with roe deer, foxes, chaffinches and wood pigeon; the rough grassland is tended for summer grazing. The six-mile-long quartz dolerite hills, rising above the moorland saddle, are best seen from the Howe of Fife, that verdant plain lying to the north of the hills. A 'howe' is a hollow, or a low-lying piece of ground, and the hills afford spectacular views of the whole county. From the east the hills rise ruggedly and steeply towards the north, but gradually and smoothly to the south. In the eighteenth century lead was worked and silver extracted on East Lomond in the region of Hangingmyre farm. A rumour of gold being found on West Lomond started a 'gold rush' in 1852; there are still relics of the old sandstone quarries and limekilns, and a keen eye can trace the medieval rig and plough-marks. At several locations over the hills stones with 'WR 1818' can be seen; these are boundary markers remembering when the rights of common grazing were taken away from the people and given to landowners in the parliamentary Act of 1815.

Set in the Lomond Hills are two interesting forts dating from the late first millennium BC to the early first millennium AD. East Lomond's Bronze Age cairn is reached from the established picnic area, and the West Lomond Fort, known as 'Maiden Castle', is reached from Craigmead car park. Around 1920 a slab bearing the Pictish figure of a bull was discovered at the south side of East Lomond Fort. Two stones feature in Lomond legend; at the foot of the West Lomond, 'Bonnet Stone' is said to cover the remains of a Pictish chieftain and may have sheltered a hermit. The 'Maiden Bower' nearby was a lovers' trysting place long thought to be the tombstone of a jilted local girl. Hereabouts too are the important reservoirs, including Harperleas, Holl and Ballo, with its castle ruin to recall the families who once worked the area.

Gateside

Many visitors enter the Howe of Fife along the A91 at Gateside, which was once known as Edenshead. Within the old village, off the main road, is an eighteenth-century smithy and adjoining houses, but the settlement is very much older, having been the site of the chapel of St Mary of Dungaitside belonging to the monks of Balmerino Abbey. The church of Edenshead, on the main road, dates from 1823. On the east edge of the village, down by the River Eden, is the Gateside Mills area, recalling how once the village was noted for its bobbin- and shuttle-mills, the suppliers of weaving factories all over the world. The bridge of Eden dates from the late eighteenth century and both Edenshead House and Gateside House go back to the eighteenth century, though the former was renovated in 1900.

The modern A91 follows the line of the old Ladybank–Kinross railway, and opposite the tourist car park stands the three-storeyed ruined sixteenth-century Corston Tower; this occupies the site of a fifteenth-century residence built by the prominent denizen of James II's court, John Ramsay. Opposite the junction with the road to Strathmiglo is Pitlour estate with its house of 1783–84, stables (c.1760), icehouse and nineteenth-century lodges. Strathmiglo was bypassed in 1969.

Strathmiglo

The old barony burgh of Strathmiglo (Eglismartin – 'the church of St Martin') has two distinct fifteenth-century districts, Kirklands and Templelands, recalling that the lands were once divided between the medieval collegiate church and pedagogy and the Knights Templar and thereafter the Knights Hospitallers. Of the former it is said that they were introduced into Scotland by David I around 1128. The templars, or Poor Knights of Christ and of the Temple of Solomon, were a religious order founded around 1120 in Jerusalem by a group of French knights. They were sworn to protect the pilgrim routes to the Holy Land, as were the Knights of the Order of the Hospital of St John of Jerusalem, who were landlords in Strathmiglo until the nineteenth century. The Templars and the Hospitallers were landowners in Fife rather than residents. Today Strathmiglo is divided in two by the River Eden which separates the more modern dwellings from the ancient heart.

Of the buildings within Strathmiglo the Tolbooth, with its open balustrade and octagonal spire, in the High Street, takes pride of place. Its stone came from Strathmiglo Castle, the mansion house of Sir William Scott of Balwearie, a courtier of James V; the house was refurbished to impress James V who, in the event, was underwhelmed and nicknamed it 'cairnie flappit' – a pile of stones that collapses; the mansion had fallen in ruins by 1734. The arms on the Tolbooth tower are of later landowners hereabouts, the Balfours of Burleigh. The village, once the home of prominent merchants who supplied Falkland Palace, has an interesting set of eighteenth–nineteenth century houses and taverns. One of the most unusual of Scotland's rights of way leads through Strathmiglo Inn; a sign above the passage door indicates the twenty-four-hour right of access to Back Dykes. By the picnic area is the California; the word means spring of cold water and the well has gushed forth here for countless generations. Although agriculture and supplying back-up services to Falkland Palace were once the staple breadwinning occupations of Strathmiglo, Skene Street still has cottages with the heavy ceiling beams once associated with the construction of handlooms. A. T. Hogg (1858–1927) was once described as the 'man who made Strathmiglo famous'; he pioneered the selling of boots by post and his 'Fife Boots' won international fame; the firm he founded still has a presence in the village as Hoggs Fife Footwear Company.

Strathmiglo manse originated in 1785 and the church with its bellcote dates from 1783–84, although there was a pre-Reformation church in the village dedicated to St Martin, Bishop of Tours. Once Strathmiglo's November Fair – to celebrate the Feast of St Martin –

was famous throughout Scotland, but James II caused it to be moved to Cupar in 1437. The pre-Reformation church was sited in the present burial ground. South of Strathmiglo are East and West Cash Feus, the eighteenth–nineteenth century dwellings and weavers' cottages; the feus once belonged to the third Marquess of Bute, the renovator of Falkland Palace.

Falkland

The village of Strathmiglo is linked to Falkland, the capital of the ancient Stewartry of Fife, by way of the A912 which cuts across the northern part of Falkland Estate. A working estate, it has a series of waymarked routes, an interesting adjunct to the enjoyment of Falkland Palace legend and history. These old royal hunting grounds have had a series of owners from the sixteenth century, but in 1820 the estate was sold by General George Moncrieff to Professor John Bruce and thereafter the estate was owned by the Bruces until its purchase in 1887 by the third Marquess of Bute. The House of Falkland, not to be confused with the Palace, lies on a plateau between the Mapsie and Mill Burns and was built during 1839–44 for Onesipherous and Margaret Tyndall-Bruce. The Tyndall-Bruce Monument on the Black Hill above Arraty Craigs is a large obelisk-type monument set up by Margaret Tyndall-Bruce in memory of her husband Onesipherous whose distinctive name is linked with the development of today's Falkland.

'A pretty little Town . . . a stately Palace' is how the Dutch engraver, John Slezer, described the weaving village when he saw it in the seventeenth century. Falkland was made a royal burgh in 1458 by James II and its buildings reflect the status and personalities of the courtiers and tradesmen who used to live in the medieval burgh.

From the A912, herein New Road and the Pleasance, the visitor enters Falkland's East Port and on the left, opposite the Palace, stands Moncrieff House. A two-storeyed seventeenth-century building thatched with Tay reeds, Moncrieff House has a marriage lintel dated 1610 and a signed plaque of the same date for Nicoll Moncrieff, King's Averiman, a servitor in charge of the royal stables of James VI. The Hunting Lodge Hotel (1607) next door also has carved and painted stones. Across Back Wynd is the steepled Georgian town house of 1801 with the arms of the burgh showing a stag sitting under an oak, remembering the forest of Falkland cleared by Oliver Cromwell's order of 1652. The town house, now a visitor centre and museum, fronts the old market square, in the centre of which is the Bruce Fountain (1856) with the arms of the burgh and those of the Keeper of the Palace who provided the fountain and the Gothic church of 1849; the manse of 1807 is in Chapel Yard. Next to the church is the memorial statue to the benefactor of all this, the ubiquitous Onesipherous Tyndall-Bruce. Around the square too are the eighteenth-century white-harled St Andrews House and Key House (1713), with its Angus roof slabs, once the Palace Inn.

Next to the town house is the Covenanter Hotel (1771) whose name related to the house in the south-west corner of the square, the birthplace of schoolmaster Richard Cameron (1648–80), the famous Covenanter – he is associated with the naming of the Cameronian Regiment in 1689.

Covenanters are well represented in Fife history and lore. The origins of the movement lie in the foolishly conceived religious, financial and prayer book policies of Dunfermline-born Charles I, pursued after his accession in 1625. The name Covenanters was given to the signatories of the resultant Scottish National Covenant of 1638, a document which pledged to uphold the Presbyterian faith against prelacy and popery. Further to this came the religious and military pact of 1643, wherein Scots Covenanters were committed to the presbyterianisation of all Great Britain and Ireland; this was known as the Solemn League and Covenant.

These engendered a following of fanatical Puritan funda-mentalists, who saw themselves as the 'Lord's Chosen People'; they also refused to sign the Oath of Allegiance after the Restoration of Charles II in 1660. Many of the main events of the Covenanting days, from the Bishops' Wars of 1639 and 1640 to the rebellion of the Covenanters in 1679, had repercussions in Fife, like the murder of Archbishop Sharp (see page 62).

Richard Cameron of Falkland was an important Covenanting leader. Son of a small shopkeeper, he became a schoolmaster and preacher and head of an extreme group of Covenanters known as the Cameronians. Pursued by government military he was defeated, killed and mutilated at Airds Moss by troops led by fellow-Fifer Andrew Bruce of Earlshall. Other Fife Covenanting personalities included Alexander Henderson (1583–1646), minister of Leuchars (1612), who helped draft the National Covenant; he was also chaplain to the Covenanting army. Sir Alexander Leslie, 1st Earl of Leven (c.1580–1661) also sponsored the Covenanting cause and became a general of the Covenanting army.

Covenanting meetings – conventicles – were held in such places as Covenanters' Glen, Glen Vale, West Lomond. Histories of such churches as Erskine Church, Dunfermline, indicate places where the National Covenant was signed (for example Dunfermline, 1638). Monuments to Covenanters can be found at such places as Cupar's old parish church of St Michael of Tarvit. A tombstone inscription:

> Here lie interred the heads of Laur[ence] Hay and Andrew Pitulloch, who suffered martyrdom at Edinburgh, July 13th, 1681, for adhering to the word of God, and Scotland's covenanted work of Reformation; and also one of the hands of David Hackstoun of Rathillet, who was most cruelly martyred at Edinburgh, July 30th, 1680.

> Our persecutors filled with rage,
> Their brutish fury to assuage
> Took heads and hands of martyrs off,
> That they might be the people's scoff.
> They Hackstoun's body cut asunder,
> And set it up a world's wonder
> In several places to proclaim,
> These monsters glory and their shame.

Falkland's Cross Wynd is lined by single-storied cottages, interrupted only by cobbled Parliament Square. Houses of varying dates and worthy of exploration are to be found in Mill Wynd, Castle Street and Back Wynd. Down Mill Wynd is the Stag Inn of 1680. The eighteenth-century Reading Room sub-station was restored by the old South of Scotland Electricity Board in 1960 and was once two houses, of which one was home to a family of thirteen. Around 1850 the lower house was used as a reading room, in which a local stonemason, Thomas Drysdale, read newspapers, tracts, pamphlets and books to the illiterate inhabitants of the burgh. Brunton House (1712), Brunton Street, was the home of the Simsons of Brunton, hereditary royal falconers.

Falkland Palace developed out of the fourteenth-century castle built by the family of Macduff, Thane of Fife. Today its site is at the back of the later palace set above the garden. In the fourteenth-century the castle passed to the Stewarts, and by 1458 it was being referred to as 'a palace'; its undoubted heyday was during the fifteenth and sixteenth centuries. The last royal resident of the

John Patrick, third Marquess of Bute, Rector of the
University of St Andrews. He supplied funds to excavate
the Augustinian priory at St Andrews cathedral site and
began a reconstruction programme. (Author's collection)

palace was Charles II in 1650, who was in Scotland for his coronation, and the palace fell into a state of disrepair after the Jacobite rising of 1715. Yet the palace retained its hereditary keeper, and it was Keeper Onesiphorous Tyndall-Bruce who was advised by Sir Walter Scott to restore the palace as a 'romantic ruin'. In 1887 John Crichton Stuart, third Marquess of Bute, acquired the keepership from the Tyndall-Bruces and undertook a massive programme of restoration. Today the palace is still in the ownership of the monarch and the Crichton Stuarts are still keepers, with the National Trust for Scotland as deputy keepers since 1952.

These days the visitor enters the palace by way of the gatehouse which dates from 1451 and bears the refurbished coats of arms of the Royal Lyon of Scotland, the Lyon of the Earls of Fife and the Arms of Stuart of Bute. Thence the visitor enters the South Range with its vaulted cellars and tapestry gallery and the most oustanding feature of all, the Chapel Royal, begun by James IV. The Crichton Stuarts are Roman Catholics and the chapel is used regularly. In the antechamber of the chapel are the colours of the Scots Guards who have had an association with the palace since Charles II 'christened' the regiment here in 1650. Part of the private quarters of the keepers of the palace may be seen in the drawingroom and the old library. The East Range dates from the days of James IV and contains the royal apartments.

Across the roofless second floor of the East Range is the king's bedchamber which was rebuilt by the third Marquess; here James V died in 1542. That year James' army was defeated by Henry VIII's forces at Solway Moss, a disaster to add to the death of his two infant sons in 1541. At Falkland James heard that his wife, Marie de Guise-Lorraine, had given birth to a daughter at Linlithgow Palace, West Lothian, on the Feast of the Immaculate Conception of the Virgin Mary, 8 December 1542. He declared the event the worst of his doom-laden life. At six days old the infant Mary became Queen of Scotland, for James turned his face to the wall of his chamber at Falkland, and as he died he muttered sourly about the fate of his family, the Stewarts; 'The devil go with it,' he said. 'It came with a lass and it will go with a lass.'

In this prognostication James was as premature as his daughter. Although the House of Stewart had been founded by Marjorie

King James VI and I. Falkland Palace was a favoured
residence of the king who made several trips to
Fife to hunt. His charters show that he gave grants for
several Fife properties to court favourites. (Author's collection)

Bruce, daughter of Robert the Bruce, when she married Walter
Stewart in 1315, their house was to be royal for years to come; the
line came to an end in 1714 with the death of Queen Anne.

Beyond the foundations of the North Range lie the palace
gardens replanted as a modern formal garden. Further back is the
1539 royal tennis court, built only eight years after Henry VIII's
tennis court at Hampton Court.

Murder at Falkland

David, Duke of Rothesay was born on 24 October 1378, the eldest
son of the weak and vacillating Robert III and Queen Annabella

Drummond. Along with his uncle, Robert, Duke of Albany (1339–1420), they were the premier dukes of Scotland. Because Scotland was in a chaotic state at the time, and Robert III was unfit to rule by temperament and disability, the Duke of Albany had real power as Guardian of the Kingdom. In 1399 the Three Estates appointed Rothesay to the post of lieutenant of Scotland to help keep order in the realm. Uncle and nephew were set on a collision course of rivalry.

Chroniclers aver that Rothesay was inadequate in character and not fitted to exercise impartial authority, being bent on thwarting his ambitious uncle. Although he was betrothed to Euphemia, sister of David, Earl of Crawford, and then to Elizabeth, daughter of George, Earl of March, in 1400 Rothesay married Marjorie, daughter of Archibald, Earl of Douglas. His flouting of the Earl of March's daughter caused the earl to switch his allegiance to King Henry IV of England, greatly to Scotland's disadvantage. So at the behest of the Earl of Douglas and the Duke of Albany, Rothesay was arrested 'between Nydie and Struthers' in Fife and via a dungeon in St Andrews Castle was finally imprisoned at Falkland Castle.

Here legend and history blend. On 26 March 1402 Rothesay died in circumstances that were suspicious. On 16 May 1402, on Albany's prompting, the Scottish Estates of the Realm examined the circumstances aurrounding Rothesay's death and issued the official declaration that Rothesay 'departed this life through the divine Dispensation and not otherwise'. Thus Albany and his clique were officially exonerated of all guilt in the matter, except amongst gossips, their court enemies and future historians.

Rothesay's death at Falkland was a story strand in Sir Walter Scott's *The Fair Maid of Perth* (1828), where he has Albany lure Rothesay to Falkland to his death. In this Scott is following the version of events set down by such historians as Hector Boece. Records show, however, that the Constable of Falkland, John Wricht of Burnturk, and Rothesay's Chamberlain in Fife, Sir John de Ramorgny (d.1403) may have been the actual murderers by starving the prince to death. John Wricht was later declared traitor for involvement in Rothesay's death. It may be added that modern historians suggest that Rothesay may have died of dysentery.

Rothesay was buried at the abbey of Lindores where 'numerous miracles' were reported at his tomb, a vault despoiled at the Reformation.

The legend of Falkland's unusual royal visitor

In the summer of 1496 a curious group of foreign soldiers and Irish hangers-on arrived at Falkland to be feasted at the court of James IV. No locals, who were used to witnessing regular entourages coming and going from the palace, had ever seen Perkin Warbeck before. But gossip soon circulated that the young man was no less than Richard, Duke of York, the younger son of King Edward IV of England, who had long been thought dead as one of the murdered 'Princes in the Tower'. The young man had proclaimed himself King Richard IV of England in 1494 and was bent on overthrowing the usurper, Henry VII. Falkland turned out to view what was to become a comic royal circus.

Perkin Warbeck was, in reality, the son of John de Werbeque (or Osbek), said to be Controller of Tournai, Picardy, and born around 1474. Although vain, foolish and incompetent, he was being used by Henry VII's Yorkist enemies in England and the continent, in a plot to threaten the Tudor dynasty. Warbeck travelled through Europe gaining support and recognition, and by 1492 he was accepted by Edward IV's sister, Margaret of Burgundy, as her nephew and he was coached in his imposter's role.

In Ireland Perkin Warbeck raised an invasion force and eventually turned to James IV for help. James saw advantages in supporting Warbeck in his ongoing thwartings of England's powers and even married him off to his cousin, Lady Catherine Gordon, daughter of the Earl of Huntly. At Falkland James and Warbeck plotted an invasion of England. This invasion ended up as hardly more than destructive raids by the Scots army in the valleys of the Tweed and Till and into Northumberland. Eventually, seeing the uselessness of the campaign, James IV returned to the hunt at Falkland, but for his own ends continued paying Warbeck a pension and funding his further exploits.

Leaving Scotland in 1497 Perkin Warbeck's last refuge was in Cornwall, where he landed at Whitesands Bay to rouse disaffected

Cornishmen. His new campaign was unsuccessful and Perkin Warbeck fled the field to seek sanctuary at Beaulieu Abbey, Hampshire. There he was captured and brought to the English court; later he was imprisoned in the Tower and was hanged at Tyburn for treason on 23 November 1499, aged twenty-five. Thus Falkland and Fife had once more witnessed events and characters whose stories would be interlarded in local legend and the nation's history.

Freuchie

The B936 out of Falkland links Newton of Falkland with the village of Freuchie. Newton had a long association with brewing and malting, and the late nineteenth-century Bonthrone Maltings, with their pagoda-like outlets on the roofs, are a reminder of the old trade. Balreavie Cottage (1735), was once a brewery too, and after that a school. There are still a few eighteenth-century weavers' cottages in the hamlet.

There is a local tradition that Freuchie was the place where French masons dwelt who worked on Falkland palace in the sixteenth century and that the village served as a place of exile for disgraced courtiers from Falkland; modern-day Freuchie folk recall that within living memory people in this part of Fife used such dismissive phrases as: 'Awa tae Freuchie, whaur the Froggies live'. Freuchie also had a linen factory founded by the Lumsdens in about 1870. The Albert Tavern is eighteenth century and the Lomond Hills Hotel in the High Street is dated 1753. The church dates from 1875.

Kingskettle

Kingskettle lies to the north-east of Freuchie and by tradition takes its name from *catel*, a battle; local legend has it one was fought between the Scots and Danes near the modern village. There is a pleasant local legend too that says the battle gave Scotland its emblem of the thistle. The tale recounts that the Scots were roused from their slumbers when one of the invading Danes trod on a thistle and let out a yell. In truth, the thistle head did not make its appearance as a Scottish emblem until the minting of the groats of

James III in 1471. The name Kingskettle first appears in a charter of 1541, by which time the lands hereabouts were crown property within the hunting forest of Falkland.

Known locally as Kettle, the old parish takes in the villages of Kettlebridge, eighteenth-century Balmalcolm, Coaltown of Burnturk and Muirhead, anciently known as Lathrisk. Although there are Iron Age hillforts in the vicinity, and Bronze Age relics have been found nearby, the earliest written record of Kingskettle is the grant of lands by Malcolm IV to Duncan, Earl of Fife, in 1166. Most of the folk of Kettle formerly earned their living from the linen industry, producing material for shirts and window blinds. The first power loom was opened at Kingskettle in 1864 and the last one was dismantled in 1929. Coal- and lime-working took place at Burnturk and Pitlessie respectively.

Once a stop on the old turnpike road from Newport to Pettycur, Kingskettle retains its mostly eighteenth-century villas and cottages set round the nucleus of the elegant Tudor Gothic church of 1832 which replaced the older church of St Ethernaseus, *circa* 1636, which itself succeeded the church dedicated by Bishop de Bernham in 1243. The former manse dates from 1792. The earliest parish church is said to have been that of Lathrisk dating from the fourteenth century, now thought to be a part of Lathrisk House of 1710–80, and there are sites of pre-Reformation chapels at Clatto and Chapel-Kater. Near Kettlebridge once stood Bankton House, the long-vanished home of James Russell, one of the murderers of Archbishop James Sharp in 1679 (see page 62).

Pitlessie

Pitlessie, the only village in the old parish of Cults, grew as a rural community with employment not only on the neighbouring estates but in the 19th century Priestfield Maltings and the lime works. Etymologists believe that Cults derived from the Gaelic *quylt*, a 'resting place'. Certainly the sandstone Cults Kirk with its small nineteenth-century session house, set at a distance from Pitlessie at Kirkton, was a place of rest and refreshment from its construction in 1795 during the ministry of the Revd David Wilkie.

The Revd Wilkie's son, also David, was born at the adjoining manse on 18 November 1785. Young David's mother was the daughter of a Pitlessie miller, and he attended the parish schools of Pitlessie and Kettle and thereafter the academy of Cupar. In 1799 he began to study art at the Trustees' Academy at Edinburgh. At the age of nineteen in 1804, he returned to the manse and began work on his first famous picture, *Pitlessie Fair* (now in the National Gallery of Scotland), which contains no less than 140 faces, many of which he sketched while attending services in the parish church. The picture contains a self-portrait and depictions of his father and siblings. In Wilkie's time there were two fairs held at Pitlessie for the sale of cattle, in May and October, and it is thought that the May fair inspired Wilkie. The site of the fairs was in the middle of Pitlessie near the house called 'Burnbrae' (once a public house). Many of young Wilkie's early drawings were to be found on the walls of the manse attic, but they were destroyed by fire in 1926. Another of Wilkie's famous pictures, *The Village Politicians*, also has its origins in Cults. In time David Wilkie won fame as a portrait painter, and in 1823 he succeeded Sir Henry Raeburn as the King's Limner (painter) in Scotland; when Sir Thomas Lawrence died in 1830 Wilkie was selected as Painter-in-Ordinary to King George IV. Wilkie was knighted in 1836; in 1841 he died aboard ship while travelling home from the Near East and was buried at sea. His memorial is by the pulpit in Cults church.

Opposite Clatto Hill, to the south of Pitlessie, is Devon Wood and the place called Torloisk; it takes its name from *tor* and *Loisgthe*, meaning 'hill of the burning', an undoubted Pictish association with the feasts of Beltane and Samhuinn, the two divisions of the Celtic year, in May and November. At these times the arrival of summer and winter were marked with bonfires. The fires of Torloisk were probably a hilltop link with the Perthshire mountains of Ben Ledi, Schiehallion and Ben More.

These hills were a popular area for the royal hunt from Falkland. Over the slopes of Kirkforthar they would race to Devon Common with its links with the *Damnonii* tribe of Roman times, to Kilmux Wood, pausing for refreshments at Mildeans and Black Tankard. These wild hills were the haunts too of the Setons, who regularly left their now-vanished stronghold of Clatto Castle to persecute their neighbours. The old gibbet tree of Clatto was still to be seen until it fell in a gale in 1927; thereafter the gibbet irons (in which the miscreant's body was hung) were long displayed at Clatto farm.

Ladybank

Known prior to the twelfth century as Moss of Monegae, Ladybank was used as a peat-cutting area by the monks of Lindores Abbey, who called it 'Our Lady Bog'. Prior to the construction of burns and drainage like the great Rossie Drain from the mid-eighteenth century, the area was very marshy with a loch. 'Lady's Bog' was changed to 'Ladybank' when the railway station was being planned: today the name Monkstown, a district alongside the B938 and the only part of Ladybank to pre-date the railway construction of the late 1840s, is the sole memorial to the holy brothers of Lindores.

The North British Railway Company's (later LNER) junction for Perth and Kinross gave Ladybank a great boost. The town was made a burgh in 1878 and was noted for its linen and maltings; Ladybank Maltings were demolished in 1986. The town's parish church was built 1874–76. In Ladybank Masonic Hall, by the railway bridge and opposite the obelisk gates to the now-vanished Ramornie House, H.H. Asquith, Liberal Prime Minister from 1908 to 1916, and MP for East Fife, made many of his great speeches. A plaque at the Masonic Hall commemorates the fiftieth anniversary of Asquith's entrance to parliament in 1886.

Along the A92 from Pitlessie the largest house in the area is Crawford Priory, set within its own wooded estate which once sported a deer park. It was built in 1813 by Lady Mary Lindsay Crawford, sister of George, thirteenth Earl of Crawford, on the site of a lodge built in 1755 by Lady Mary's father, Viscount Garnock. The style of the house is Gothic, with castle-monastic overtones which reflect Lady Mary's interest in things medieval. Noted as an eccentric, Lady Mary died in 1833 and was buried at Walton Hill (to the south-east of the priory) in the isolated mausoleum in the form of a Roman temple, built by the twelfth Earl of Glasgow in 1758. Lady Mary's obsession with animal welfare caused her to set an elaborate gravestone near the Priory stables to her pet deer. The estate passed to the Earl of Glasgow in 1833 and he made alterations and improvements in 1871; his son-in-law Lord Cochrane of Cults lived at the Priory until his death in 1951. The Priory is now a forlorn shell. Across the way from Crawford Priory ruins at Edenwood can be seen the elevations of a Roman marching camp.

Fernie Castle

Just north-east of Letham, in the Bow of Fife, stands Fernie Castle, which incorporates the old sixteenth-century tower of Fernie which legend says was on the site of a keep belonging to the equally legendary Macduff, Earl of Fife. With the barony of Fernie went the titles of Forester of Falkland and Constable of Cupar. Fernie Castle fell to the Balfour family of Mountquhanie around the fifteenth century and was held by a cadet branch of the Balfours up to 1965, after which it became a hotel. The castle is constructed on an L-plan but has been much altered, although its sixteenth-century fortalice is discernible.

The stables and icehouse date from the 1820s. Fernie Castle's neighbour, the old estate of Cunnoquhie, sports a classical mansion remodelled in 1852. Another aristocratic neighbour is Over Rankeillour House built between 1796 and 1800 by John Hope, fourth Earl of Hopetoun, who died in 1823. The surrounding area is dominated by The Mount, which displays a monument of 1826 to the said John Hope, a lieutenant-general in the Peninsular War of 1808–14. The Mount is associated with Sir David Lindsay (c. 1486–1555), poet and Lyon King of Arms. Sir David was born in Monimail parish, spent much of his life here, and passed his latter days in the shelter of Mount Hill in seclusion. Educated at Cupar Grammar School and St Andrews, Sir David Lindsay's poems may be described as 'tracts of the times', and perhaps his most famous is *Ane Satyre of the Thrie Estaitis* which castigates the evils of church, state and society.

Monimail

Its name is thought to derive from the Gaelic *monadhmaol*, 'the bare hill': Monimail village and its environs were once owned by the See of St Andrews and there was an episcopal residence here from the days of Bishop William Lamberton (1298–1328), of which

Monimail Tower remains as a relic. Certainly John Hamilton, the last medieval archbishop of St Andrews, still used it as a residence in the mid-sixteenth century. While at Monimail, an old legend goes, the archbishop was tended by one Girolamo Cardano of Milan, an astrologer and physician, who is purported to have used water from a local well in his potions to cure the asthmatic archbishop; this mineral well was long described as 'Cardan's Well'.

Monimail Tower, excavated in 1987, is ascribed to Archbishop Hamilton's predecessor, Cardinal David Beaton, and is all that remains of a larger edifice overlooking the parish graveyard in which are buried the earls of Leven, the Balfours and the Melvilles. Monimail Church was built 1794–97 to replace its ruinous pre-Reformation predecessor, and its Gothic tower dates from 1811.

Once dubbed the most important Renaissance building in Scotland after Holyrood, Melville House at Monimail dates from 1692. Built for George Melville, first Earl of Melville, who was imprisoned at Burntisland for his support of the exiled Charles II, its mile-long beech-lined approach avenue was formerly considered one of the finest entries of any mansion. Work on the main house continued until 1703. Ownership of the house and estate went out of the Melville family hands piecemeal during 1938–50 and the property has functioned as a private school and a Fife Council property from 1975 to 2001, wherein it was bought by property developers. The gardens of 1697–1825 were also sold off in the 1980s.

Collessie village was long an agricultural centre with handloom weaving as a subsidiary industry and relics of Bronze Age settlements are to be found in the vicinity. A local legend has it that Collessie was one of the regular haunts of James V when he was resident at Falkland Palace; he was fond of wandering about the countryside incognito as 'the guid man of Ballengeich' – the latter being a gulley at the foot of Stirling Castle used by the king as a secret exit. Many tales are told of the king's encounters with his subjects who failed to penetrate his disguise as he walked along the shores of the now-drained Rossie Loch from which eighteenth-century Rossie House takes its name. The modern village of Collessie has several interesting eighteenth- and nineteenth-century weavers' cottages, all clustering in narrow roads round the square-towered church of 1839. In medieval times the neighbourhood supplied part of the living of the abbey of Lindores and the see of St Andrews.

Auchtermuchty

In medieval days wild boars rooted in the oaks, swamps and forests of Auchtermuchty and gave their name to the Pictish settlement called *uachdarmuc*, 'high ground of the wild boar'. The area was deemed important enough for the Roman legionaries to construct a 60-acre temporary camp at Auchtermuchty wherein the modern A91 road to Cupar cuts its northern boundary. Historians date the camp to the campaigns of the Emperor Septimus Severus and his son Caracalla, 208–210 AD, with the suggestion that Pictish Auchtermuchty was on a route Severus took through Fife from the Forth, at North Queensferry, to the River Tay at Carpow camp. Artefacts found on site in 1988 suggest that the folk of Auchtermuchty used the ditches of the Roman camp as rubbish tips in medieval times. Granted a charter in 1517, which elevated it into a royal burgh, Auchtermuchty exhibits its antiquity in crow-stepped gables, red pantiles, thatched roofs and bridges. Macduff House, named after a previous edifice on the site belonging to the earls of Fife, stands on the west side of the main square and is the oldest house extant, dating from 1592. From this house, legend has it that Lord Sempill was married to Mary Livingstone, one of Mary, Queen of Scots' ladies.

Auchtermuchty Church was built in 1779–81 and enlarged in 1838. A curious Fife legend is associated with the church. It appears that the folk of Auchtermuchty were once noted for their piety; so much so that they attracted the attention of the Devil bent on corrupting them. So he visited the village one day disguised as a Presbyterian minister and so inspired all that heard him with the eloquence of his sermons that he was much fêted. A local, one Robin Ruthven, was harder to convince of the new preacher's probity, and was moved to raise the hem of the minister's gown to reveal his cloven feet. Unmasked the Devil made a hasty retreat. Thereafter wrote poet James Hogg, it was difficult to convince Auchtermuchty folk by sermonising. Said Hogg, 'for [*an Auchtermuchty man*] thinks aye that he sees the cloven foot peeping out from beneath every sentence'.

Auchtermuchty Tolbooth dates from 1728. The bell of the Tolbooth was said to be one of those purloined from Lindores Abbey after the Reformation. Auchtermuchty is on record as having gone bankrupt in 1818 when creditors sold up the assets of the burgh.

Sixteenth-century Myers Castle, just south of Auchtermuchty, was built by John Scrymgeour on the estate given by James I to his English page Robert Croxwell for faithful service, and enlarged in 1822 and 1890. The castle was restored in the 1960s. Part of the old Myers estate now forms the village of Dunshelt; according to legend, the name is a corruption of 'Dane's Hold', a local encampment of invading Danes who were defeated at Falkland Moor.

3
THE EASTERN HEARTLAND

Cupar

The historic route of entry into Cupar, by the West Port is still traced by way of the A91 from Stirling to West Fife. That medieval way carries the much expanded modern traffic down Hangman's Road, past the ruin of Carslogie House (1590), erstwhile home of the Clephane family, into Cupar. Legend recalls that Alan Clephane of Carslogie fought alongside Robert the Bruce at Bannockburn, losing a hand in the conflict. The king ordered a steel artificial limb made for him which was preserved as a family heirloom to be mentioned in the will of Margaret Clephane, Marchioness of Northampton (d.1830).

Historically Cupar was the centre of the judiciary for the county of Fife as well as being the county town; from the Middle Ages people travelled from afar to have their wrongs redressed at Cupar. From this time too Cupar was a prominent commercial centre; cattle and sheep were brought here for the flesher, hides for the cordwainer, wool for the tailor and weaver, and grain for the miller and baker. Linen manufacture was also a prominent trade. When financially embarrassed, monarchs sought help from the thriving little town run as a tight ship by the burgesses and enterprising Merchant Guild.

Once Cupar had a thriving trade with Holland, and from 1428 James II confirmed for the burgh the already established freedom of the Water of Eden and the right to use 'the Port of Mottray', modern Guardbridge, 'without any impediment or obstacle'. Cupar was granted a charter as a royal burgh by Robert II in 1381, but the town had been a place of importance much earlier. Here in 1275 died Alexander III's wife Margaret, daughter of Henry III of England, and a year later Alexander held an assembly of the three estates: clergy, nobility and burgesses – forerunner of the Scottish parliament.

For many centuries Castlehill, on which the Thanes of Fife had their stronghold, was the focal point of Cupar. Castlehill Centre (school of 1727 and 1846) is on the site of the ancient fortress, and here it is said that Sir David Lindsay of the Mount gave the first performance of his *Ane Satyre of the Thrie Estates*. J.G. Mackay, in his *History of Fife and Kinross*, leaves a picture of the first production: 'On the 7th of June at seven in the morning every man, woman and child who could get there gathered at Castle Hill and the play began. It consisted of seven parts or interludes loosely slung together. It took nine hours to perform, but the audience, who had breakfasted well in the old Scots style, were allowed intervals for refreshment and if they followed the advice of the messenger who announced the play, "With gude stark wyne your flagons see ye fill", they were probably well sustained throughout.' The performance was in the open air, so those who tired could leave, but probably few left so rare an entertainment, for Lindsay's satire went straight to the heart of current opinion; it cut to the quick. It was a piece of history, and an acted sermon. As Sir Walter Scott said of Lindsay's work:

> The flash of that satiric rage,
> Which, bursting on the early stage
> Branded the vices of the age,
> And broke the keys of Rome.

An English envoy who saw the play performed before the Court at Linlithgow wrote that James V after seeing it 'called upon [Gavin Dunbar] the Bishop of Glasgow, being Chancellor, and diverse other bishops and exhorted them to reform their fashions and manners of living, saying that unless they did so he would send some of the proudest of them unto his uncle [Henry VIII] in England'. A shock had been sent through society that day at Cupar.

Many of the landed gentry had their town houses in Cupar, like the Prestons of Preston Lodge (1623) and Lord Balmerino in the Bonnygate (Boudingait of 1580) and the Earl of Rothes at Millgate. Cupar's four old ports (town gates) have vanished, but the street layout to the north of the Eden is largely as it was in medieval times; Crossgate (the medieval *Vicus Crucis* of 1505) and Bonnygate being the most ancient 'ways'.

Standing at the corner of St Catherine Street (the A91) is Cupar's Mercat Cross of 1683; it was placed here in renovated form to commemorate Queen Victoria's Diamond Jubilee in 1897. For decades the cross stood at a site further into Crossgate, but at the end of the eighteenth century it had fallen into such a dangerous state of disrepair that it was to be broken up. The pillar and unicorn, however, were rescued by Colonel Wemyss of Wemysshill who caused it to be set up on Wemyss Hill to mark the spot where the treaty of 1559 was signed between the Queen-Regent Marie de Guise-Lorraine and the Protestant Lords of the Congregation; here it remained until 1897. Between the present site of the cross and St Catherine Street stood the old Tolbooth, and the story of its demolition is worthy of note as a tale of civic pride and unity between burgesses and the council. The Tolbooth had three floors: the lowest was a flat, foul, noisome den, almost entirely subterranean, which served as a jail and was known as the 'Black Hole'. The middle floor, called the 'Weigh House', contained the public weigh beam, while the top floor housed those imprisoned for debt. The debtors endured many hardships but were slightly better off than the miscreants in the 'Black Hole', but the debtors depended for sustenance on the alms of charitable citizens which were placed in bags raised and lowered from the windows. The provost of the day put forward the proposal that the whole dreadful place should be removed, but there was opposition from local law officers, and a messenger was sent to Edinburgh to secure an interdict from the Court of Session. In the meantime the provost called up the burgesses who, by the light of torches and bonfires, destroyed the Tolbooth before the interdict could arrive.

A large part of the old town has been swept away at different times to satisfy the demands of modernisation, and these demolitions included the old closes and outside stairs that gave the town so much of its character. One relic of the past does exist, though, in the parish church. Records show that there was a church dedicated to the Blessed Virgin some distance to the north of the present site in Kirkgate. The church was in decay by 1415 and the church dedicated to St Christopher was erected as a substitute; this was demolished in 1785 to make way for the present structure which was remodelled in 1882; the spire of 1620 remains. Nearby is the old churchyard which legend says contains the severed heads of the Covenanters Laurence Hay and Andrew Pitulloch who suffered for their religious beliefs. Other buildings of note in Cupar are the County Buildings (1816 and 1925), the Town Hall (1817) and the steeple of St John's Church (1877) and the Corn Exchange (1862).

Burgh schools were mentioned at Cupar from the early fourteenth century and the modern Bell–Baxter School evolved from two local educational foundations, the Madras Academy founded by Dr Andrew Bell in 1831 and the education institute 'for young ladies' founded in 1871 by Lady Baxter of Kilmaron Castle. An interesting school, however, was set up at the medieval Dominican monastery, which was located at the foot of Castlehill. Dedicated to St Catherine, the fourth-century virgin and martyr, the monastery was founded by Duncan, Earl of Fife, in 1348; the house was merged with the Dominican property at St Andrews in 1519 and the land of the friars was given to the burgh by James VI in 1572. It seems that nursery accommodation was located in the monastery precincts for the care and education of the royal children. The monastery buildings fell to Michael Balfour, dubbed a traitor in 1579 for his part in the murder of Henry Stuart, Lord Darnley, and the now-vanished monastery was the mansion of the Lord of Balgarvie.

On 5 October 1785 the folk of Cupar were agog at the arrival of one Vincente Lunardi. He had appeared in a most unorthodox way, alighting from a balloon in a field at Coaltown of Callinge, near Ceres, after a 46-mile flight from Edinburgh. Lunardi, born at Lucca, Italy, in 1759, was a pioneer balloonist; conceited, foppish yet sophisticated, Lunardi was a daring adventurer who astonished the Fifers of his day. Fife aristocrats such as Lord Balgonie, who had made the Grand Tour, were all conversant with the world's first aeronauts, Pilâtre de Rozier and the Marquis d'Arlandes, who made a test flight in a balloon from the Château de la Muette, Paris, on 21 November 1783. Now aeronautics had come to Fife. Writing from the library of his host Lord Leven's mansion of Melville House, Lunardi left the first ever description of Fife from the air. Cupar fêted him well, including a dinner with the provost and magistrates and a presentation, Lunardi said, of the Freedom of the Burgh. To this he added the Freedom of St Andrews, honorary membership of the Royal and Ancient Golf Club – he took twenty-one strokes at the first tee – several Fife agricultural societies and drinking clubs as well as the attentions of 'upwards of a hundred beautiful ladies' at a St Andrews Assembly Ball. Lunardi died at the convent of Barbadinos, Lisbon, on 31 July 1806, but his flight to Fife was never forgotten. As the Revd Mr Arnot of Ceres observed at the time for the *Edinburgh Evening Courant* 'succeeding generations would venerate those who saw and spoke to Lunardi'. Indeed mementoes of Lunardi were much sought after from medallions with his head to fragments of ribbons with which he decorated his balloon. In Fife in 1832 one old lady, in great distress, advertised a large reward for her lost fragment.

Cupar's railway station and bridge date from 1847, and by the bridge is one of Fife's very few public statues; this honours David Maitland Makgill Crighton of Rankeillour, born 1801, a well-known radical politician. Remembered too in the property known as 'The Chancellor's House' is John Campbell, son of the parish minister, who attained the highest legal office in Britain. Created Lord Campbell in 1841, he held the offices of Lord Chancellor of Ireland and Chief Justice of England, and became Lord Chancellor of Great Britain in 1859.

To the north-west of Cupar lies Kilmaron Castle site, built in 1815 on the fifteenth-century estate of the Pitblado family by Admiral Maitland on ground long considered to be sanctified by the presence of a chapel dedicated to St Roan. The property was formerly the home of the educational philanthropist Sir David Baxter of Dundee, who died at Kilmaron in 1872.

Fife assassins

Property owners at Cupar, Kilconquhar and Rankeillour were involved in two famous Scottish assassinations. David Rizzio, an Italian musician, had come to Scotland in the entourage of the ambassador of Savoy, Rizzio becoming secretary to Mary, Queen of Scots. His supposed influence over the queen was disliked by the Protestant courtiers, including Mary's husband, Henry Stewart, Lord Darnley, and Protestants in general looked upon Rizzio as a papal spy. Consequently a group of Protestant lords, together with

Darnley, murdered Rizzio in the pregnant queen's presence at Holyrood, 9 March 1566, to the applause of such as John Knox. His body was left with over fifty stab wounds.

Perpetrators of the murder were identified as Patrick, third Lord Ruthven; Andrew Bellenden (the Bellendens held Kilconquhar estate until 1634); George Douglas (the Douglases had a wide range of property in Fife) – he struck the first blow with Darnley's dagger; Thomas Scott; Henry Yairr (later executed; he also murdered a Dominican priest on another occasion).

Many were party to the crime by implication; one such was James Makgill of Nether Rankeillour, a lawyer who later sat as Lord Rankeillour of Sessions; he also became Scots ambassador to the court of Queen Elizabeth I and died in 1579.

Henry Stewart, Lord Darnley, was born about 1545 and married Mary, Queen of Scots on 29 July 1565. It was when Mary was a guest of Sir John Wemyss at Wemyss Castle that she first met Darnley. Described by one Scots courtier as 'an agreeable nincompoop', Darnley's petulant arrogance made him many enemies amongst the nobility. By 1566 he was estranged from the queen. While recuperating from a bout of syphilis at Kirk o'Field, Edinburgh, his residence was blown up on 10 February 1567. Darnley's body was discovered in the garden; he had been strangled.

Amongst the key players in the murder plot were, James Hepburn, fourth Earl of Bothwell (*c.* 1535–78), who became Mary's third husband.

Amongst the lesser fry was Michael Balfour, eldest son of Sir James Balfour of Pittendreich, who owned properties in Cupar which had belonged to the *Fratres Predicatores* (preaching friars); these properties were forfeited when Balfour was declared a traitor.

Dairsie

Dairsie village, with its nineteenth-century cottages, is set in rolling farmland. The village was formerly one of linen weavers, many from Flanders, and Dairsie was once called Osnaburg after the Flemish linen. It is thought that Dairsie was part of a twelfth-century *thanage* with a church of that date re-dedicated to the Blessed Virgin in 1243 by David de Bernham, Bishop of St

Dairsie Bridge across the River Eden dates from around 1530.
On the hill stands the Church of St Mary, built by Archbishop
John Spottiswood in 1621. (STARALP)

Andrews. In historical terms the real focus of Dairsie is to the
south. Standing above the River Eden, Dairsie Church and castle
are the historic core of the parish. The church, with its hexagonal
belltower, remains essentially as it was when completed for John
Spottiswoode, Archbishop of St Andrews, in 1621, although its roof
was changed around 1800. Above the doorway is the armorial
cartouche with the archbishop's coat of arms and the motto set in
lead: *Dilexi de corum domus Tuae* – 'I have loved the habitation of
this house', from Psalm 26:8. The church interior was refurbished
in 1900. Today Dairsie folk worship in the plainer former United
Free Kirk (erected 1843, restored 1877) in the village.

From the thirteenth century the bishops, and after 1475 the
archbishops of St Andrews, had a residence at Dairsie; probably a
fortified house on the foundations of the present reconstructed
castle abutting the church. Certainly a 'parliament' of nobles was
held here in 1335, and it is said that David II spent part of his
boyhood at Dairsie. In the sixteenth and seventeenth centuries

Dairsie became associated with the Learmonths and the Spottiswoodes who served the crown and church to great personal advantage. Archbishop John Spottiswoode rebuilt the late fourteenth-century bridge over the Eden, which had been restored by Archbishop James Beaton, and added towers to the castle to give it a Z-plan structure. It is said that the archbishop composed a large part of his *History of the Church of Scotland* (1655) at Dairsie Castle.

Balmullo

The busy A91 leads to Balmullo past Pittormie. The house dates from 1867 with a 1764 pediment, but the steadings are of 1855 and the icehouse is dated 1862. On the hill above Muirhead stands the sixteenth-century L-shaped fortified house of Pitcullo restored in 1971. Balmullo sits at the foot of Lucklawhill. The redstone quarry at the side of Lucklawhill is a landmark for miles, and paths and drives all over this part of the country are laid with Lucklaw chippings.

At one time Balmullo was the home of Martin Anderson, who won national reputation as a cartoonist under the pseudonym of Cynicus. He was one of the pioneers of the picture postcard and his factory at Tayport reproduced his satirical lampoons. An eccentric socialist, Anderson built his redstone Cynicus Castle as a folly on the grand scale and it had commanding views of the area. Although the dwelling was never completed, Anderson packed it with treasures from ancient Egypt. Anderson died in 1932 and his castle was demolished in 1939. Some of the older Balmullo houses contained handlooms for weaving the locally grown flax.

Leuchars

Below Balmullo stands Leuchars junction station, across the Mottray Burn, which joins the Moonzie Burn to empty into the River Eden at Guardbridge. Once the junction for trains to St Andrews and the East Neuk, Leuchars station won national fame when it was 'attacked' and set afire by suffragettes before the first World War. Although bypassed today the village of Leuchars retains a historical jewel in its twelfth-century church with arguably the

The Norman apse and eastern elevation of
Leuchars Church, with fine examples of blind
arcading. (STARALP)

best Romanesque features in Scotland. Sited on a mound in the
centre of the village, the church appears to have been built between
1183–87 and was dedicated in 1244 to St Athernase. The chancel and
distinctive apse remain and a new nave was added in the nineteenth
century; the church's arcaded decoration is a delight. Within is the
memorial to Sir William Bruce who fought at the Battle of Flodden
in 1513 and lived to found Earlshall Castle in 1546.

Earlshall stands a half a mile to the east of Leuchars and is still a
private home. In the fourteenth century this area was the estate of
the Duke of Albany, as Earl of Fife, but in time part of it was
granted to the Moneypennys of Pitmilly; the estate came into the
ownership of the Bruces by 1495. Later it passed to the Hendersons
of Fordell who sold the castle and estate in 1852. The whole fell into
decay but was acquired by R.W.R. Mackenzie of Stormontfield
who commissioned Sir Robert Lorimer to restore it. The building
still retains the distinctive long gallery with its painted ceilings.

Earlshall Castle. The building was started by Sir William Bruce
in 1546. The castle and gardens were restored by Sir Robert Lorimer
in 1891. (J.R. Baxter)

Thomson, the head gardner at Earlshall Castle (right) with
new lawn mower. (J.R. Baxter)

One bedchamber is pointed out as the 'Royal Bedchamber' to recall
the visit of Mary, Queen of Scots in 1561. Since the 400th
anniversary of Mary's execution in 1987, Fife has been very much
on the 'Mary Queen of Scots Heritage Trail': Earlshall, Falkland
Palace, Balmerino Abbey, Dunfermline Abbey and Palace and
several other sites can all be viewed from the perspective of Mary's
life.

The old castle of the Norman de Quinceys, earls of Winchester,
at Leuchars, which is remembered in the name of a farm, stood on
a knowe to the north of the modern village, set within an area of
once treacherous marshes. The original wooden pallisaded motte
and bailey was replaced with stone and rebuilt several times; the last
castle here was torn down by Robert Lindsay, sixth Earl of
Balcarres, in the 1790s. At the predecessor of nearby Pitlethie House
Mary, Queen of Scots and James VI came to hunt.

Leuchars is known today for its RAF base. It was the Royal
Engineers who started aeronautics here, when in 1911 they experi-
mented with balloons. During the First World War an airfield took
shape and the Royal Navy started a Fleet Training School; in 1920
this was taken over by the RAF. By 1938 Leuchars airfield became
fully operational as a base for Coastal Command, and it so

Earlshall Castle *c*.1870. (J.R. Baxter)

remained until 1950 when it was transferred to Fighter Command; 1968 saw it evolve as Strike Command.

Across the Lundin Burn, and surrounded by the Tay, St Andrews Bay and the estuary of the River Eden, Tentsmuir was a wild, marshy, enchanted and isolated region which the medieval chronicles filled with *diaboli, urses et bos primiginius* – 'devils, bear and oxen'. Tentsmuir was an area inhabited by Stone Age and Bronze Age people whose chief diet was mussels and clams; the banks of the River Eden have a long history of mussel cultivation, used as bait by fisherfolk in many parts of East Scotland. In time Tentsmuir was inhabited by shipwrecked mariners and became a sanctuary for vagabonds and outlaws. The courtiers of Malcolm Canmore hunted here out of Leuchars Castle and introduced the rabbit, which at one time earned the estates of Scotscraig, Reres and Kinshady lucrative annual income.

Guardbridge sits at the estuary of the River Eden, and takes its name from *gaire*, the triangular piece of ground hereabouts. The six-arch *gaire-brig* was built here, at great expense, by Henry

Wardlaw, Bishop of St Andrews and, with its repairs of 1685, remains a good example of a Scottish medieval bridge. On either side are panels bearing the arms of James Beaton, Archbishop of St Andrews. A modern bridge was built alongside in 1939 and the piers of the old railway bridge to St Andrews are still to be seen; the line was closed in 1969. This area was a gathering place for medieval pilgrims so that they could journey to St Andrews under guard through the wild places of Kincaple.

The Guard Bridge Paper Company was founded in 1873 and set on the site of the old Seggie Distillery, which had been founded by William Haig around 1810. From 1898 to 1960 the company reclaimed land from the River Eden and the Mottray Burn to make up the modern complex. A village was created here to accommodate the paper-mill workforce between 1887 and the late 1930s. The paper-mill still functions as a commercial entity. It is interesting to note that well into the Victorian era large schooners and sloops sailed far into the now-silted mouth of the Eden. The anchorages of Guardbridge were once an important port: known as 'The Water of Eden' this was the main medieval port for the Metropolitan See of St Andrews.

Strathkinness

The village of Strathkinness appears on record for the first time in 1144 when Bishop Robert gave the lands to the Priory of St Andrews and a settlement was established by 1160. After the Reformation the lands fell to the Balfours of Burleigh and they were forfeited to the crown because the Jacobite Balfours were involved in the 1715 rebellion. The policies were purchased by the Melville family in 1724 and so remained until 1900 when the properties were sold to James Younger of Alloa.

The Youngers built Mount Melville mansion house (1903); in 1947 the grounds of the house were sold to Fife County Council and the mansion was used first as a maternity hospital, then as a geriatric hospital. It is now a golfing complex. The grounds with the Dutch model village (1918) and Japanese, English and Italian gardenscapes were made into Craigtoun Country Park.

Set on the hill in the form of a T, Strathkinness lay between medieval roads leading to St Andrews and was an agricultural community with a considerable amount of weaving in the eighteenth and nineteenth centuries. Quarrying also was an important local industry up to modern times. A Free Church was established in Strathkinness in 1843 and the much altered church of 1867 is now the village hall. The parish church dates from 1864; the manse of 1873 is now a private house.

To the east of Strathkinness lies Strathtyrum, another estate in ecclesiastical hands until the Reformation. It fell to the crown and was conferred on royal favourite the Duke of Lennox. Archbishop James Sharp purchased the property in 1669 and thereafter it passed to the Cheape family who continue as owners. The modern mansion dates from 1720–40 with a frontage of about 1805. In the early 1990s the sea washed up to Strathtyrum gates: the saltmarshes and rivulets are now golf courses. In Victorian times the mansion was rented by Tory publisher John Blackwood (1818–79) who regularly entertained such eminent figures as the historian, James Froude, the writers Charles Kingsley and Anthony Trollope and the painter, Sir John Millais.

To the south of Strathkinness lies Magus Muir, over which the old Bishop's Road ran, and here on 3 May 1679 nine Presbyterian fanatics hacked to death James Sharp, Archbishop of St Andrews and primate of all Scotland.

An archbishop's murder

Born in 1618, James Sharp was the episcopalian archbishop of St Andrews. He taught for a time at St Andrews University and in 1649 was minister of Crail. During Covenanting times he supported the Royalist Resolutioners and acted as their spokesman in discussions with Oliver Cromwell in London. On the return of King Charles II he saw that episcopacy could once again be renewed in Scotland and he was consecrated Archbishop of St Andrews on 15 December 1661. To those of strong Covenanting beliefs Sharp was a 'traitor'. An attempt was made on his life in 1668; six years later his assailant James Mitchell was arrested and promised leniency in exchange for a confession. But Mitchell was executed in 1678, and this sealed Sharp's fate; a group of fanatics shot and stabbed him to death in front of his daughter at Magus Muir as he made his way to St Andrews.

Today a cairn marks the spot where the archbishop was murdered, and there is also a monument in Holy Trinity Church, St Andrews. Nearby are the graves of one of the assassins and the Covenanters who were captured at the Battle of Bothwell Bridge in 1679 and executed as part revenge for the murder. Fife properties associated with Sharp in Fife include Randerston (1659), Scotscraig, Tayport (1661) and Stathtyrum, St Andrews (1669).

Beyond Magus Muir is Drumcarrow Craig with its prehistoric settlement.

Kemback

Strathkinness High Road continues along the crest of the hill overlooking Guardbridge and Dairsie to Kemback. The parish has as its focus the Gothic church of 1814, perched above Dura Den, close to its neighbour the post-Reformation church of 1582, which was originally a rectory given to St Salvator's College by Bishop James Kennedy in 1458. The people of Kemback once earned a living from the flax industry whose mills were powered by the Ceres Burn in the gorge. The relics of this industry lie in ruins or have been converted to modern housing.

At Kemback lived one Myles Graham, a purported prominent regicide. James I, second son of Robert III, was born at Dunfermline on 25 July 1394. He became heir apparent on the supposed murder of his elder brother David, Duke of Rothesay, at Falkland. A conspiracy formed around Walter, Earl of Atholl, James I's uncle, Atholl's grandson Sir Robert Stewart, and the disgruntled Sir Robert Graham, and led to James' assassination at the Dominican Friary at Perth on 21 February 1437. Sir Robert Graham was uncle of the Earl of Mentieth and the senior representative of the issue of Robert II's second wife; he bore the king a grudge, and with the assistance of Sir John Hall and his brother Thomas stabbed the king to death. All the main perpetrators were caught and executed. Myles Graham was implicated in the murder and forfeited his Fife estate.

The Schevez family obtained the estate of Kemback and in 1478 supplied an archbishop of St Andrews in William Schevez. Beyond Kemback wood lies Blebocraigs, once the centre of thirty red sandstone quarries. The estate belonged to the Earl of Douglas in David II's time and in the fourteenth century fell to the Traills, whose famous son was Bishop Walter Traill of St Andrews.

Old folk in the Kemback area used to tell how a man and a woman, probably itinerants, once sought refuge in the cave high on the cliff opposite Kemback Bridge and the nineteenth-century Mill House. There they lived until one day the smell of oatcakes burning accidentally on their fire brought their pursuers and the couple were murdered. To this day, the story goes, you can smell burned oatcakes on the air from time to time at Kemback. Kemback House has nineteenth-century gatepiers, a sundial of 1784 and a doocot of 1710, while the mansion is eighteenth-century, pre-dating nearby Blebo House by almost a century.

At Pitscottie lived Scotland's first vernacular prose historian, Robert Lindsay (*c*.1532–80), who wrote his credulous and picturesque *Historie and Cronicles of Scotland* covering the period 1436 to 1575. With its eighteenth-century bridge, Pitscottie was an old posting station along the way from Ceres.

Ceres

First mentioned in the twelfth century, in the reign of William the Lion, Ceres was formerly a burgh of barony (1620) within the control of the Hopes of Craighall, whose scion Sir Thomas Hope was the King's Advocate exiled by Charles I for his Covenanting sympathies, but recalled to public life by virtue of his legal wisdom. Weaving, bleaching, brewing and agriculture have all earned Ceres its daily bread. The seventeenth-century Weigh House forms the entrance to Fife Folk Museum and once served as a burgh tolbooth and a venue for the pre-eighteenth-century Barony Courts. Here are displayed the *jougs* for the restraining of miscreants during market days. Above the doorway a stone tablet, set with the scales of a medieval merchant proclaims the pious hope GOD BLESS THE JUST.

Opened in 1968 and administered by the Fife Folk Museum Trust the museum displays a wide range of artefacts of relevance to any study of Fife's history and legend. As the museum is in the old weigh-house it is relevant that the displays offer a selection of weighing machines from butter and confectionery scales to chain measures and metal gauges. It was only in 1661 that an attempt was made to regularise the wide diversity of Scotland's weights and measures. Irregularities in weights were still to be found up to 1824 when a uniformity of weights and measures was statutorily established. In medieval Fife at least three standards of weight would be used: English pounds (of sixteen ounces}, Dutch pounds (seventeen and a half ounces) and Tron pounds (twenty-two ounces). English measures were used to weigh flour, bread and barley; Dutch for meat and meal; and Tron weights for flax, wool, butter, cheese and tallow. Gone too are the names of some of the old measures, from *lippie* (2 pounds in weight) to *firlot* (2 stones), and from *boll* (8 stones) to *chalder* (128 stones), the latter measure commonly used by Fife coal merchants. Fife public houses sold their ale and spirits in *mutchkins* and *chopins*.

Within Ceres Museum too is pointed out the trapdoor that leads into the old tolbooth prison, a useful introduction to the display telling the story of the last public hanging in Fife, at Cupar in 1852. Here too is the Cupar Weavers' banner: made in 1727 it represents the area's once-dominant trade and is one of the oldest trade-union banners in Britain. Outside the museum sports a wide range of agricultural machinery and implements to illustrate the history of Fife's yearly cycles.

A stroll around Ceres reveals that its layout is rare enough in Scotland, a community around a village green. Near the museum, in the High Street, is the figure known as 'The Provost'. He sits within his alcove 'merry as a Toby Jug' and is local sculptor John Howie of Sauchope's conception of a church provost, the Revd Thomas Buchanan, the last holder of the office. Set beneath the statue is the Howie panel, said to commemorate the Battle of Bannockburn, 1314.

Ceres church dates from 1805–06 and within its vestibule is a fine fifteenth-century crusader effigy which reminds us of the pre-Reformation church of St Ninian on the same site. The church spire was added around 1870. The seventeenth-century vault of the Lindsay earls of Crawford stands in the kirkyard. Ceres – perhaps a corruption of the medieval Latin *syrs*, a marsh – was long famous for its fairs, held in March and October, of which the 'Plack and Penny' fair was distinctive and thought to date from the fourteenth century when the men of Ceres marched out with Sir William Keith of Struthers Castle to support Robert the Bruce at Bannockburn. They crossed the ancient village bridge near to where Sir William had taught them archery at the Bow Butts, and across a successor of this bridge trundled the carriage of Archbishop Sharp only minutes away from his assassination. By the seventeenth-century bridge is the old house with its garden vaults known as St John's Lodge, once the house of the local Freemasons; it was built around 1765 and restored in 1964. Ceres' conservation area also includes Baltilly House (*c*.1780) and cottages. Ceres Games, which are still held, are thought to have derived from the celebration after the victory at Bannockburn.

Signposted from the centre of Ceres, Craighall Den and the site of Craighall castle were gifted to the local authorities by Colonel Hope of Luffness. Demolished in 1955, the mansion of Craighall was built in 1637 by Sir Thomas Hope, incorporating French Renaissance styles with the Scottish baronial of an earlier edifice. A prominent feature of the modern Den walk is the large kiln built in 1814 from stone from the ruins of Craighall castle; the kiln, which processed lime to be use as fertiliser, went out of production in 1837. Beyond Craighall are the curiously named policies of Teasses (1879), and by Craighall Burn are the house (1750) and bridge (1769) of Teasses Mill.

Craigrothie

Nearby Craigrothie is a village which was once a coaching stop. Craigrothie's old inn is eighteenth century and the earliest cottages hereabouts date from 1735; its mansion house is eighteenth–nineteenth century, but the coach house is dated 1668 and the icehouse is contemporary with the mansion. Craigrothie's neighbour is Chance Inn, once known as 'Change Inn' because it was a stagepost where coach horses were changed for the last leg to Cupar. Some two miles to the south sits ruined L-plan Struthers Castle which dates from the end of the fourteenth century with seventeenth-century additions. Originally belonging to the Ochter-Struthers in the twelfth century, the property fell to the Keiths, Grand Marischals of Scotland. In time the property belonged to the Lindsays and Crawfords and in 1633 the title of Lord Struthers was conferred on the first Earl of Lindsay. Charles I was entertained at Struthers in 1651, and two years later the castle was occupied by Cromwell's troops.

Between Craigrothie and Cupar are sited Scotstarvit Tower and the Hill of Tarvit. Scotstarvit Tower was also associated with the Struthers and is a five-storey construction. In 1611 Sir John Scott bought Scotstarvit estate and built his tower on the site of a previous building mentioned in a charter of 1579. A keen antiquary, the outspoken Sir John was Director of Chancery and author of *The Staggering State of Scots Statesmen*, containing illuminating comments on contemporary politicians and administrators, and he encouraged the study of topography in Scotland. He sponsored the work in this connection of Timothy Pont, finished by Sir Robert Gordon of Straloch and his son, and published in Amsterdam in 1654 by John Blaeu as an atlas of Scotland. He also edited *Delitiae Poetarum Scotorum*, and an anthology of Latin verse by Scots (1637). Sir John's tower was abandoned in 1696 and his descendant, the Duchess of Portland, sold the estate to Oliver Gourlay of Craigrothie. A new dwelling was constructed nearby after 1696 to the design of Sir William Bruce, Master of Works to Charles II, and called Wemyss Hall. When Frederick Sharp, a scion of a Dundee family of 'jute princes' bought the property in 1904 he had it radically altered by Sir Robert Lorimer as a family dwelling and as a home for his collection of antiques. The house, re-dubbed 'Hill of Tarvit,' was bequeathed to the National Trust for Scotland on the death of the last owner, Miss E.C. Sharp, in 1948.

4
ST ANDREWS: CITY OF LEGEND

Not long after he ascended the throne of the Scots kingdom, Alexander I, known as 'The Fierce', of the House of Dunkeld, rode into the little thatched hamlet that would grow into St Andrews. On that day he gave a curious gift to the bishop of the diocese and his clergy, at the earliest of the cathedrals that would grace the triangle of land atop the beetling cliffs of the religious enclave. To the Glory of God he handed to the bishop the reins of 'his comely steed of Araby' caparisoned in 'many a precious fair jewel'. It was the first of several such generous gifts. Yet Alexander was to set in motion a series of events that would bring the legends of the founding of the holy place at St Andrews into fine focus and link them with a new lease of life for his realm of Scotland.

Alexander recognised the power of holy relics on the minds of his people. He saw in St Andrews a place where Christ's earthly kingdom could have new meaning to his Scottish subjects. The king knew well the story of the coming of the corporeal relics of St Andrew, apostle and martyr, to this holy place by the grey North Sea. Alexander had been the only layman present when the tomb of the seventh-century abbot-bishop of Lindisfarne, St Cuthbert, had been opened at Durham in 1104; the ceremony had moved him deeply and inspired him to call upon St Andrew to be his spiritual helper in a plan he had in mind.

In the days of the Pictish heathendom the place now known as St Andrews was called Kilrymont, that is to say 'the head of the king's mount'. Here, by at least the sixth century, Christianity had a foothold. The 'Legend of the Coming of St Andrew's Bones' to St Andrews has several conflicting sources, manipulated by many a monastic hand for political and economic advantage. Suffice it to say this: the elder brother of St Peter, and like him a fisherman, Andrew was a disciple of John the Baptist and was the first to be called to Christ's apostleship. Tradition has it that he evangelised Asia Minor and Greece, and that he was crucified at Patras in Achaia some time in the first century on a *crux decussata*, which as a symbol would become the central feature of the Scots saltire flag. Apostle Andrew's feast day was set in the general calendar of the Roman Catholic Church as 30 November.

The chroniclers averred that some time around AD 345 the bones of St Andrew were to be taken from Patras to Constantinople by the grandson of Constantine the Great. By divine revelation, one of the custodians of the bones, the canonised bishop Regulus, known as St Rule, was warned beforehand and secured a portion of the bones. Far away, in the north of Britain, Angus MacFergus, King of the Picts, was amassing an army to face King Athelstan at the mouth of a river dubbed the 'Tyne'. In a dream Angus was promised a great victory by St Andrew and that his relics would be brought to Angus' kingdom as a sign of favour. Revealing his vision, King Angus roused his army and dedicated each man as a warrior of St Andrew. Angus was victorious and Athelstan's head was severed as a trophy of war. Yet a more powerful symbol was in the offing.

The Legend of the Bones goes on: Bishop Regulus received another divine revelation that he must go to the 'uttermost edge of the world' with the relics he had saved. Where his ship finally came to rest he must build a church and dedicate it to St Andrew. So Regulus set sail and finally came to rest in the territory of the Picts. At Kinrymont, Angus gave Regulus and his party land for a church to celebrate St Andrew, and thus the relics of the saint became the spiritual focus for a new foundation of Celtic Christianity.

By the time Alexander I was making his plans the relics of St Andrew were lodged in the noble Romanesque mid-eleventh-century church of St Regulus which still towers in ruin 108 ft above the St Andrews cathedral cemetery. The church was thus the precursor of its neighbour – the medieval cathedral – and was the first church of the Augustinian Priory of St Andrews. The Augustinian clergy were to figure in the next phase of Alexander's legendary plans.

Alexander wanted Scotland to be a special part of Christendom, with a certain degree of independence in matters of religion. For centuries St Andrews had been the headquarters of bishops of the

St Rule's Tower, St Andrews. The first cathedral
of St Andrews. (Author's collection)

St Andrews cathedral; the nave and gable of the east window looking
towards St Rule's Tower. (STARALP)

old Celtic Christianity. Alexander did not think they were up to the job of helping to spearhead the European Catholic Orthodoxy he believed was the way forward for his kingdom. To this end he founded the priory of Scone around 1120, and the priory of Inchcolm, three years later, and handed them over to the Augustinians, whose ordained clergy followed the programme of religious life drawn up by St Augustine, Bishop of Hippo.

The appointment and consecration of bishops for the St Andrews diocese had been long a matter of dispute in Alexander's day. The first of the Anglo-Norman bishops of St Andrews was Turgot, Prior of Durham, who was consecrated to the See in 1109. On the death of Turgot in 1115, the See was to have gone to Eadmer, a monk of Canterbury, but Alexander was keen to secure the liberty of himself from English influence and his kingdom from the religious pressures of the archbishops of York and Canterbury who both claimed Scotland as a religious vassal. Just before Alexander died in 1128, Prior Robert was elected Bishop of St Andrews; he was Alexander's own man from his foundation at Scone. Thus the diocese of St Andrews and the kingdom of Scotland were given an atmosphere of self-reliance from immediate outside influences.

Bishop Robert is an important player in the traditional foundation story of the burgh of St Andrews. Since around 1140 Bishop Robert established the burgh of St Andrews centred on an L-shaped *vil*, acreage given to him for the purpose by Alexander I's brother, the new King David I. Its focal point is likely to have been a simple castle-palace where the present ruined castle stands. From here St Andrews expanded westerly until by 1560 it extended to the extant West Port to link with the age-old hamlets of Argyle and Rathelpie. For his new burgh Bishop Robert chose its first *praepositus* (provost), a Fleming from his family home of Berwick-upon-Tweed, one Maynard. Thus from its very conception the burgh of St Andrews has had a cosmopolitan flavour.

For four centuries after Bishop Robert founded his burgh, the great medieval cathedral was the focal point of the city of St Andrews and the ecclesiastical capital of Scotland. When Bishop Robert died in 1159 his successor, Arnold, Abbot of the Tironesian house at Kelso, founded the new cathedral around 1160. With the encouragement of Malcolm IV, the building of the cathedral,

The West Port, the only surviving gateway into the heart of medieval
St Andrews, in a late Victorian photograph. The gateway
was reconstructed in 1589 and renovated in 1843–45. (STARALP)

which would in time be the largest medieval building in Scotland,
was laid out to a length of 391 ft. The cathedral was finally all of a
piece in the fourteenth century and was consecrated on 5 July 1318.
In 1472 St Andrews was erected into the dignity of an
archiepiscopal and metropolitan see, and St Andrews's relics made
it one of the great pilgrimage sites of European christendom.

Today the skeletal ruins of the reliquary chapel, set behind the
site of the high altar of the cathedral, belie the sumptuous setting
the relics of the Apostle had enclosed in the Celtic *morbrac*
(reliquary) on its own catafalque. The shrine was the focal point for
the cathedral's rich treasure trove of painted gilded statues,
tapestries, ivory crucifixes, mass vessels of gold and silver and the
brightly decorated tombs of such as the long-dead bishops of the
diocese and Archbishop Alexander Stewart, illegitimate son of
James IV, who died with his father at the Battle of Flodden in 1513.

Legends of Scots people, places, facts and faces, scenes and
memories long forgotten, were all to be found in St Andrews
cathedral and its precincts: the history of St Andrews was the

history of Scotland. Within the cathedral, with its Augustinian priory to the south and the whole encompassed by the 20-ft wall built with thirteen towers by Prior John Hepburn (d.1522) and his nephew Patrick, Bishop of Moray, the Augustinian canons regaled visitors with legends of the artefacts they could see. Here was the silver-encrusted spear shaft of Alexander I, the crystal cross from the field of Bannockburn and the curious duo of boar's tusks chained to the high altar. The latter was a memory of the Pictish hunting grounds which spread south of the cathedral's precinct into the nearby heathland where the clergy still hunted boar. Indeed memories of the Picts were everywhere, their burial cairns and mounds ringing the burgh, and they were to keep their secrets and burial goods intact until rediscovered by archaeologists' trowels in the 1980s.

The treasures of the cathedral were plundered when the building was sacked by the mob incited to violence by John Knox's fiery sermon in Holy Trinity Church and the stage-management of the Protestant Lords of the Congregation on 15 June 1559. Over the

The wall to the 30-acre cathedral and priory precinct at St Andrews was reconstructed by Prior John Hepburn (d.1522). The walls are fortified by thirteen attached towers. (STARALP)

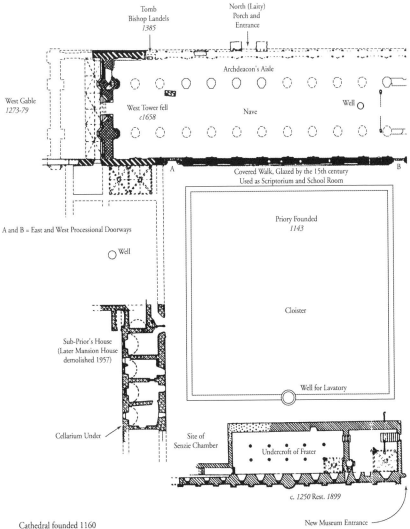

Tomb
Bishop Landels
1385

North (Laity)
Porch and
Entrance

Archdeacon's Aisle

West Gable
1273-79

West Tower fell
c1658

Nave

Well

A and B = East and West Processional Doorways

Well

Covered Walk, Glazed by the 15th century
Used as Scriptorium and School Room

Priory Founded
1143

Cloister

Sub-Prior's House
(Later Mansion House
demolished 1957)

Well for Lavatory

Cellarium Under

Site of
Senzie Chamber

Undercroft of Frater

c. 1250 Rest. *1899*

New Museum Entrance

Cathedral founded 1160
Consecrated 5 July 1318
Sacked 15 June 1559
In original form
cathedral 320 feet x 168 feet
extended to 391 feet
current length 357 feet

Ground plan of St Andrews Cathedral

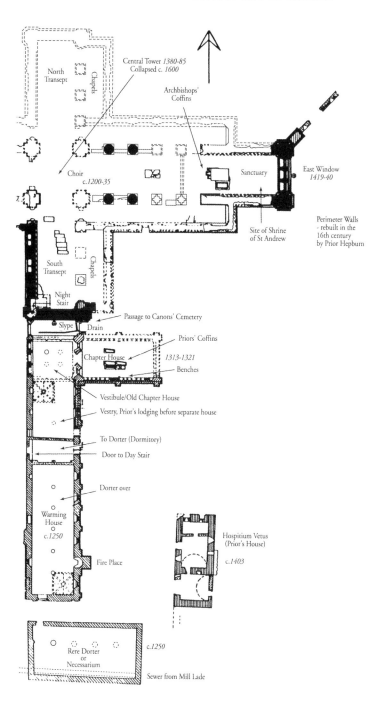

North Transept

Chapels

Central Tower *1380-85*
Collapsed c. *1600*

Archbishops' Coffins

Choir
c.*1200-35*

Sanctuary

East Window
1419-40

Site of Shrine
of St Andrew

Perimeter Walls
- rebuilt in the
16th century
by Prior Hepburn

South Transept

Chapels

Night Stair

Slype

Drain

Passage to Canons' Cemetery

Priors' Coffins

Chapter House

1313-1321

Benches

Vestibule/Old Chapter House

Vestry, Prior's lodging before separate house

To Dorter (Dormitory)

Door to Day Stair

Dorter over

Warming House
c.*1250*

Fire Place

Hospitium Vetus
(Prior's House)

c.*1403*

Rere Dorter
or
Necessarium

c.*1250*

Sewer from Mill Lade

years the fabric was reduced to a quarry for the townsfolk; still today carved stones from the cathedral precinct appear in gardens and walls to recall the legendary past of the great church. In 1826 the barons of the Exchequer assumed ownership of the ruins of the cathedral, while in 1946 the priory was given to the then Ministry of Works by John Patrick Crichton-Stuart, third Marquess of Bute. Although St Andrews ceased to be the ecclesiastical capital of Scotland in 1559, the university and burgh continued to supply St Andrews with new legends.

St Andrews had many other church buildings, though some have completely disappeared and others are in ruins. The aisle of the sixteenth-century Blackfriars' Chapel remains in South Street, in

Tomb of Archbishop Sharp at Holy Trinity Church, St Andrews. The archbishop was murdered in 1679. (STARALP)

the grounds of Madras College (1832), and the well of the fifteenth-century Greyfriars monastery is still to be found in Greyfriars Garden, which runs parallel with the wall which linked to the Marketgait port, one of the main gates into the medieval burgh. Holy Trinity Church in South Street, opposite the Town Hall (1861), was built in 1412 to replace the twelfth-century parish church whose site had been next to the south-east gable of the cathedral; the parish church in South Street was remodelled in the eighteenth century and 1907–09. The original tower of the church remains and inside is to be found the Dutch-built (1681) monument to the murdered Archbishop James Sharp. For the ecclesiastical architecture buff there is also the fifteenth-century chapel of St Leonard's College, reached down The Pends, and set by St Leonard's School for Girls (1877).

The history and legend of St Andrews was given a boost in the nineteenth and twentieth centuries by the work of four men, Sir Hugh Lyon Playfair (1786–1861), George Bruce (1825–1904), David Hay Fleming (1849–1931) and William T. Linskill (1855–1929). All different in character and idiosyncratic of motive these men put flesh on the bones of medieval St Andrews to give it a new lease of

The Pends gateway, St Andrews. This entrance to the old priory precinct dates from around 1350. (STARALP)

life. As provost Playfair set the tone for the development of modern St Andrews; philanthropist Bruce is remembered for his sponsorship of the Bruce Embankment; Hay Fleming for bringing the history of St Andrews into a new focus; and Linskill, as Dean of Guild, for his imagination as a keen ghost-hunter and for his 'howkings' in the cathedral.

In medieval times St Andrews was a town within a town, and it was divided into four quarters – those of the merchants, the fishermen, the prelates and the university, all set on the main highways, which fanned out from the west door of the cathedral. Market Street, with its Tolbooth (demolished 1862), buttermarket, Mercat Cross (removed 1768) and Tron, was the domain of the merchants. North Street had at its eastern end the Fisher Cross

Example of fisher house with forestair, St Andrews.
(STARALP)

denoting the area of the fisherfolk, and further down was the nucleus of the university, while The Scores linked with the medieval castle. South Street was a great processional way to the cathedral and down this wide street merchants built their houses, many of which had 'riggs', or long narrow gardens, some of which have remained since they were first laid out in the fifteenth-century. A fine example of such a dwelling is at 49 South Street with its sixteenth-century painted ceilings. So the layout of St Andrews streets retains the features of a medieval town, and despite the extensive housing developments to the south and east, the burgh pattern has changed little over 300 years. St Andrews is a perfect blend of wynds, courtyards, streets and closes, typically conveying the mood of an old Scottish burgh.

The colour and splendour of St Andrews' medieval craft guilds and merchants is remembered each year in the town at the Lammas Market. The oldest surviving medieval market in Scotland, it takes place in early August and people come from all over the UK to set up stalls and perform shows in Market Street and South Street. Once held on 'the Day of St Peter's Chains' (1 August), the colourful and joyful religious overtones were swept away at the Reformation. At the turn of the twentieth century Lammas Market was a hiring-fair for ploughmen seeking work, but today it is bright, noisy holiday carnival.

One relic which many visitors miss is the 'Blue Stane', formerly set in the centre of the road. Once the rendezvous of the Whiplickers (the Carters' Society) on the day they held their annual races, the whinstone boulder is now set within the gardens opposite Hope Park Church (1864) in St Mary's Place.

At the end of The Scores, medieval Swallowgait, which derives its name from the old Norse *scaur* (a ridged clifftop), stands St Andrews' courtyarded castle. Built around 1200, probably on the site of an earlier fortification, it has a long history of demolition and rebuilding and makes good use of the cliffs for its north and east defences. Down the centuries the castle's role has been fourfold – a fortress, a prison, an episcopal residence and an archiepiscopal palace. The stonework seen today dates in the main from the last rebuilding by Archbishop John Hamilton of 1547–71. The castle contains the famous Bottle Dungeon of around 1386 and the mine

St Andrews Lammas Market as it appeared
in 1947. It is still the oldest surviving medieval
market in Scotland. (Alex B. Paterson)

and counter-mine dating from the siege of 1546–47. The castle
declined in importance after the Reformation and in 1654 the town
council ordered that part of the stonework be used to repair the
harbour.

Outside the castle's frontal entrance, and set in the roadway, are
the stone-block initials 'G.W.'; these are in memory of the
Protestant reformer George Wishart (1513–46), the intimate friend
and teacher of John Knox. Wishart was arrested on a charge of
heresy by the order of Cardinal David Beaton (1494–1546) and
brought from Edinburgh Castle to St Andrews.

One of the most prominent clergymen of any age, Beaton, born
at Markinch around 1495, held a multitude of important positions
in church and state, reaching the position of Chancellor of
Scotland in 1543. He was invested as Archbishop of St Andrews in
1538.

Legend has it that Wishart was imprisoned in the 25-ft deep
Bottle Dungeon. He was later strangled and burned outside the

castle; it is said that the cardinal watched Wishart's incineration from a window of the castle on 1 March 1546. Wishart had probably been involved in the attempted assassination of Beaton in 1544; his fellow conspirators murdered Beaton at St Andrews Castle less than three months after Wishart's death. Beaton is thought by some to have been first buried in the Dominican monastery of Blackfriars, South Street. At the Reformation this tomb would be destroyed, so vilified was his name in local memory.

John Knox retains a high profile in the history and legend of St Andrews, and if ghosts walk his shade must be deemed to appear in the environs of St Andrews Castle and Cathedral – indeed one chronicler wrote that Knox berated the Devil in an impassioned impromptu sermon in the cathedral graveyard. Little is known of Knox for the first thirty years of his life; he is thought to have been born around 1512 and attended Haddington Grammar School. From there he went to St Andrews University, but left without a degree to be ordained a Roman Catholic priest in his local church of the Greyfriars, Haddington. Knox said that George Wishart 'touched and wakened him' to Protestantism and he long retained a deep affection for St Andrews – 'where God first opened my mouth', he said.

By the end of June 1547, Knox was at St Andrews and played a role in defending the Reformer-held castle from attack by a French force under Admiral Leone Strozzi, Prior of Capua, and backed by the troops of Queen Marie de Guise-Lorraine under Monsignor Lorge de Montgomery. From the tower of St Salvator's college the garrison at the castle was bombarded by cannon. Plague broke out in the castle and the beleagured Reformers eventually surrendered. Knox and the lesser men and servants were transported to Nantes, on the Loire, as galley slaves, and Knox languished aboard the *Notre Dame* until 1549. St Andrews had not heard the last of Knox. Ten years later he was back as a leader of the Reformation. Here he rang the death-knell of the cathedral and St Andrews' role as the ecclesiastical capital of Scotland. With the burgh occupied by Protestant Lords, on Sunday 11 June 1559 Knox preached an inflammatory sermon at Holy Trinity Church. Hardly had he finished speaking than the mob attacked the cathedral, and popery was expunged from its heart.

The Protestant 'martyrs' have a high profile in St Andrews' memorials, for instance on The Scores – above the Bruce Embankment – stands the Martyrs Monument of 1842, erected to the memory of Patrick Hamilton, George Wishart, Paul Craw, who was burned near the Market Cross in 1433 and Henry Forest and Walter Myln, who were burned on the north side of the cathedral in 1533 and 1558 respectively.

Along from the castle, past the cathedral and down Kirkhill, the harbour has a pier nearly 300 yards long. Still a working harbour, once full of sea-going merchantmen and fishing boats, the eighteenth-century inner harbour sits on older foundations. Originally there would have been a wooden pier, built around 1100, with a stone pier of 1560. Rebuilt in the seventeenth century with

Students' Pier walk to St Andrews harbour.
(STARALP)

stone from the castle the harbour saw the bustle of exports of grain, coal, potatoes and iron until the 1920s. Apart from golf, St Andrews is today essentially a university town, with the university as the main landlord and employer in the old burgh. The University of St Andrews is the oldest in Scotland, founded in 1410. A high standard of education was offered at the school attached to the Augustinian priory of the cathedral and a charter of incorporation was given to the school by Henry Wardlaw, Bishop of St Andrews, during 1411–12. The activities of the school were officially recognised by the Avignon Pope Benedict XIII in 1413 and thus the school became recognised as equivalent to the other prominent educational establishments in Europe. At first the university was no more than a society of learned men concerned with the study of arts, divinity and canon law. Within a few years they acquired their first building, the pedagogy in South Street on the site of the old University Library, and by the end of the Middle Ages three endowed colleges had been founded: St Salvator's (1450); St Leonard's (1512) and St Mary's (1537). Throughout the sixteenth century almost all of the leading figures of church and state in Scotland were educated in St Andrews.

At the Reformation the university was stripped of its 'popish' influences and was the centre of a new national scheme of education grounded in parish schools. St Mary's College became a seminary of Protestant theology. University life was regularly interrupted by the political troubles of the sixteenth and seventeenth centuries. It survived through the burgh's decline of the eighteenth century and achieved a slow recovery in the nineteenth century when the town underwent a commercial revival. The university expanded rapidly from 1886 to 1915.

Following the separation of Queen's College, Dundee, to form its own university in 1967, the University of St Andrews is again limited to the town of its birth. The university buildings are easily viewed and a visit to St Salvator's collegiate church and tower, which dominate North Street, is particularly recommended. The church was built 1450–60 by James Kennedy, Bishop of St Andrews, and the spire was added to the tower around 1550. Within the church is the tomb of the bishop, who is remembered too in a colourful pageant which forms a highlight of the university year.

Thought to originate in 1849 as an end-of-term 'rag' by final-year students, the Kate Kennedy Pageant is a colourful costume display in which sixty or seventy students (members of the Kate Kennedy Club) process through the streets dressed as characters associated with the town and university, from Mary, Queen of Scots to Field-Marshal Earl Haig (a former Rector). The pageant takes its name from the following circumstances. The old bell in the tower of the collegiate church of St Salvator has long been known as 'Katherine', supposedly named after the niece of Bishop Kennedy. During the rag one student is thought to have dressed up as Kate and capered at the centre of the noisy masquerade; the rag was successful and repeated until it became a tradition. As the professors attempted to suppress it, the tradition became a symbol of undergraduate freedom. It was almost totally banned from 1874 to 1926 when it was revived as a historical pageant.

The matriculated students of St Andrews University have always had a say in the government of the university through their ancient right to elect a rector. The rector holds the position for three years, is the chairman of the university court and is spokesperson for

Characters in the Kate Kennedy Procession, University of
St Andrews. (STARALP)

students both within and without the University. The students have been thus represented down the decades by famous people of history from philanthropist Andrew Carnegie and writer-dramatist Sir James Barrie to explorer Fridjof Nansen and inventor Guglielmo Marconi. In 1982 the students elected their first female Rector in journalist Katherine Whitehorn.

Each street, wynd and close of St Andrews offers a great diversity of architecture to cater for all tastes, be it the fifteenth-century 'Roundel' at the east end of South Street and its neighbour, Deans Court, recognised as the oldest extant domestic site in the burgh with a twelfth-century core, or the West Port of 1589 and the Victorian Hope Street and Howard Place. St Andrews too has the Byre Theatre, rebuilt and reopened in 2001, which evolved from the St Andrews Play Club, founded in 1933.

St Andrews' western approaches are dominated by its golf courses. The earliest note on golf in St Andrews is dated 1552 and the oldest golf course in the world is the Old Course, purchased by the town council in 1894. Throughout the world the rules of golf are administered by the Royal and Ancient Golf Club which had its origins in a meeting of enthusiasts on 14 May 1754. The present clubhouse was opened in 1854, twenty years after King William IV agreed royal patronage of the club. Thus golf and academia have been the life-force of the history and legend of St Andrews for hundreds of years.

Today, the history and legend of St Andrews can be assessed and enjoyed at three main locations. First there are the visitor centres at the castle and cathedral, then the burgh museum at Kinburn and the Preservation Trust Museum in North Street. Both the burgh and Trust museums offer interesting stories in themselves.

The burgh museum is sited in castellated Kinburn House, set on the northern boundary of a medieval development outside St Andrews called Argyle. The house was built by the Buddo family in 1854–56 on land bought in 1852 by Dr David Buddo of the Indian Medical Service. Named after a Russian fort captured by a Franco-British naval force during the Crimean War, the house was bought by the old St Andrews town council in 1920 and developed as a public park.

St Andrews Preservation Trust was established in 1937 to, in the words of the Trustees, 'secure and safeguard the valuable amenities and historic character of St Andrews and its neighbourhood'. Today its collection of historical artefacts, extensive photographic portfolios and rotating exhibitions are housed at 12 North Street. The building is a sixteenth-century town house, once the home of fisherfolk in the heart of the burgh's old fisher quarter. The property was saved from demolition in 1937 and was finally acquired by the Trust in 1962.

5

THE EAST NEUK AND ITS NEIGHBOURS

'I never saw so many good houses of people of family and fortune as in this part of Fife'. So wrote Sir Walter Scott of the East Neuk. He visited the area during the weekend of 13–16 June 1823, with Sir Henry Raeburn and the Blair Adam Club. Scott had first visited St Andrews in 1793 and several of his books from *Guy Mannering* (1815) to *The Heart of Midlothian* (1818) contain hints of East Neuk history and legend. Today the East Neuk has changed relatively little in aspect since Scott's time, but Sir Walter would hardly recognise the descendants of the folk he met.

The A918 from St Andrews lies almost parallel to the coastal path to Crail, now developed as a nature walk. The trail runs by such volcanic rocky outcrops as the Maiden Rock, the Rock and Spindle and Buddo Rock, all favourites of Victorian and Edwardian painters and geologists; the trail has exit points at Boarhills and Kingsbarns. The character of the area has however altered recently with the development of the St Andrews Bay golf and hotel complex. Once this area was swampy forestland of oak, pine and beech; and from the time of the eighth-century Pictish monastery at St Andrews, wild boar, deer, wolves and bears were hunted by both prelate and laird alike on the Boar's 'Raik', or run.

Today Victorian and Edwardian hands are still to be seen in the architecture along the way. The houses of Kingask and Pitmullen show a characteristic feature of habitation in East Fife – a big house and estate which once gave life and employment to a small village or hamlet. Round by Kinglassie, on a Sunday morning, the bellcote of the church at Boarhills bids the visitor welcome to the East Neuk; 'neuk' being the old Scots word for niche, nook or corner. Boarhills Church is set on the ridge of a hill just off the road before the sharp turn-off to the village proper. Once upon a time the folk of this area worshipped in the schoolhouse of the village, but in

1866 it was decided to build a church to serve the parish in 'keeping with the tastes and requirements of the age'. The church was set alongside a cemetery, which pre-dated it by many centuries; it was linked with the parish of Dunino in 1966. The older gravestones near the west wall of Boarhills cemetery emphasise the local sense of mortality; drownings were a common occurrence along these shores. The most famous was the wreck of the Swedish brig *Napoleon* off Boarhills in 1864. All hands perished and lie with this Victorian sentiment above:

> The waters compassed me about even to the soul
> The depths closed me round about
> The weeds were wrapped about my head.

Just north of the church, at Chesterhill, was erected the first lifeboat station in these parts. Its early presence, it was uncharitably said, owed nothing to humanitarianism; the guidfolk of Boarhills 'negotiated' with the shipwrecked and would rescue only those able and prepared to pay. One chronicler actually accused the Boarhills folk of setting up false beacons to encourage wrecks.

Boarhills itself is a scattered parish. Dating from 1789, but marked with 1815 on a skew-end, Boarhills Primary School was taken from local heritors in 1928 and absorbed into the county system. The heritors of Fife's schools in past ages had a wide range of responsibilities from employing and paying the schoolmasters to succouring the poor.

The delightful country mansion of Kenly Green derives its name from the *ken* (promontory) made here by Kenly Water. Above the polluted stream where salmon were once rifle-shot as they leapt the weir, two man-made hillocks invite the archaeologist's spade. One of them may be the lost castle of Draffan, which the Revd James Roger averred was built here by the Danes. The twenty-odd acres of wooded policies lie partly in the old parish of Kingsbarns and partly in the parish of St Leonard and St Andrew, recalling that they were monastic acres in medieval times. In front of the house, across the burn, the seventeenth-century (restored 1987) doocot is the oldest extant building hereabouts. Yet by the time the present Kenly Green house was built in 1791, the land had come into the ownership of the university. It is believed that the house is on a much earlier foundation, a hunter's shelter or a pilgrims' retreat. Designed by the Adam brothers, Kenly Green House exhibits their characteristic decorations and mantelpieces. From the 1920s, Kenly Green was the home of Sir Alexander Nairne Stewart Sandeman, jute spinner of Dundee and Liberal MP (1923) for the Middleton and Prestwich division of Lancashire. When he died in 1940, the house fell to his widow and thence her relatives; since 1960 it has been modernised. Near the front door is a hunk of Gothic masonry from the old Palace of Westminster, brought by the redoubtable Sir Alexander. Nearby historic Peekie Bridge dates from the early sixteenth century and bears the arms of the Hepburns on the north side.

All over the East Neuk ruined farm cottages, windows and doors agape, wantonly display intimacies of past life around the couthy hearthstones. Layers of peeling wallpaper tell of the labourers' fight against damp, while the nettle-ridden earth closets tell their own story: these privies were as good an indication of the character of the owners as anything. Some were noisome holes, others passably decent; others had seats scrubbed to snow-whiteness and polished wooden floors. A guidwife might even go as far as to nail up a popular Victorian religious text on the back of the privy door, like 'Thou God seest me' – or impale a wholesome, inspiring scene from a soap advert or even a portrait of, First World War leader, Field-Marshal Kitchener. The East Neuk inhabitant of past ages was nothing if not continually bent on broadening the mind.

Dovecotes, or doo cots in fourteenth-century Scottish parlance, are an essential part of Fife's social history because of their style, character and presence. Their design was to reflect the pinnacles of Fife's builders' skills and often they are the only clues to a vanished castle, mansion, estate or hamlet.

Dovecotes were probably introduced to Lowland Scotland, in particular, by the Romans, who placed their pigeons and doves in *columbarii*. In 1503 an Act of the Scottish Parliament required landowners to erect dovecotes on their properties; after 1677 the right to erect dovecotes was limited to those whose land produced an annual rent of one and a quarter hundredweights of grain, and the dovecote had to be built within two miles of the main dwelling it was to serve. It was considered a serious offence to steal pigeons or break into dovecotes.

There are around half a dozen basic shapes of Scottish dovecotes: cylindrical, or beehive, turreted, horseshoe and conical or lectern. The most popular feature of the Scottish dovecote was the saddleback, with a pitched roof and crow-stepped gables. Their architectural interest today is that they were never quite identical.

It was Fife's lairds and ministers who mostly erected and used dovecotes. But they were very much a part of the poorer tenant farmer's economy. For dovecotes were strictly practical and a part of the business of keeping alive. They ensured a supply of fresh meat. Wood pigeons, for instance, were not easy to catch before the invention of the shotgun, so to have them in a dovecote made them easier to trap. Pigeon eggs were considered a great delicacy, as was the meat, particularly of 'squabs', that is young birds. Not forgetting too, that dovecotes were a fine source of fertiliser for fields and gardens.

The pigeons kept in Fife were mostly rock doves or rock pigeons, which normally mate for life. Dovecotes went out of fashion during the eighteenth century. At this time the turnip was introduced and this made the winter feeding of livestock practicable. Thus with the development of cold storage techniques the need for pigeon meat vanished.

Representative examples can be seen in Fife at these places: Bow Butts House, Bruce Terrace, Kinghorn (eighteenth century); Durie House, Leven (octagonal); Melville House, Ladybank (converted windmill); Kenly Green, Boarhills (seventeenth-century, gabled, a possible relic of episcopal manor of Inchmurdo); West Pitkierie (two-storey, octagonal); Balcaskie House (twin circular dovecotes); Bogward Dovecote, St Andrews (Beehive); Garden of St Mary's College, St Andrews (early eighteenth century; there is also a tower pigeon loft).

On from Kenly Green the road to Crail swings past the Gallows Law, where miscreants, guilty or innocent, kicked their heels into eternity. Falside Farm lies on the right, and facing the road is an intriguing agricultural relic in the lee of the modern farm buildings.

Horse-mills were once a common sight in Fife; these are low, circular or octagonal buildings – as at Falside – with conical roofs which used to house and protect the timber horse engine that drove the threshing drum in the adjoining barn. Generally the Fife horse-mills had several openings, usually spanned by a timber ring-beam, in turn supporting a very intricate core of roof timbers. The rafters diminished in size towards the apex of the roof in the older examples, and are clad with slates on the outside and usually finished in a large knop finial. Internally the horse-mill would be dominated by a large, square cross-beam traversing the centre of the mill parallel to the barn wall. This beam was formerly used to support the central shaft of the engine. On the floor would be a corresponding soleplate to take the base of the shaft. At one time horse-mills were an essential part of a farm's economy, replacing the tedious job of threshing by flail and allowing larger quantities of grain to be threshed and cleaned by a smaller labour force. There's another round conical horse-mill nearby at Bonnytown Farm.

Next to Falside is Pitmilly, the old mansion now only represented by its lodges. These policies were owned in the twelfth century by the priors of St Andrews Cathedral, and certainly by the fifteenth century by the Monypennys, who were lairds for over 700 years with the title 'Barons of the Barony of Pitmilly'. There is a persistent local legend, which seems to have originated in William Tulloch, Bishop of Moray's history of the family (now seen as clearly forged). As it is a fragment of attested local folklore it is worth retelling.

The story recounts how the Monypennys received their name from Malcolm Canmore (r. 1058–93). In the days when Malcolm was fleeing from the wrath of Macbeth, the king asked a stranger for the loan of a few pennies. The str.anger replied: 'Nae sire, no a few pennies, but mony pennies'. When Malcolm triumphed he officially dubbed the stranger 'Monypenny' and endowed him with properties; such tosh has long outlived Pitmilly. The policies and mansion were sold in 1928 and subsequently the mansion became a hotel. The mansion was demolished in 1974 when the latter enterprise failed. Nevertheless the estate is remembered in the weather jingle:

> Blaw the wind where it likes
> There's bield about Pitmillie dykes.

Kingsbarns

Kingsbarns is divided into two of the old land 'quarters', north and south. Originally called North Barns, the village became Kingsbarns after the extensive barns, now vanished, which were used to store the monarch's grain for use at Crail, or Falkland Palace. Land here was given to the Black Friars of St Andrews in 1519 and dues from it supported Dominican friars who preached at St Monans and Dominican students at the university. In 1592 James VI bestowed the land on his former family nurse, Helen Little, in gratitude. The original church of Kingsbarns was built in 1631 when it became dissociated from that of Crail; the church was enlarged in 1810–11. The Old Manse (1847), now called West Lodge, has been divided into two private houses and lies behind the primary school (1822). The church spire, which was added in 1865–66, has circular windows, some blind, and showing the marks of many hands.

Eighteenth-century and Georgian houses mark Kingsbarns' history, and the village owes much to an eighteenth-century laird called John Corstorphine who built Kingsbarns House in the square for his own use in 1794. Once the partan (crab) yawls put into Kingsbarns but the village was formerly known for its Osnaburg sheeting and shirting. Down by the seashore are relics of the breakwater a farmer in the late nineteenth century built for the shipping of local potatoes to England. Probably the breakwater and the dykes of the fields were built from the stones of the now-vanished castle of Kingsbarns, which lay to the west of the coastal walk to Crail.

In the hallway of the Erskine family home at nearby Cambo House, the Fife Hunt gazes collectively from the montage of the 1880s, and in a corner of the picture is a lively cameo of what Cambo House used to look like before the disastrous fire of 8 July 1878. The old house with its central tower was swept away; Wardrop and Reid's design of 1879–81 remains, although it was divided into flats in the late 1950s. In its tower rests Kingsbarns' old public clock. Cambo, once linked with Kellie, was a twelfth-century foundation and stronghold of the Norman de Cambhous. The Myretouns (Mortons) held it from 1364 to 1668 when Sir Charles Erskine, Lord Lyon King of Arms, bought the property; the

Erskines have lived here ever since.

Local folklore recalls how the Kingsbarns inhabitants looted the Erskine wine cellars in 1878 during the fire; the locals were drunk for weeks on the best of the French vineyards. At a distance from the house a Regency mausoleum contains the tombs of the Erskine family and the earls of Kellie.

Associated with the history of Cambo are the boundary-linked estates of Randerston and Wormiston. There was an estate and castle at Randerston in the thirteenth century owned by Sir John de Randolfstoun, thence the Myretons by 1429. The present house was built in the sixteenth century. Today the neighbouring house of Wormiston has a fourteenth-century foundation with its main architecture being of the sixteenth century with nineteenth-century additions. The property belonged to the Spens family who were Constables of Crail. Once the Spens lived in Crail Castle, but when this was abandoned the family moved to Wormiston, the centre of the crown barony. The house was owned sporadically by the Balfours and the earls of Lindsay who sold the property in the 1950s to Lady Erskine as a dower house; she died here in 1958 and the house remained empty until the late 1960s when it was purchased and renovated.

Crail

Crail's history and legend is best honed-up on at the local museum in Marketgait. Its home lies in the shadow of the Old Tolbooth and its door carries the marriage lintel for TM and IP with the date 1703. Here all the clues to Crail's past can be found from its beginnings as a royal burgh in 1310; it remained an independent unit until 1975. The burgh's charter was confirmed by Robert I which gave the burgh the right to trade on the Sabbath. But the place was old even then for Countess Ada de Warren, mother of Malcolm IV and William I, often dwelt here in the 1160s when the burgh was but a hamlet around its harbour. From holiday resort and medieval port trading with the Low Countries, to an ecclesiastical suburb of St Andrews, Crail, 'the corner town', was long a portal to European riches and ideas.

The railway came to Crail in 1886 (the old station is now a

Cobbled street and fisher houses, Crail. (STARALP)

garden centre), and brought a sense of wider horizons which had not been known since the town lost its monopoly as the fish market for Forth and Tay catches. In Marketplace the much-altered sixteenth-century Dutch-influenced Tolbooth was centrepiece of a medieval market, one of the largest in Europe. On the thick-set tower, with its upper tiers dating from the 1770s, sits a fish weathervane as a constant reminder of the famous Crail capon (a haddock, split and dried) which made the burgh celebrated. The Tolbooth bell was made in Holland in 1520 and once belonged to the church.

In the Marketgate, across from the Mercat Cross with its unicorn and seventeenth-century shaft (sited here in 1887), are the Regency town house of the Inglis family called Kirkmay (1817) and the much earlier and well-preserved Friar's Court (1686), restored in 1938. A memorial fountain celebrating the Diamond Jubilee of Queen Victoria sets off Marketgate. All around are hints of the medieval church and its officers' titles in Crail's place-names: Prior's Croft, Priory Doocot and Prior's Well hint at the priory of St Rufus and the properties of the nuns of Haddington in Nethergate. The latter is now a treelined backwater which used to be furnished with

Dating from the twelfth century the Church of St Mary, Crail, was expanded in the sixteenth century; it was renovated in 1963. The fine memorial gates remember the dead of two World Wars. (STARALP)

weavers' cottages; the bleaching yards and cloths were once spread around the greens of the town.

Crail's parish church, the old Kirk of St Mary, was first consecrated in the twelfth century, but has been considerably altered, particularly in 1796, 1815 and 1963. It became a collegiate church in 1517, had nine altars and was rich in ornamentation, vestments and books. In June 1559, John Knox preached in the church and the kiss of death was placed upon its medieval ecclesiastical heritage. Within the church lobby is the Sculptured Cross dating from the ninth century.

Crail kirkyard is a good place to pause and think of how Fife's past inhabitants still speak to us in stone. The study of graveyard epitaphs is a much underrated source of clues as to who the Fifers of the past were and what they did. Fife has a plethora of public and private graveyards with tombstones, mausoleums, vaults, wall plaques and memorials to offer vital insights to the ancient kingdom's history and legend. A study of Fife's epitaphs can also reveal old parish and place-names, vanished hamlets and farms and estates, as well as instances of bubonic plague (fourteenth–eighteenth century), typhus (1140, 1694–1707), smallpox (1610–

eighteenth century) and cholera, together with data on miscellaneous causes of death and life expectancy.

The first true epitaphs to be expected in Fife would be of Roman date, and are yet to be identified; nevertheless the very close neighbour to Fife's boundary is the vexillation-fortress of Carpow (environs of Newburgh) which produced fragments of commemorative slabs. The earliest epitaphs after the Roman form a mixture of runic and Latin characters, with the Anglo-Norman use of Latin and Norman French in a short formula like 'Pray for the soul of . . .'. Many fine early medieval tombs were destroyed at the Reformation. By the sixteenth century epitaphs had taken on a more sentimental to cloying content, but by the seventeenth century they were beginning to show more literary merit. Eighteenth-century epitaphs were flowery and gloomy, while Victorian examples are sickly.

The objective of Fife's headstones is to give details of the persons buried below, but the range of information for those in search of

Fife's older graveyards are rich in informative
headstones giving details of local Fifers.
(Author's collection)

Detail of the kind of grave carvings found in many of Fife's older
graveyards. (Author's collection)

family roots or local social history can be quite wide. Here's an
example of what can be revealed:

	HERE LYETH ENTOMBED
Name	JOHN GOURLIE
Occupation	SCHOOLMASTER
Birthplace	A NATIVE OF CERES PARISH
Date of death	THE 7 APRIL 1787
Age	AND OF HIS AGE: 58
Marriage	HIS WIFE MARY WATTERS
	PLACED THIS STONE
Deceased's interests	Ah John what changes since I saw thee last
	Thy fishing and thy shooting days are past
	Thy pen and pencil thou cans't weild no more
Deceased's character	Thy nods, grimaces, winks, and pranks
	are o'er.
Wife's dates	AND TO MARY WATTERS
	WIFE OF THE ABOVE
	BORN: 1731 DIED: 1798
Decendant	AND ONLY DAUGHTER
	MARY
	BORN: 1751 DIED: 1803

Many of Fife's older epitaphs reveal long-vanished trade names from baxters (bakers) to fleshers (butchers) and from souters (shoemakers) to mantymakkars (dressmakers). Surmounting, or around the gravestones may be emblems of the deceased's work, say, hammers and nails for a blacksmith, or a shuttle and wool card for a weaver. Some have a touch of humour. At Crail is this:

Here lies my good and gracious Auntie
   Wham death has packed in his portmanty
   Threescore and ten years did God gift her
   And here she lies, wha de'il daurs lift her?

And another at Crail:

Here ALEXANDER MAPSIES corpse doth ly
   In death
   Death snatched him of most suddenly
   The King of Terrors made him fall
   A solemn warning unto all
   In friendship good and peace livd he
   With all mankind
   And thus he died a presant Ballie of
   This Burgh the good of which he always sought
   He died the twenty-ninth of June
   In Anno one thousand and seven hundred and
     fifty nine
   He hurried was from this stage in the
   Fiftieth year of his age

Near the kirk gate stands the Blue Boulder which used to be kissed by Crail folk leaving the burgh for work elsewhere, to ensure their return. The bolder retains a more sinister legend. It is said that the Devil flung this rock from the Isle of May to demolish the church as it was being built. It missed and the boulder split in two, one part landing at Balcomie beach and the other where it is now – it still exhibits his dark lordship's thumbprint. At the Kirkgate too stood a school, demolished in 1890. Sir William Myretoun founded two schools in Crail in the 1500s where music and grammar were a particular forte.

The harbour at Crail. (STARALP)

Crail's most ancient neighbourhood is around the harbour. Above the anchorages stood the royal castle of David I until its walls fell into the sea. Here the king feasted on '9,850 herrings and two porpoises' on one occasion, and made a special pilgrimage on 18 December, the feast day of St Rufus of Antioch, whose name blessed the castle chapel. The site of David's castle is occupied by a Victorian mansion, divided into flats. The King's Mill was sited next to the harbour.

The origins of Crail harbour are lost in antiquity, but there have been extensive repairs to it since the 1500s, and the west pier was added in 1826–28 to the design of Robert Stevenson. Fisherlore notes that in 1803 the harbour was home port for '6 ships and barks and about 80 fishing boats'.

Crail Harbour looking west. (STARALP)

Fronting the principal quay in Crail is the crow-stepped Custom House of the 1690s, which was repaired by the Crail Preservation Society in 1964. The relic of the excisemen who chased the fleetfoot smugglers who plied the Fife coast hereabouts was acquired by the National Trust for Scotland. All around Crail are relics too of local craftsworkers. Spinning lint-yarn was an eighteenth-century cottage industry in Crail, but coal was once mined here and shoes were made. Crail craft market was legendary: pots, cloths, silverware, copperware, wood and leather objects were sold and displayed in booths presided over by the various deacons of the crafts and guilds. In passing it is noted that golf was an early pastime for Crail folk: the Crail Golfing Society was instituted on 23 February 1786.

In Victoria Gardens, St Andrews Road (A918), is the early Christian relic known as the Standing Stone of Sauchope, dating from the ninth century. It was moved to this location in 1929. The gardens were opened on 1 July 1914 and were presented to the town by an expatriate, one George A. Gay of Hartford, Connecticut.

From Marketgate the main road leads to Fife Ness, the most easterly part of Fife. An old airfield lies along this road. Here functioned a busy airport during the First World War; in the

Second World War the site was a Royal Naval (Fleet Air Arm) operation unit for light torpedo bombers such as HMS *Jackdaw*. In 1946 it became Scotland's Royal Navy Boys' Training Estate as HMS *Bruce*; the MD vacated the site in the 1960s. Provosts of Crail once added 'Rear Admiral of the Forth' to their civic titles.

As the road bends right, Balcomie Castle, centrepiece of a modern farmstead, lies to the left. Privately owned and not open to the public, Balcomie Castle is an E-plan structure of the late sixteenth century with a nineteenth-century mansion and agricutural complex attached. The fine gatehouse remains, decorated with interesting panels showing the arms of the Learmonth family and the Myretouns.

Fife Ness, a now-vanished settlement, is best explored on foot. The area is dominated by Balcomie Golf Links. At Craighead farm the road sweeps round to the Coastguard Station: where the road skirts the farmstead, the Dane's Dyke runs down to the sea. Local legend ascribes it to Danish invaders, and the dyke once enclosed the whole promontory of Fife Ness. At the sea end of the dyke Long Man's Grave marks the supposed tomb of a Danish hero.

Round Foreland Head, towards Lochaber Rocks, the old anchorage can be seen where Marie de Guise-Lorraine, the bride of James V, landed on 10 June 1538. Her fleet captain had mistaken Balcomie Castle for that of St Andrews, and she rested a few nights at Balcomie on her way to St Andrews and her nuptial blessing at St Andrews Cathedral. These were the days when Fife Ness was a royal burgh through the new owner of Balcomie, Sir James Learmonth of Dairsie, who was a joint master of the royal household with Patrick Wemyss of Pittencrieff.

Out to sea the North Carr Beacon gives light and sound warnings to shipping. These rocks have claimed many vessels and lives, the most famous wreck in local lore being that of the passenger steamer *Windsor Castle* in 1844. All round are relics of the salmon-fishing cottages. One feature to look out for is Constantine's cave, with its walls decorated with incised crosses and primitive animals. Constantine II, King of Alba (903–943), became an abbot of the Culdee monastery at St Andrews.

About three miles from Crail is Airdrie House, whose fourteenth-century policies became a major seat of the

Lumisdaines. The privately owned Airdrie House incorporates the tower of a castle of 1586 and has seen much modernisation; it was probably originally a hunting lodge for Crail Castle. The A917 hugs the coast from Crail to Anstruther and a few hundred yards along the way to Kilrenny it passes the old Salt Pans. Fishing and agriculture gave Kilrenny its character and the street names show the old structure of the village. Kirk Wynd led to the commercial heart of Trade Street which once rang with the hammers of the farriers and the shoemakers. Yet most folk worked on the land and lived in the cottar houses like those in the curiously named Routine Row – undoubtedly a corruption of *route de roi*, 'king's way'. Kilrenny once had political importance in that it had its own MP in the Scottish parliament. In 1578 the village was given a charter by Patrick Adamson, titular Archbishop of St Andrews, to erect a market cross and hold a weekly fair.

Modern historical scholarship and archaeological work have added to the early Kilrenny story, wherein the legends and history surrounding two Pictish stones are relevant. In 1993 and 1997 respectively fragments of the artefact known as the 'Kilrenny Stone' were found on Kilrenny beach and at Cornceres farm. They form part of an eighth-century cross slab bearing a Celtic cross and a fabulous fox-like beast. The earlier 'Skeith Stone'. with its eight-pointed cross and Chi-Rho (an early symbol for Christ's name), are thought to have marked the boundaries of a monastery dedicated to St Ethernan, a companion of St Adrian of the May Island: Kilrenny means 'church of Ethernan'. All along this coast are Pictish pagan–Christian symbols at various sites from Crail Kirk and Chapel Cave, Caiplie, to Lundin Links and Scoonie. The landlords of Kilrenny area were once the monks of Dryburgh Abbey, who were given the policies of *Kilrethni* by Ada de Warenne around 1177. They sponsored a church on the site of an ancient edifice and it was rededicated in 1243. This church was demolished in 1807–08 when the present one was built; the tower is all that remains of the earlier building. It was renovated in 1933 and retains its plain interior, but with a fine reredos.

Abutting the foot of the tower is the huge eighteenth-century tomb of the Lumisdaines of Innergellie, and around the corner is the equally massive mausoleum set up by the Duchess of Portland in memory of her father, General Scot of Balcomie, *c.*1776. Local legend has it that the bones of the murdered Cardinal David Beaton lie somewhere around the Beaton burial enclosure, brought here by his nephew John Beaton of Balfour in 1546.

Kilrenny's old manse is not in the heart of the village, but lies across the main road: built in 1818, it stands foursquare and stolid with a part-moat effect. Some windows are blocked up, not as is popularly supposed, to avoid the window tax of 1697–1851, but simply according to an incumbent's wishes.

Cellardyke evolved around a crofter–fisherfolk community at the old creek of Skinfasthaven at Nether Kilrenny. The extant harbour dates from the sixteenth century and was rebuilt between 1829–31. Many of the core eighteenth-century houses remain. Once Cellardyke had its own castle, built by Bishop James Kennedy of St Andrews by the harbour; nearby was the anchorage for Bishop Kennedy's barge, the Bremen-built *Salvatour*, which plied regularly to the Hanseatic ports; the vessel was wrecked off Bamburgh in 1473. Here too Cardinal David Beaton enjoyed the episcopal residence, descending the 'Cardinal's Steps' to join the barque ferrying pilgrims to St Andrews Cathedral. The town's almost parallel two main thoroughfares of East Forth Street and George Street are linked by the town hall of 1883 in Tolbooth Wynd. Cellardyke's first town hall was built in 1624, but below the dedication plaque of the later building is the iron-clamped old cross of Kilrenny dated 1642.

Anstruther

Modern Anstruther is divided into two, Easter and Wester, by the Dreel Burn. Past the long curve of Edwardian houses, the A917 from Crail sweeps past Cunzie House. Here Robert Louis Stevenson spent some time in 1868, ostensibly to help his father who had been put in charge of harbour works. In 'Random Memories' from *Across the Plains* (1892) RLS says, 'he lodged with Baillie Brown in a room filled with rose-leaves'. A carpenter by trade, Brown was vouchsafed young RLS's secret: 'I came as a young man to glean engineering experience from the building of the breakwater. But indeed I had already my own private determination to be an author . . . Though I haunted the break-water by day . . . my only industry was in the hours when I was not on duty!'

In the evenings RLS wrote *Voces Fidelium*, his dramatic verse dialogues. A verse of his is now weathering to extinction on the plaque of Cunzie House:

> Nor one quick beat of your warm heart,
> Nor thought that came to you apart,
> Pleasure not pity, love nor pain
> Nor sorrow has gone by in vain.

Stevenson also strolled across the road to the aptly named Burial Brae leading to Anstruther Easter parish church. The T-plan kirk is dated 1634 by the door and was dedicated to St Adrian of May. On the south wall of the church is the memorial of 1898 which contains the longest epitaph word in Europe, *Tetuanireiaiteraiatea*, which translates as 'The great God whose power extends to the heaven of heavens'. Such was the cognomen of Princess Tetuane Marama of Tahiti who married George Dairsie of Anstruther. She lived near the top of Kirk Wynd in Johnstone Lodge.

Abutting the church is Anstruther Town Hall (1871), a fine centrepiece for a characterful area of two-storey dwellings and narrow streets. The burgh sports another town hall, that in the High Street, a house of 1795 converted in 1912; it lies near St Andrew's Church Hall with its sixteenth-century steeple in the High Street. School Green and High Street, with its Masonic temple, impart the flavour of the past. In High Street too, was born William Tennant (1784–1848) in a narrow building next door to a tavern known as the 'Smuggler's Howff': the house was demolished in the nineteenth century, but the site is marked by a blue plaque.

Anster Fair

William Tennant was born at Anstruther on 15 May 1784, son of a local merchant and small farmer. Largely self-taught after he left St Andrews University without a degree, Tennant was much taken with the idiosyncracies of the Scots tongue and steeped himself in local lore, legend and historical tradition. While working as a clerk to his corn-merchant elder brother, Tennant toiled on his first major work *Anster Fair*, after the publication of which in 1812 he was appointed schoolmaster at Dunino. His private studies in oriental languages in St Andrews University library stood him in good stead, for by 1819 he was appointed teacher of classical and oriental languages at Dollar Academy. He continued writing and produced a whole portfolio of long poems, verses and articles; these include *The Thane of Fife*, 1822 (a story of a Norse invasion) and *Papistry Storm'd*, 1827 (the destruction of St Andrews Cathedral by the Protestant mob in 1559). By 1834 he was appointed Professor of Oriental Languages at St Andrews University. Tennant died at his home, 'Davengrove', near Dollar on 15 October 1848, to be buried at his native Anstruther.

Tennant derived his inspiration for *Anster Fair* from the Fife folk-song 'Maggie Lauder' in which Maggie, a local beauty, is wooed by the celebrated Border piper, Rob the Ranter. With a background of Anstruther Fair, to which Maggie Lauder invites Rob, Tennant interweaves Fife folklore and legend and the supernatural world of wizard Michael Scott to produce one of Scotland's finest comic poems.

The poem begins:

> While some of Troy and pettish heroes sing,
>   And some of Rome, and chiefs of pious fame,
> And some of men that thought it harmless thing
>   To smite off heads in Mars' bloody game,
> And some of Eden's garden gay with spring,
>   And hell's dominions terrible to name,
> I sing a theme far livelier, happier, gladder,
> I sing of ANSTER FAIR and bonny MAGGIE LAUDER.
>
> What time from east, from west, from south, from north,
>   From every hamlet, town, and smoky city,
> Laird, clown, and beau, to Anster Fair came forth,
>   The young, the gay, the handsome, and the witty,
> To try in various sport and game their worth,
>   Whilst prize before them MAGGIE sat, the pretty,
> And after many a feat, and joke, and banter,
> Fair MAGGIE's hand was won by mighty ROB the RANTER.

Tennant is buried at St Adrian's church, where his inscribed obselisk is near the north-east corner.

Anstruther's link with the sea

Past the church and along School Green is Melville's Manse. Named after James Melville (1556–1614), whose *Autobiography and Diary* is a valuable account of his ministry at Anstruther; he was the nephew of the founder of Scottish Presbyterianism, Andrew Melville (1545–1622). Melville began to construct his manse in 1590. The story is still recounted how Melville acted as a negotiator when survivors of the Spanish Armada supply ship *El Grand Grifon* arrived at Anstruther on 6 December 1588. One of the Spanish grandees, General Don Juan Gomez de Medina, came ashore with his retinue and explained what had befallen the Spanish fleet; de Medina had himself been wrecked on Fair Isle and made his passage in a hired ship to Anstruther. The Anstruther folk gave sincere hospitality to the Spaniards which was to be repaid in a fortuitous way. On his way home de Medina called in at Cadiz where he found a shipwrecked Anstruther fishing crew impounded by the authorities. The Commander pleaded the case of the Anstruther fishermen to King Philip II of Spain and obtained their release.

The history and legend of modern Anstruther is best assessed by visiting the Scottish Fisheries Museum. The museum was opened in July 1969 at St Ayles on the harbourside. Fish trade has been conducted on the site since 1318 when a land charter and fish-market rights were granted by the Norman de Candelas family to the monks of Balmerino Abbey. Thereafter a community of fishermen, brewers, coopers and salt dealers settled nearby; their spiritual needs were catered for by St Ayles Chapel, built in the fifteenth century, whose window-head is still preserved. Today the oldest building on the museum site is the accommodation for the representatives of Balmerino Abbey, now restored and colloquially known as 'Abbot's Lodging'. The museum presents a panoramic picture of the fishing communities of Scotland, and includes a recreation of a net-loft, a fisher-family dwelling of around 1900 and the restored herring drifter *Reaper* (1901). Here too is the memorial to Scottish fishermen lost at sea.

Originally called Kinstrother, 'end of the marsh', and a royal burgh from 1567, Anstruther was until the 1940s the capital of the herring fishing industry in Scotland during the winter months. Rich shoals of herring arrived in the waters of the Forth annually and Scots fishermen based themselves at Anstruther in January and remained until March. The shoals deserted their traditional waters in the Second World War. Once it was said to be possible to walk from one side of Anstruther harbour to the other by stepping from boat to boat.

Anstruther once had its anti-pirate squad, and was a rich recruitment ground for the press gangs of the Royal Navy. Records show that Anstruther sailors played a vital part in the victory over the Dutch fleet at the Battle of Copenhagen in 1801, during the first war with Napoleon.

Opposite the Old Murray Library (1908) is the Burgh Cross. Standing some 9 ft high, only the shaft is original, dating from 1677. Further along Shore Street, on the gable end of a shop, is an inset of 1885 showing the carefully preserved masonic tools of the Lodge St Ayles No. 95. Along the harbourside the late medieval merchants' houses still stand, and the buildings have been restored to retain their historical appearance.

Out of Castle Street runs Wightman's Wynd, a narrow dank passage jostling the site of the Castle of Dreel, built by the time of Robert the Bruce. The 'dumb-bell' loop in the wall is considered to be a fragment of the old fortress. The Wynd emerges near the Post Office Close, a stone's throw from the birthplace of Thomas Chalmers (1780–1847), the first Moderator of the Assembly of the Free Church of Scotland.

Round into Crail Road the way leads past the Smugglers Inn where Jacobite conspirators met during the 1715 rebellion. In the town archives was a letter written on behalf of Charles Edward Stuart's secretary, James Murray of Broughton, thanking Anstruther folk for quartering his troops in 1745. The road leads over the Dreel bridge: the sixteenth-century wooden bridge was replaced in 1795 and is the entrance to a quarter redolent of Fife legend and history.

At the corner is St Nicholas's Church with its sixteenth-century tower. St Ethernan founded a church here in the seventh century, dedicated to St Adrian. The site was dedicated to St Nicholas, patron of the sea in 1243. Here John Knox preached destruction and the last vestiges of popery were swept away. According to local legend St Nicholas tower carried the first landward sea beacon ever lit in Fife.

Two town houses here stand out in local lore. Buckie House, reconstructed by the National Trust for Scotland, is seventeenth century in origin and displays the buckie (shell decoration) of local worthy Alexander Batchelor, who died in 1866. Across the way a blue plaque marks the home of Captain John Keay who won fame as master of the tea-clipper *Ariel*, which held the all-time record on the famous China Run of 83 days from Gravesend to Hong Kong. *Ariel*'s great rival was Captain MacKinnon on the *Taeping*, owned by Alexander Roger of Cellardyke.

A close neighbour property is the sixteenth-century Dreel Tavern with a plaque which reads: 'James V, 1513–42, travelled incognito through Fife as the "Guid Man o'Ballengeich", coming to the Dreel Burn and fearful of wetting his hose, he was carried across at this point by a stout gaberlunzie woman, who was rewarded with the King's Purse'. 'Gaberlunzie' is an old Scots word meaning tramp or beggar. Along from the Dreel Tavern is the Craw's Nest Hotel whose name recalls a visit by Charles II. When entertained by Sir Philip Anstruther, the king remarked: 'Such a fine supper I have gotten in a craw's nest' – Charles was referring to a meal taken in a lofty tower at Dreel Castle. Local tradition recalls that Anstruther was once famous for less respectable entertainment. In the burgh at Card's Wynd met the Regency club known as the 'Beggars' Benison', which continued until 1836; it was a bawdy, self-indulgent institution for the delight of its aristocratic members.

'Anster lore' and Fife's superstitious fisherfolk

Of all the trades of Fife that of the fisherman attracted most superstitions, probably as a consequence of trying to earn a living against the dangerous capriciousness of the sea. The old folk still talk of 'Anster lore', that curious folk philosophy that suggests that actions and artefacts can bring bad luck or good omens. Fiercely superstitious Fife fishermen saw bad luck looming if they encountered a clergyman whilst *en route* to their ship, or saw a rat, a pig or a rabbit before setting sail. A dog howling near a ship was deemed a bad omen, as was a white cat by a berth – a black cat, though, was never chased from a vessel.

A whole range of seabirds from the albatross to the stormy petrel were considered to be the souls of doomed seamen. Not surprisingly most Anster lore concerned the seagull, a bird that should never be wantonly killed. A seagull flying against the window of a house was a warning of misfortune for any household member then at sea. Three gulls flying together overhead was an omen of death. Omens of doom and fatality far outweigh any others in Anster lore, from a candle blowing out indicating a drowning at sea, to a shipwreck forecast by a ship's bell tolling on board untouched by human hand.

Fife fishermen considered it very unlucky to lose a mop or bucket overboard. Many other actions were also deemed unlucky. For instance, to sing and laugh before an early morning sailing was deemed ill-fortune, as was whistling. Every Fife fisherman's child knew that witches could summon up storms by whistling. Again a ship was doomed if its launch name was changed, or if any figurehead it might have be damaged. Children who lived by the sea were warned if they made grotesque faces at the moment the tide turned they ran the risk of finding the grimace fixed permanently. The state of the tide was also deemed to affect lives and actions of those who lived by the shore; births were thought most likely to occur with the flowing tide, and death with the ebb.

A whole range of taboo vocabulary grew up. It was bad luck to say such words as drowning, hare, eggs, pig or anything to do with magic or witchcraft either on land or sea – all would bring bad luck, as would the wearing of, or uttering the words, green or orange.

Perhaps the most curious superstition of all along the Fife coast was that certain families were 'unlucky', and consequently their family names. This might well have something to do with a fisherman who might be considered accident-prone. It was said that certain surnames ending in double consonants were unlucky, like Kerr or Watt. Some Anstruther folk were not happy to voyage with a mate called Melville – after all one Andrew Melville was arraigned on a charge of witchcraft in St Andrews, and everyone on Fife's southern shore knew that witchcraft ran in families.

Pittenweem

A town of Flemish gables and designs, Pittenweem – the name
derives from *pit* meaning farm and *uamh* meaning cave – is proud
to tell its visitors by road sign that it is the 'East Neuk Fishing
Centre'. All the narrow streets lead to the steep inclines down to the
harbour, yet for the visitor the basic tone of Pittenweem's legend and
history is at first ecclesiastical. The two buildings which stand as the
main road snakes from the east into town are modern 'holy' places.
On the left is the Church of Scotland manse built in 1838, while on
the right is the Roman Catholic Church (a villa of 1830 converted in
1935) and Presbytery of Christ the King, supporting above its door a
sculpture (1952) by the craftsman Hew Lorimer.

The street names reflect Pittenweem's religious past, like
Marygate and Abbey Wall Road, and the visitor cannot but notice
the great sacerdotal heart of the town. Off Marygate and down by
the old folks' cottages by Priory Court, past the Episcopal church of
St John the Evangelist, 1805 (reorientated 1869–70) lies the fine old
priory gateway.

Pittenweem harbour was in ruins by the sixteenth century,
but was repaired in 1687, and around it houses were established
by brewers, shipbuilders, fishermen, tobacco merchants and ship-
masters. At the harbour breakwater, 'The Gyles', is a seventeenth-
century house owned by the other Captain James Cook, the one
who took Charles II to France after the Battle of Worcester in 1651.

Pittenweem's general market was justifiably famous, particularly
the fairs of Ladyday (26 March) for linseed and shoes; Lammas (1
August, also known locally as Gooseberry Market) for wool, and
Martinmas (11 November) for cattle.

North of Pittenweem lies Grangemuir House, in the centre of
the Prior of St Andrews' ancient hunting grounds. Built by Robert
Bruce of Grangemuir around 1807, the house was enlarged in the
1870s by Lord William Keith Douglas. Chesterhill House was once
the home of the nineteenth-century Fife biographer, M.F. Conolly.

The land abutting and including the site of the Priory of
Pittenweem, dedicated to the Blessed Virgin and St Adrian, was given
to the medieval church authorities by David I, about 1143. Some time
between 1290 and 1307 the Priory of the Isle of May was transferred

to the Pittenweem lands to be called variously 'the monastery of Pittenweem alias of the Isle of May'. The priory became a dependency of the Augustinian priory at St Andrews by 1318.

The early history of the priory foundation at Pittenweem is vague and legend links it to a Culdee site of the seventh century with a local hagiography glorifying St Adrian, St Margaret, St Fillan and St Monan to the foundation (see page 117). By the early fourteenth century the Priors of Pittenweem are starting to be mentioned prominently as papal judge-legates and adjudicators. From the fifteenth century the priory began to lose importance, with various archbishops and bishops holding the foundation *in commendam*; one such was Andrew Forman, Archbishop of St Andrews 1514–21. By 1487 the priory was described as non-conventual and of little importance as a place 'dependent on the *virtuosis laboribus* – honest toil – of the poor fishermen inhabiting the burgh and barony of Pittenweem'. In 1452 Pittenweem had become a burgh of regality, raised to a royal burgh in 1543.

At the Reformation only six canons dwelt on site, and by 1567 the priory had been passed into the ownership of Sir James Balfour of Pittendreich by the Commendator of Pittenweem, James Stewart, Earl of Moray. This being so James VI confirmed to the magistrates and commonalty of Pittenweem the right to use certain of the priory properties for their corporate duties. In 1606 the lands of Pittenweem were erected into a temporal barony in favour of Frederick Stewart, and by charter he was created a lord of parliament as Lord Pittenweem; the title died with him in 1625. Thereafter the priory site and lands went through various hands until David Low, Bishop of Ross and Argyll, bequeathed them to the church of St John the Evangelist.

A relic of the legends of the priory's history can be found down steep Cove Wynd. Here is St Fillan's Cave in the care of the Episcopal church; legend has it that the sixth-century Fillan of Glendochart lived in the cave during his mission to the early dwellers of the East Neuk.

The Culdees of Fife

In almost every medieval parish of Fife – and Pittemweem is no exception – there are mentions of the Culdees.

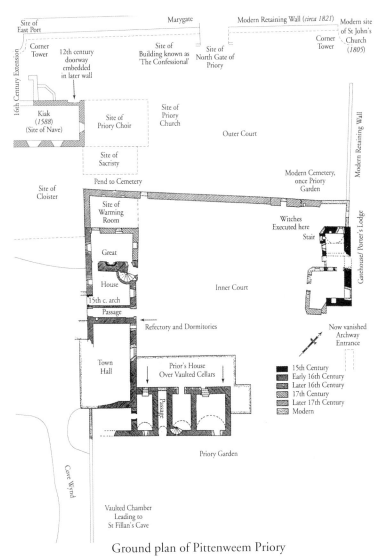

Ground plan of Pittenweem Priory

The term Culdee comes from the Old Irish *Célé dé*, meaning a companion, or servant, of God. This was rendered in Scottish medieval Latin as *Keledei* in such texts as those of the late twelfth century. The Culdees flourished during the early ninth century to the early thirteenth century as members of an ascetic movement within the Celtic Church.

The Culdees had two religious capitals outside their strong community at Iona, one at Dunkeld and the other at St Andrews, where they had become established by 943; they were to survive in St Andrews as a separate unit until the 1180s but their lore lived on for many decades. Broadly during the reorganisation of the church in the twelfth century the Culdees were absorbed as canons, regular and secular.

In their early form the Culdees lived a secular life in companies of around a dozen with their own head, variously dubbed provost, prior or abbot. They do not appear to have been celibate and their positions were often held on a hereditary basis. Their work was to succour the poor, study the scriptures and conduct worship. There was an element of education too, with an appointed Culdee as *ferleiginn* (man of learning) to oversee the studies of the *scoloqs* (scholars) in training for church duties. At St Andrews the Culdees elected the Celtic bishops of the earliest diocese and assisted in their work.

At St Andrews the Culdees were still in existence when the Augustinian Order founded their priory (1141) as a chapter of the cathedral church. Thereafter, as ordained by Pope Eugenius III, as the Culdees died out their places were taken by the Augustinian canons as beneficiaries of Culdee properties. It is known though that by the early thirteenth century there was a group of clergy at St Andrews enjoying papal, royal and episcopal protection as a community of secular canons of the collegiate church of St Mary at St Andrews. These canons were confusingly called Culdees although their Celtic counterparts had died out. Before 1290 the Culdee church at St Andrews was a chapel royal called the College of Our Lady of the Rock at the Kirkheugh St Andrews, with clergy acting as royal and episcopal clerks.

Thus the Culdees were early Fifers with properties, rights and privileges from their establishments at St Serf's, Culross and from Dunfermline to St Andrews. Various Fife churches also boasted Culdee foundations like Scoonie Church, Leven, and those at Markinch and Abdie.

Withcraft in Pittenweem

Within the priory ground at Pittenweem were enacted the great cruelties against local 'witches'. In no other place in Scotland were witches hunted with such fervour as in Pittenweem. All of the nonsensical trials for witchcraft in Pittenweem occurred after the Presbyterian Reformation, the first cases taking place between 3 November–13 December 1643. In his *Annals of Pittenweem*, Cook cites three cases in which John Dawson, Thomas Cook and John Crombie were 'ordanit' to pay the expenses of executing their relatives for witchcraft. Pittenweem goes down in the history of witchcraft in Scotland for the great trials of 1704–05, largely underlining the bigotry of the ministers of the Scottish kirk which fanned the flames of superstition and persecution and incited mob violence.

Largely these witchcraft cases grew out of the ramblings of a deranged youth called Patrick Morton, who made accusations against various people who displeased him. One such was Janet Corphat who was tortured, tried, convicted and thrown into Pittenweem tolbooth jail. Eventually she was released as no real evidence could be sustained against her. Alas for her, the paranoid Pittenweem minister the Rev. Patrick Cowper incited the mob to attack her.

In his *Tracts on Witchcraft* (1677) John Webster tells the story: 'During the night of the 30 January 1705, a mob of Pittenweem folk dragged her from the house in which she had been staying and took her, bruised, bleeding and bound to the beach. There she was tied to a ship's mooring hawser and stoned; half dead, the last breath was crushed out of her with heavy stones laid on her chest.' John Webster concludes: 'And to be sure it was [that she was dead], they called a man with a horse and a sledge, and made him drive over her corpse backward and forward several times'. The Revd Cowper made no attempt to intervene and denied her broken corpse burial in Pittenweem kirkyard; none of the mob were prosecuted for Janet Corphat's murder.

The table below summarises the cases of witchcraft in Fife over 163 years.

CALENDAR OF FIFE WITCHCRAFT CASES 1542–1705

Abdie, 1662
Aberdour, 1622, 1650, 1654, 1661,
    1668
Anstruther, 1643
Anstruther Easter, 1701
Auchtermuchty, 1662
Auchtertool, 1662

Balmerino, 1648, 1649
Burntisland, 1597, 1598, 1649

Carnbee, 1666
Collessie, 1662
Crail, 1599, 1621, 1625, 1643
Creich, 1645
Culross, 1624

Dalgety, 1649
Dunfermline, 1563, 1628, 1643,
    1645, 1648, 1650
Dysart, 1626, 1627, 1630, 1632,
    1637, 1638, 1639, 1644

Falkland, 1661, 1162
Flisk, 1662
Forgan, 1662

Inverkeithing, 1621, 1623, 1649

Kilmany, 1662
Kinghorn, 1643
Kirkcaldy, 1604, 1621, 1632,
    1633, 1638, 1639

Luthrie, 1662

In all there were around
109 main witch trials in
Fife during 1542–1705.
The largest number (thirteen)
was at St Andrews.
One 'notable', Sir William
Stewart, Lord Lyon King
of Arms, was executed for
witchcraft at St Andrews
in 1569. And on 28 April
1572, John Knox took a
direct part in the trial
of Richard Bannatyne at
St Andrews.
The exact number of witch
executions in Fife is not
known. In 1643 alone,
some 40 people were
executed in Fife.

Case called at Dysart for
bewitching a cow, 5 May 1626.

In 1633 the Town Council of
Kirkcaldy spent £7 1s on
witch trials, rials, and the Kirk,
£17 10s.

Markinch, 1643
Monimail, 1648

Newburgh, 1610, 1653, 1661, 1662

Pittenweem, 1643, 1644, 1704, 1705

St Andrews, 1569, 1572, 1575, 1581
          1588, 1595, 1613, 1630,
          1643, 1644, 1645, 1667
Torryburn, 1624, 1630, 1666, 1703,
          1704

Wemyss, 1626, 1627
Wemyss, Wester, 1626, 1630

The 'Markinch Curse', to be
intoned by witches:

Our Lord forth raide,
His foal's foot slade:
Our Lord down lighted,
His foal's foot righted;
Saying: Flesh to flesh,
Blood to blood,
and bane to bane.
In Our Lord's name.

The kirk of Pittenween (1588) nestles alongside the distinctive burgh tower with its lock-up at the foot where Janet Corphat and others languished; along from the barred window stands the Town Cross, and although its capital bears the date 1711, it is likely that the shaft is sixteenth century. In the graveyard of the kirk are many interesting stones. Here lie the Hendersons of the Henderson Shipping Line, and one John Smith, the eighteenth-century horologist who made the church clock. In the High Street are a number of seventeenth-century properties including Kellie Lodge, the town house of the earls of Kellie.

At the end of Marygate, Routine Row branches off; at the corner of the Row the yellow-painted house bears a shield-plaque of unusual interest. It tells how near the site in 1736 the Kirkcaldy exciseman, James Stark, was robbed by two men, Andrew Wilson and Geordie Robertson. At their subsequent trial in Edinburgh, their courage and demeanour won popular admiration and their attempted escape while on their way to execution gave rise to the famous Porteous Riots immortalised by Sir Walter Scott in *The Heart of Midlothian* (1818).

St Monans

Formerly known as Abercrombie, which is in reality today a small village a mile or so away, St Monans lies between the Dreel Burn and St Monans Burn. Folklorists note that St Monans was one of the most superstitious villages in the East Neuk.

On the eastern outskirts of St Monans is an archaeological site which has played a significant part in local history. In the mid-eighteenth century the site was worked by the Newark Coal and Salt Company, established by local landowner Sir John Anstruther and his business partner Robert Fall. The coal mined nearby, known as 'panwood', was used to evaporate the sea water for salt reclamation. Today the windmill by the shore and the Coal Farm policies recall the nine busy salt pans that operated here. The industry was abandoned by 1823.

A burgh of barony since 1621, St Monans depended upon the fish trade for its prosperity, and the sea was writ large in its lifestyle, history and legend. The individuality of St Monans fishermen was seen in the 1860s and 1870s when they personally raised the finance to make considerable improvements to their sixteenth-century harbour. At the harbour are located the successors of Messrs J.N. Miller and Sons who have built boats here since 1779, although the Miller family had established themselves as boatbuilders in 1747.

West Shore leads via the Clapper Bridge to Scotland's kirk 'closest to the sea'. Dedicated to Monan, the Irish missionary companion of Adrian of May, the church was founded in 1265–67 by Alan Durward, Earl of Atholl and Chief Justiciar, but was built in its present form during 1362–70 with monies donated by David II, whose arrow wounds received at the Battle of Neville's Cross in 1346 were deemed healed through prayer at the shrine of St Monan. The kirk was once a royal votive chapel, in the gift of the monarchy until the nineteenth century.

The church has fought the sea for nearly 800 years, was burned by the English in 1544 and shaken by mines in 1944. The kirk, first used as a parish church in 1646, is very much a place of worship for Calvinist fisherfolk: their marks are everywhere in trenchant opposition to the relics of the Dominican friars who once intoned their divine offices here. Ruined by 1772, the church was restored in 1826–28 and renovated in the 1960s to a modern, clinically bright state, although it retains some fourteenth-century features. Although the pre-Reformation altars were swept away, a trefoil sedilla and piscina remain on the south wall of the choir around which are set twelve consecration crosses, one for each Apostle. The north gallery holds the Sailors' Loft, and a full-rigged model ship of 1800 hangs from the ceiling by the south transept. St Monan's Cave, a stone's throw from the church, marks the old shrine and hermitage.

A few hundred yards along the cliffs from the triptych of cemeteries lie the remains of Newark Castle. Originally in the possession of the Sandilands family, who became the Lords Abercrombie, the castle had one really distinguished owner. He was General David Leslie, first Lord Newark, who defeated the Marquis of Montrose at the Battle of Philiphaugh in 1645; he bought the property in 1649. Leslie's bones rested in the choir of St Monans kirk until 1828 when they were unceremoniously thrown over the sea wall by the zealous renovators. Newark passed to the Anstruthers and then the Bairds of Elie and is now a lonely ruin above the Long Shank rocks. Within sight of Newark lies the almost vanished Ardross Castle, built by William Dishington in 1370 when he was Sheriff of Fife and agent of David II for building the kirk.

The tiny village of Abercrombie, with its white harled cottages, sits less than a mile north of St Monans. Abercrombie farm (1892) lies on the site of the old mansion which had been built by Richard Cocus in 1260. The date of the founding of Abercrombie chapel is not known, but by the mid-twelfth century it was in the hands of the monks of Dunfermline. It was consecrated by Bishop David de Bernham in 1247, but was deserted exactly 400 years later when the seat of the parish moved to St Monans. Long used as a burial place of the Abercrombies and their retainers, the chapel stands ruined in Balcaskie Wood.

The shell of Balcaskie laird's tower was old when Sir William Bruce of Kinross rebuilt it in 1668–74. Today Balcaskie House is an oblong block of three stories, reached by a long straight drive from eighteenth-century gates. Bruce bought the property in 1665, and the house and lands of Balkaskie are traceable to Juan Cook's ownership charter of 1223; and probably Bruce's architectural teeth were really cut here before he went to restore and rebuild Holyrood Palace (1671–79) for Charles II. Much work was done at Balcaskie and its policies in Victorian times, but today the New Zealand laburnums, the Indian strawberry and petrified Roman emperors add ambience to a house that would be stark without them. Bruce sold the property in 1684 and it was purchased in 1698 by Sir Robert Anstruther, whose family has owned the property ever since. The Fife family of Anstruther of Dreel Castle have long flourished as powerful land- and shipowners and have intermarried with many Lowland families.

Elie

Elie House lies on the east boundary of the twin royal burghs of Elie and Earlsferry, between Elie East Links and Kilconquhar Loch. It is a house worth noting for the fascinating local stories about it. Its nucleus is an L-shaped towerhouse built by Sir William Anstruther in 1697. In 1366 the lands hereabouts belonged to Andrew Anstruther and Elie House's main entrance was once at the west side (it is now located at the east) with a perron (an external stone stairway) leading to a beautiful statued garden now swept away. William Adam had a hand in certain design features. Around 1853 Elie House passed from the Anstruthers and William Baird, of the prominent coal and iron family, occupied it into the twentieth century. It was then taken over by Michael Nairn in 1924; on Sir Michael's death in 1954 the house and immediate policies were bought by the nuns of the order of the Convent of Marie Reparatrice, an order founded in Paris and Strasbourg in 1855 by a Belgian widow, Baroness Emilie d'Hooghvorst. The nuns sold the convent in 1982 and the house is now a private development.

Elie House and its occupants have added much to Fife and Scottish folklore. Take for instance the story of Lady Fall, who married Sir John Anstruther in 1750. Janet Fall was the second daughter of Charles Fall, Provost of Dunbar and descendant of the gipsy Faa's. She was the famous Jenny Faa' mentioned by Thomas Carlyle as being 'a coquette and a beauty'. The said Jenny was peeved at the presence of the poor hamlet of Balclevie, which stood to the north of Elie House. Her dissatisfactions may have arisen from the fact that the tinkers who dwelt therein reminded her of her own lowly birth, so she pestered her husband to have the hamlet razed to the ground 'to improve the view'. This was carried out and the eviction of the inhabitants possibly inspired Sir Walter Scott to weave the actuality around the fictitious eviction of the gipsies from Derncleuch by the Laird of Ellangowan in *Guy Mannering* (1815). Local legend has it that a spey-wifie (fortune teller) from the doomed hamlet cursed the Anstruthers (as Meg Merrilies cursed Ellangowan) and forecast that only six generations of the family would live in the house. The prognostication was proved true. Incidentally, the old ruin which can be seen on the approach road to Elie from St Monans is also connected with the haughty Janet. The ruin is called Lady's Tower. It was intended as a summerhouse, but was used as a dressing-room for Janet after sea-bathing. It is said that when she went bathing a bellman went round Elie to warn villagers to keep away.

A mile-long strip of coast used to be four separate communities: from east to west, Elie, Liberty, Williamsburgh and Earlsferry. Since 1929 all four have been united as the burgh of Elie and Earlsferry. Elie – 'Ailie of Ardross' in passed times – had its burgh of barony status confirmed by James VI in 1589, and began to develop as a middle-class holiday resort after the boatbuilding, the fishing and the weaving had died out. The High Street has a tree-lined square. Stenton Row and Rankeillour Street lead down to the harbour constructed in 1589.

Standing at the centre of Elie is the old parish church built by Sir William Scott of Ardross Castle in 1639. The distinctive campanile was added by Sir John Anstruther in 1726. In the kirkyard is an interesting range of tombstones; one worth noting is to be found set in the east-end wall of the kirk dedicated to the second daughter of Thomas Turnbull of Bogmill. There is a lifesize skeleton, covered from breast to ankle in a scroll shroud. In South Street is the house called 'The Castle', a fine example of late sixteenth-century Scottish architecture with seventeenth-century renovations: this was the town house of the Gourlays of Kincraig, whose lands stand further along the coast above Shell Bay. The Gourlays, who have been here since the days of William I, The Lion (1143–1214), had a family tie with the Sharps, whose famous kinsman, Archbishop James Sharp, was murdered at Magus Muir in 1679. In the castle Margaret Sharp grieved over her father's assassination.

Above the doorway of Gillespie House is a rich stone lintel (1682) bearing the marriage initials of its builders, Alexander Gillespie of Newton Rires and his spouse Christina Small. Once it was called 'The Torret', or 'Muckle Yett' (that is, big gate) of an earlier house on the site, the residence of the Duke of York, who became James VII and II and who was Governor of Scotland 1679–82.

Earlsferry

Earlsferry is a royal burgh of greater antiquity than Elie. Ferries to the Lothians, mostly to and from North Berwick and Dirleton, began a long time before their recognised foundation by Alexander II in 1223 to facilitate the pilgrim routes to St Andrews.

Above where the sea-swell batters the small islands of West Vows and Chapel Ness, at Earlsferry's western extremity, stand the remains of the Ardross hospice for the poor, travellers and pilgrims, run by the Cistercian nuns of North Berwick whose benefactor was Duncan, fourth Earl of Fife and his eponymous son the fifth earl. Crossing the Forth was a perilous business in medieval times and the nuns set up lamps to guide the doughty travellers. Behind the chapel lie Earlsferry Links, on which golf has been played since the sixteenth century; eighteen holes were set out in 1895. Beside them is The Grange, founded by the Cistercian nuns. The house passed into the hands of the Revd Alexander Wood, son of the famous seaman, Sir Andrew Wood. For many centuries the lairds of Grange maintained a dispute with local people on rights to the use of the links. Particularly out of step with his neighbours was Walter of Grange, a fervent Jacobite who assisted John Erskine, Earl of Mar, when he landed at sixteenth-century Elie harbour by way of prelude to the 1715 Jacobite rebellion.

Over this land, too, trundled the waggons of the fish 'cadgers' bound for the royal palace of Falkland (see pages 36–37). Next to The Grange is Kincraig hill with its interesting caves of Devil, Doo' and Macduff. The last is reached by a delightful walk along the foot of Earlsferry Brae. Local legend has it that the probably fictitious Macduff, Thane of Fife, hid here while awaiting a ferry to flee from Macbeth. Modern Rires Farm, between Balcarres and Flagstaff hill, has within its policies the site of Macduff's (now vanished) supposed East Neuk Castle.

Kilconquhar

Kilconquhar village, pronounced 'Kinucher', stands on the shores of a lovely loch, the only loch in Fife's Lowlands, which, local legend has it, was formed in 1624 after a storm blocked a natural drainage channel. Court records, however, suggest the loch was there before 1599 and in Kilconquhar churchyard is an epitaph which records the death in 1593 of one James Bellenden who drowned while skating on the loch.

Formerly the neighbouring villages of Barnyards and Kilconquhar were separate, but now they are one. Set on a knoll by the shores of the loch, the parish church was built in 1819–21 and its distinctive 80-ft tower is a landmark. There was a church here as early as the twelfth century which was in the care of the nuns of North Berwick from Ardross. Some historians have suggested that the name of the village comes from *Kil*, meaning cell, and Conquhar, the Latinised name of Connacher the Hermit; the loch was once called Redmire and its environs were formerly an important source of fuel (peat) and turf for village and ecclesiastical granaries. The oldest religious relic is the fragment of a nave by the church filled with the tombs of the earls of Lindsay and the Anstruther-Thompsons. Opposite the church stands the early eighteenth-century Kinneucher Inn.

The cottage of one Robin Gray stands near to Kilconquhar. He had been a cowherd at Balcarres estate and was immortalised by Lady Anne Lindsay (1750–1825), daughter of the Earl of Balcarres in the ballad *Auld Robin Gray* (1771) which Sir Walter Scott thought 'slightly improper'. The verse began:

> When the sheep are in the fold, and the kye's come hame,
> When a' the weary world to rest is gane,
> The waes o' my heart fa' in showers frae my e'e,
> Unkent by my gudeman wha sleeps soundly by me.

To the east of the village lie Kilconquhar House and the remains of an earlier castle. The original fortress was built in 1547 on the lands of Sir John Bellenden, Lord Justice Clerk in the reign of James V. It then passed to Sir John Carstairs in 1634, and until modern times the L-shaped house, with enhancements of 1831 and 1839, was the

Local parlance calls this 'Auld Robin Gray's Cottage'. Immortalised
by Lady Anne Lindsay in her eponymous ballad of 1771, Robin Gray
was a cowherd on the Balcarres estate. This cottage is to be seen at
Colinsburgh, but in reality Robin Gray lived in a cottage deeper
within Balcarres estate. (STARALP)

seat of the earls of Lindsay. The castle was badly damaged by fire in
1978, but was restored as the centrepiece of an estate of multi-
ownership holiday villas.

Balchristie, the 'Town of the Christians' after a supposed Culdee
chapel here, was once the hunting range of Malcolm Canmore, and
via the monks of Dunfermline and the Duncans of Balchristie the
estates descended to the Bairds of Elie. Today the whole area is a
mixture of scattered farms and nineteenth-century mansion houses
like Lahill House which belonged in an earlier form to Sir Andrew
Wood of Largo, and then the Glasgow merchants the Rintouls.
Nearby Coates House was the seat of the Beatons of Creich and
Sir John Leslie (1766–1832), professor of mathematics at
Edinburgh. Charleton House, with its surrounding woods named
after Boer townships, was built in 1749 by John Thomson and
descended to the Anstruthers of Balcaskie. Additions were made to
the house in 1832, and in 1906, when Colonel Anstruther covered
the open areas and made the north entrance to the design of Robert
Lorimer.

Largo

Westward towards Largo lies the now almost deserted parish of Newburn. Its decline was brought about by the drift of the rural population to the towns. Its ruined church was first erected by the monks of Dunfermline in 1166. Today its shell is a mausoleum for local families, and the stones around testify to the more prosperous days when the folk of Newburn engaged in milling, handloom weaving, shoemaking, quarrying and salmon fishing. In the west corner of the windblown graveyard lie the Lorimers, of whom the architect Sir Robert Lorimer (1864–1929) left an indelible mark on Fife. A new parish church was built in 1815. This parish was once the home of the 'Royal Cadger'; it was his duty to carry fish from Earlsferry to the royal palace of Falkland. In recompense for such duties he had a free house at Newburn with the right to graze a cow and pig in the parish.

Modern housing developments have linked historic Upper or Kirkton of Largo, Lower Largo and Lundin Links into a single entity. The old two-storeyed cottages, harled with red roofs, have given way to less picturesque slated buildings. The Largo Stone (now in the churchyard) shows that this area once saw extensive Celtic activity, but Largo first entered recorded history when it was given over to the convent at North Berwick by Duncan, Earl of Fife, in the twelfth century. As its centrepiece Upper Largo has the twelfth-century kirk, with chancel of 1623, tower of 1628 and enlargements of 1688 and 1817, and restoration of 1894. Down its main artery (the A915), the coaches once came from St Andrews to Largo Pier to link with Newhaven. Largo's chief industry was formerly linen manufacture, and there were once extensive bleaching greens.

Largo is said to have derived its name from the Gaelic *leargach* meaning 'a sunny seaward slope'. Undoubtedly the most famous son of Upper Largo was Sir Andrew Wood (c.1460–1540), who became a merchant trader of the busy port of Leith. Wood has been dubbed 'the Scottish Nelson', and the exploits of his ship the *Yellow Carvel*, with its 500 crew and fifty guns, are legendary. In this ship Wood defeated the English fleet in the Forth in 1498. All that remains of his castle is Wood's Tower. After heavy rain a 'canal' which was constructed by him can still be traced from the tower in the orchard of old Largo House, through the park behind the manse (1760). Down this waterway Wood sailed from his home to church. Largo House is now a ruin, but a pair of Durham eagles are still spread-winged on the gateposts of the South Lodge. Here lived the Durhams of whom the first was Sir Alexander Durham, Lord Lyon King of Arms, who acquired the estate in 1659. The house, of which the shell only remains, was built by John Adam in 1750. After 1945 it was inhabited by the Polish army and the roof was removed soon after they vacated it. North of the church is a terrace of houses known as Wood's Hospital (Wood's Houses in local parlance). The benefice of John Wood of Orky, the hospital was founded in 1665 and was rebuilt in 1830 to become modern sheltered housing.

Upper Largo is still linked to the sea by a footpath known as 'The Serpentine'; this leads to Temple Hill, denoting that the lands hereabouts once belonged to the Knights Templar. Their lands included those of mid- or late eighteenth-century Strathairly House, the family home of the Briggs, who bought it from the Lundins in 1789; the house was refronted c.1830.

Visitors to Lower Largo – Seatown of Largo – cannot miss the statue of Alexander Selkirk (formerly Selcraig), who inspired Daniel Defoe to write the great adventure story *The Life and Surprising Adventures of Robinson Crusoe* (1719). Dressed in the recognisable garb of Defoe's hero, the memorial marks the site of the home where Selkirk was born in 1676, and was set up by David Gillies of Cardy House in 1885. Selkirk was the hellraising seventh son of a tanner and shoemaker who ran away to sea. His wildness led him to rebel against Captain Thomas Stradling of the vessel *Cinque Ports*, one of veteran buccaneer William Dampier's booty-seeking fleet. Selkirk was placed ashore in 1704 on the deserted island of Juan Fernandez, 600 miles from the shores of Chile and now dubbed Isla Robinson Crusoe. After four years Selkirk was rescued in 1709 by Captain Woodes Rodgers of *The Duke*. Selkirk now joined another treasure-hunting expedition and his share from the sacking of a Spanish galleon made him a rich man. A return to Lower Largo and a hasty marriage were not successful. He went to sea again and died in the Gambia in 1721. Daniel Defoe (c.1660–1731) toured Fife as part of his promotion of the Act of Union and as a 'spy' for Robert

Harley, Earl of Oxford and English Secretary of State, in 1706. In particular Defoe wrote of the Jacobite murmurings in the county and produced his remarks on Fife in his *A Tour through the Whole Island of Britain* (1724–27). Cardy House at Lower Largo was built by Alexander Selkirk's descendant, David Selkirk Gillies, in 1871. He had built a net factory at Largo in 1867 on the site of an eighteenth-century netting house.

Near the eighteenth-century harbour of Lower Largo is the characterful area of Drummochy by the splendid but now redundant railway viaduct (1856) across the Kiel Burn; hereabouts lived the flax spinners and the employees of the linseed oil mill. Also linked with the Largoes in past years is the village of New Gilston, three miles away; it was a community which once supported a school but no church. To the north are the remnant mining villages of Largoward, Lathones and Radernie. Coal from their defunct mines was once transported to the royal palace of Falkland. Here coal was still being hewn in the 1920s for mine owners like the Lindsays. Between New Gilston and Largo stand the ruins of the late fifteenth-century castle of Pitcruivie in the delightful Kiel's Den. The fourteenth-century estate came into the Lindsay family in 1498 and the early sixteenth-century castle fell into disuse following the tenancy of James Watson, Provost of St Andrews.

On the north side of Largo is volcanic Norrie's Law with its defensive enclosures and settlements dating from the late first millennium BC at a height of 965 ft. For generations the legend has been recounted of the treasure found here. Around 1819 a tumulus on Norrie's Law was opened to reveal a prehistoric burial site containing several silver articles. No one knows how certain of the items came into the ownership of a cadger called Forbes who sold them for scrap to various people, including Robert Robertson, a Cupar jeweller. In due time a portion of the Norrie's Law hoard came into the possession of General Durham of Largo House. Again there is a confusion as to whether Durham's pieces were from the cadger's items or later discoveries on Norrie's Law. What survives today is but a portion of the original hoard, but includes penannular brooches, Pictish symbol plaques, pins, a Roman spoon and artefacts which might date from the time when the Romans were still at Carpow. Historians believe that the items now in the National Museum of Scotland in Edinburgh were deposited on Norrie's Law around the late seventh century, possibly during the time of the Northumbrian invasion of Fife in 655. Was this a Fife native, a descendant of the local *Votadini*, hiding former ritual relics of his tribe from the Anglian invaders? We shall never know.

Lundin Links stands in the old parish of Largo. The ruined Lundin Tower is all that remains of the Lundin estates founded by Philip de Lundin in the days of Malcolm IV (1153–65). The lands passed through the Erskines of Torry and the Wemysses in 1840 to the Gilmours of Montrave, but the associated mansion was demolished in 1876. Here too are the celebrated standing stones set within the course of the Ladies Golf Club.

Colinsburgh came into being in 1705 and was formerly known as Nether Rires, but was later named after Colin, third Earl of Balcarres (1652–1722), an ardent Jacobite who went into exile with the Stewarts between 1693–1700. When he returned to Balcarres he founded Colinsburgh as a hamlet of single-storey homes for his disbanded soldiers. He was placed under a kind of house arrest after his dabbling in the 1715 rebellion.

The village remains small and tranquil, with examples of the Victorian philanthropy and local independence engendered by the Presbyterian work ethic. A library was founded here by public subscription in 1899, and a church was erected in 1843 to be reunited with Kilconquhar in 1925. The Balcarres Arms hotel was once an important posting house. Balcarres House lies to the north-west of Colinsburgh and was built by Secretary of State John Lindsay, Lord Menmuir, son of the Earl of Crawford, in 1595. The mansion is mainly nineteenth century but incorporates some sixteenth-century work which was old when Charles II was entertained here in 1651. The sundial at Balcarres is seventeenth century and was brought from Leuchars Castle. Within the grounds, too, stands a roofless Renaissance chapel (1635), long a vault for the earls of Crawford and Balcarres. Perhaps the oldest Lindsay property which can be titled is still the extant Balbuthie Farm of 1456.

The neighbouring parish of Carnbee holds two small villages, those of Arncroach and Carnbee. The villages are backed by 557-ft Kellie Law, and the modern lands of Carnbee were long owned by the Melvilles of Raith. Carnbee's old mansion house was demolished in 1813, and the church, which was under the charge of the abbey of Dunfermline in medieval times, was rebuilt in 1793.

Some three miles north-north-west of Pittenweem, Kellie Castle offers a rare sight of an unspoilt sixteenth–seventeenth-century laird's house. The castle, restored garden and some 16 acres of land were purchased in 1970 by the National Trust for Scotland, and the main contents were acquired 'for the nation' by the government.

The estate began as a *messuage* in the eleventh century, held by the Saxon family of Seward and the oldest part of the extant castle is thought to date from 1360. The estate was held by the Oliphants for over 200 years when it was sold to the Erskines in 1613, who were to become earls of Mar and Kellie. The castle was given its present form around 1537–1605 when the orginal tower house developed into a T-shaped building. The lands and castle of Kellie were dissociated in the late eighteenth century and there followed a period of neglect, ruin and virtual abandonment. In early Victorian times the whole deteriorated, but in 1876 a lease was granted to Professor James Allan Lorimer of Edinburgh. The Lorimers were associated with Kellie until the end of the twentieth century, having bought the castle in 1948. Members of the family restored its furnishings and fabric using the talents of such as Sir Robert Lorimer. The castle interior includes the Great Hall (now the drawingroom), the Withdrawing Room (now a dining room) with its waterfall panels, kitchen, study, the Earl's Room and the Vine Room with its ceiling painting of Mount Olympus by the Dutch painter Jacob de Wet.

The fourteenth-century estate of Pittarthie retains a sixteenth-century castle remodelled as a fortified house in 1682. The last family to actually live in the castle around 1700 seems to have been the original builders, the Bruces; later the property passed to the Hannays of Kingsmuir. From nearby Lochty the Scottish kings' hunting ground stretched to the sea. David II appointed *cunningares* (keepers of the rabbit warrens) and foresters to look after the wildlife hereabouts. James V conceded Kingsmuir House to Charles Murray for services rendered.

Dunino

Antiquarians still argue over the origin of the name of the ancient parish of Dunino; a derivation from *dunningheanach*, 'the hill of the daughters', is favoured, as a nunnery was said to have been founded here, and the Priory of St Andrews owned land hereabouts in the twelfth century. That Dunino was a Celtic community is further argued by those who suggest a Celtic translation of Dunino as 'fort of the hill'. In the woods by Dunino Den is the 'Celtic pothole' set on Bell Craig, locally associated with pagan worship and ritual atrocities, and below the aperture there is a Pictish cross cut into the rock. Maybe there were Druids at Dunino, but the pothole, the ritual sacrifice and the romantic sylvan location smack of a Regency or early Victorian imagination. Undoubtedly there was a Celtic community of some sort near, for the church (of 1826) is neighbour to the site of a stone circle; and there are fragments of Celtic hewn stone in the walls scattered around. The original church of Dunino was consecrated in 1240 by Bishop de Bernham, and there has been continuous worship to the present day. A manse has stood on the site of the extant building since 1564 and it was put into good order in 1780 and 1819. Opposite the manse lies a katabatic garden in whose walls are bee-boles set with shelves for skeps.

The principal private estate of the parish is still Stravithie. On the secularisation of ecclesiastical properties in the sixteenth century, the lands fell to Margaret Erskine, the lady of Loch Leven, who became Mary, Queen of Scots' jailor in 1567; subsequently she gave the lands to her illegitimate son by James V, the Lord James Stewart, the famous Regent Moray.

West of Dunino lies the estate of Kinaldy which came into the possession of the Scoto-Norman Aytoun family around 1539. The Aytouns, members of whose family were captains-general of Stirling Castle and sub-priors of St Andrews Priory, owned properties from Kippo to Wilkeston, and from Carthurlie to Lochton. The prophetic Thomas the Rhymer wrote of them: 'That none of woman born should succeed to the estates of Kinaldy and Kippo save of the Aytoun Blood'. Perhaps the most famous son of the house was Sir Robert Aytoun (1569–1638) who attached himself to the court of James VI and I, to whom he had addressed a Latin panegyric. In royal service until his death, Aytoun's most famous verse was *Diophantus and Charidora*. Writing both in Latin and English, Aytoun wrote verses which begin:

> I do confess thee sweet, yet find
> Thee such an unthrift of thy sweets . . .

which Robert Burns reworked as:

> I do confess thou art sae fair
> I wad been o'er the lugs in love

– the latter for his entries in *The Scots Musical Museum* (1797–1803). Aytoun too worked on an old ballad which features in the controversial origins of Burns's reworked 'Auld Lang Syne' in 1788.

The Aytouns held the lands and castle of Kinaldy until the turn of the eighteenth century, after which it passed to the Monypennys; but the Aytouns were to maintain a presence when their descendant, Roger Sinclair of Inchdairnie, was elected MP for Kirkcaldy Burghs in the nineteenth century. In 1778 the property was acquired by Colonel Robert Patton (1742–1812) of the Honourable East India Company, who had been secretary to Warren Hastings, 'nabob' and Governor of Bengal. Patton became Governor of St Helena, and when he died the estate was bought by Alexander Purvis; the Purvis family held the property until 1966. The present house was built in 1839 and extended in 1854 from stones from the ancient Kinaldy Castle whose foundations are under a nearby stockyard.

North-west of Kinaldy, and founded in 1645, the parish of Cameron, with its church of 1803, remains in an area of dispersed farmsteads with, as its focal point, the reservoir, which is a haunt of local anglers and birdwatchers.

> In a wee cot-house far across the muir,
> Where peeweeps, plovers, and whaups cry dreary,
> There lived an auld maid for mony lang years,
> Wham ne'er a wooer did e'er ca' 'Dearie'.
> A lanely lass was Kate Dalrymple;
> Nae music, exceptin' the clear burnie's wimple,
> Was heared round the dwellin' o' Kate Dalrymple.

Thus the 'peasant poet and precentor' William Watt (1792–1859) celebrated the unattractive but hardworking spinster, Kate Dalrymple, who is thought to have lived in her 'cot-house' in Cameron parish by the 'wimple' of Cameron burn. Kate, it seems, was transformed from rags to riches by a legacy; tradition has it she took up residence at 129 South Street, St Andrews. The song says she entered polite society and wed the 'sarkin weaver "Willie Speedyspool"'. Her cottage has now vanished from Cameron but a field still bears her name.

Once the lands around Cameron belonged to the priory of St Andrews, but by the sixteenth century private estates like that of Feddinch had become established. Undoubtedly Lathockar has the most continuous proprietary history, being granted to Sir John de Wemyss of Rires in 1383. The old mansion of Lathockar is now ruined.

Delivering the mail in Fife

Up to the year 1800 and beyond, the roads of Fife were in a very bad state, many no more than muddy tracks, and almost impassable in winter. The quickest means of transport was by horsebrack, with the bulk of Fife's domestic produce being carried by cadgers and packmen. In 1669 the Scots parliament passed an Act to impress Fife folk to voluntarily work three days a year to repair roads in their localities; fines were set out for non-co-operation, but as the means of carrying out the Act were inefficient the legislation for these 'statutory Labour Roads' was ignored. A series of new Acts from 1774 charged Fife's landowners and local leaders to raise money to pay for repairs. Great benefits came with the Fife Turnpike Act of 1790 which assured the maintenance of a 'Great Road' through Fife for the passage, mainly, of mail and stage coaches. This Great Road linked Woodhaven and Newburgh on the Tay with Pettycur and the Forth, with links to such places as Kirkcaldy and Cupar. From this the network of Fife's roads began and today relics of tollhouses, cast-iron guide plaques, bridges and milestones can still be seen.

By 1845 the *Edinburgh Evening Courant* was advertising direct coach routes to Dundee and the north; one advertisement read –

'Union Light Post Coaches through Fife daily at half past 1 o'clock, via Burntisland, Kirkcaldy, New Inn and Cupar to the Royal Hotel, Dundee'. For the convenience of travellers a relay of post houses emerged, like those at Old Inn, Kirkgate, Dunfermline and Craigrothie, for relaxation as the teams of horses were changed.

Because of the regular royal presence in Fife, royal messengers were not an uncommon sight on Fife roads up to the sixteenth century, carrying royal proclamations, parliamentary messages and summonses to all parts of the realm, or even state missives for France or the papal court. The messengers were fee earners (1p per day in the fourteenth century) with a shoe allowance; their royal duties offered them special privileges of passage, lodging and authority. By 1603 Scotland had the beginnings of a national postal service and by the sixteenth century Fife had its own network of postmasters and post offices, many in shops and inns. In 1793 the parish minister of Cupar, one George Campbell, noted that Cupar post office was one of the busiest in Fife with an annual revenue of 20 pounds sterling. The nineteenth century produced a whole flurry of new post office buildings like that of Dunfermline (1889–90), and some long-vanished mail centres are remembered in street names like Old Post Office Close, Anstruther. By 1834 steamboats made regular runs to and from Kirkcaldy, Kinghorn and Burntisland with the mails.

6
THE ISLANDS OF THE FIRTH OF FORTH

One of the most prominent of Scotland's eleven mainland firths, their names redolent of Norse origins, the Firth of Forth has had a major influence on the history and legend of south coastal Fife. The River Forth, widening from river to firth by Alloa, provided the vital link for ports of southern Fife with the Continent and ensured Scandinavian influence from Culross to Crail, and beyond, mainly from the sixteenth to the eighteenth centuries.

A journey across the Forth Railway Bridge in particular provides many visitors with their first glimpse of the islands of the Forth which have played a part in the Fife story. From the foot of the bridge the islands may be identified eastwards as Inchgarvie,

Forth Railway Bridge under construction. This bridge linked Fife
with the south, and was opened on 4 March 1890 by
Albert Edward, Princes of Wales (Alex B. Paterson)

Inchcolm, Inchkeith and the Isle of May. To the west is Preston Island in Torry Bay.

Preston Island lies a mile off Fife's southern shore as it curves by Low Valleyfield and Culross. Here the wealthy Sir Robert Preston, sixth baronet of Valleyfield (d.1834), and a former naval entrepreneur for the East India Company, sank three pits; they were abandoned in 1811 after a fatal explosion. There are the relics of salt workings too, which Sir Robert established after he eschewed coal mining on the island. Local lore remembers the island as a haunt of smugglers; after Sir Robert's death a few of the incumbent salt panners were forced to flee after excisemen suspected them of illicit liquor distillation.

The small rocky island or *inch* of Inchgarvie forms a footing for the central cantilever of the Victorian Forth Railway Bridge. Today rail passengers can look down on a range of wasted buildings whose history can be traced to the time when it was a royal possession. The fourteenth-century historian John of Fordun tells us that here in the eighth century Angus, High King of the Picts, displayed the head of the vanquished leader of the invading Angles as a warning to other foolhardy incursors. Legend gave way to fact, for in the late fifteenth century merchant vessels plying the Forth were being harried by English and Scandinavian privateers. So James IV granted a charter to John Dundas of Dundas, on 14 May 1491, for Inchgarvie on the proviso that the Dundases fortify the island against the privateers. By 1492 the privateers were forced to concentrate their plundering into what they could catch nearer the mouth of the Forth.

Inchgarvie became an important fort in the days of the governorship of Scotland by John Stewart, Duke of Albany, during the minority of James V. In this period the Inchgarvie fortalice had a stated captain (in Alan Stewart of Upsettlington for instance) and a constable (in Andrew Towris in 1517). For a while in the early sixteenth century the buildings were used as a state prison; housing prisoners such as Patrick Paniter, archdeacon of Moray and former secretary of James IV. Although rebuilt in the 1540s as a safe haven for ships of Scotland's French allies, after being razed to the ground in the invasion of Scotland by Thomas Seymour, Lord Hertford, the fortress was abandoned around 1550. By 1580 it was a quarantine station for plague-infected ships.

Inchgarvie rose to historical prominence once more when Oliver Cromwell marched north to subdue Royalist insurgents. Scotland's Royalist general of artillery, Sir James Hacket of Pitfirran, set up a battery on Inchgarvie to support General David Leslie, doomed to defeat at the Battle of Dunbar on 3 September 1650. As Cromwell moved his army along the southern shore of the Forth to attack Scottish Royalist redoubts at South Queensferry, he was harried by the guns of Inchgarvie. When Cromwell bettered the Royalists at the rout of Inverkeithing on 20 July 1651 the garrison on Inchgarvie surrendered.

With the Inchgarvie battery removed on Cromwell's orders, the island saw little activity for some 130 years, until a legendary figure caused alarm along the Fife coast. In 1779 the American naval officer, John Paul Jones, (born in Kirkbean, Galloway) acting as commodore of a French squadron under the American flag, sailed the *Bon Homme Richard* for the Forth, intent on threatening Leith. The four 20-pounder guns set up on Inchgarvie to thwart such an attack were not used, as Jones was defeated by the weather and was swept into the North Sea. Refurbishment of the battery took place in 1791, but after the Wars of the French Revolution Inchgarvie became a safe anchorage for merchantmen and fisherfolk.

Until the 1880s, Inchgarvie was in the possession of the Dundas family, who sold it to the Forth Bridge Railway Company for £2700. Inchgarvie became a workplace for the gangs fabricating the railway bridge, and in the First World War the Royal Garrison Artillery staffed the island. In living memory the sprats fished around these island waters were called 'garvies'.

Inchcolm, with its ruined abbey, lies a mile and a half west of Aberdour across the curiously named expanse of water known as Mortimer's Deep, marked on modern maps between Braefoot Point and Meadulse Rocks. The de Mortimers, possessors of the castle and barony of Aberdour, were constantly interfering with the affairs of the abbey. Of one denizen of this noble house, Sir Alan de Mortimer, the antiquary Sir Robert Sibbald had this to say in his *History Ancient and Modern of the Sheriffdoms of Fife and Kinross* (1710): 'Sir Alan being dead, the monks carrying his corpse in a coffin of lead by barge, in the night-time, to be interred within the church, some wicked monks did throw the samen [*same*] in a great deep between the land and the monastery, which to this day by the neighbouring fishing men and salters, is called "Mortimer's Deep".'

Local folklore recounts that Sir Alan's daughter was saved from being swept off by the Fife fairies by the Abbot of Inchcolm. The *Ballad of Sir Alan Mortimer* by the sailor poet David Vedder recalls the fable:

> Anon he shook his rosarie.
>   And invoked St Mary's name,
> Until sweet Emma's voice was heard
>   Chantin' the virgin hymn;
> But when he brandished the Holy Rood
>   And raised it to the sky,
> Like a beam o'light she burst on their sight
>   In vestal purity.

Fife folklore recalls a Latin riddle regarding the foundation of Inchcolm Abbey:

> M, C ter I, bis et X, literis a tempore Christi,
> Emon, tunc, ab Alexandro fundata fuisti,
> Scotorum primo, structorem Canonicorum,
> Transferat ex imo Deus hunc ad astra polorum.

The riddle's solution may be deduced from this doggerel:

> An M, a C, three Is, and Xs two
> These letters keep the year of Christ in view
> When Alexander, first, gave, Emon's isle
> His kingly gift a rich monastic pile.
> May God translate the noble founder's soul
> To regions high above the starry pole.

Thus in the year 1123, wrote Walter Bower, Abbot of Inchcolm, in his reworking of Fordun's *Scotichronicon*, King Alexander I's barge was driven upon the rocks at Inchcolm during a storm. To offer grateful thanks for his safe deliverance he founded a priory for clergy of his favoured Order of St Augustine, who would give care and prayers for shipwrecked mariners; the priory was erected into an abbey in 1235.

Unlike Alexander, modern-day pilgrims can take a safe seasonal ferry to the island. Inchcolm is around a mile and a half long and consists of two hill areas reaching ninety feet above sea level and is connected by a narrow isthmus sometimes mantled with a veil of water.

When Alexander I came to grief on its shore Inchcolm had long been inhabited by hermits who gave the king succour and sustenance at the place they called Emonia, 'island of the Mon tribe'. This was Inchcolm's name in the earliest extant charter of the house, but its decades of sanctity were to be redubbed in the name of the sixth-century Brito-Celtic priest Columba O'Donnell, known as St Colm (dove), Abbot of I-Shona (Iona).

Legend weaves in and out of fact in the early records of Inchcolm. The Dundee-born chronicler, Hector Boetius, repeats the legend that in 1033 Danish raiders entered the Forth to be vanquished by Macbeth. Negotiations to bury their dead on Inchcolm were conducted between the raiders and Macbeth's forces. Shakespeare used the legend as an incident in *Macbeth*:

Ground plan of Inchcolm Abbey

> Now
> Sweno, the Norway's King, craves composition;
> Now would we deign him burial of his men,
> Till he disbursed, at St Colm's Inch,
> Ten thousand dollars to our general use.

The Augustinian House of St Columba became rich from royal gifts of land, property and goods and mills at Aberdour, Fordell and Cramond. The clergy, known as the Black Canons of Inchcolm because of the colour of their habits, also had a brewhouse at Newton. Their peaceful life was, however, regularly disrupted. In 1335 an English vessel of Edward III's fleet landed near Inchcolm and soldiers plundered the abbey, removing the revered statue of the beloved St Columba. The statue and other plunder were returned by the raiders after they had been caught in a terrific storm which they had interpreted as the wrath of St Columba for their sacrilege. Indeed each summer brought the threat of pillage by the English, so much so that in 1340 a special prayer was added to the Inchcolm prayer book petitioning St Columba to intercede for their protection with the words *te laudantem serva chorum ab incursu anglicorum* ('from all hostile English raids, save this choir which sings thy praise'.)

Many of Inchcolm's clerics rose to high office as royal advisors and envoys to Rome; perhaps the most celebrated of all, and a notable 'Fife worthy', was Walter Bower. Born in 1385, possibly son of John Bower, deputy-custumar of Haddington, Walter Bower is thought to have begun his career as a novice at St Andrews followed by induction into the priesthood of the Augustinian canons of St Andrews. After studying theology in Paris, Walter Bower held several important court positions and became Abbot of Inchcolm in 1418. In his later years Bower started to compile his great work, the *Scotichronicon*, furthering the work of John of Fordun. Bower expanded the historical record within to the year 1437 and the end of the reign of James I. During Bower's abbacy the abbey was fortified and used as a royal prison for prisoners such as Euphemia, Countess of Ross, considered by James I to be a dangerous *agente provocatrice*. Here too Patrick Graham, the first Archbishop of St Andrews and great-grandson of Robert III, was imprisoned for a time in 1478. In Bower's lifetime Inchcolm was part of the Fife cockpit of Scotland's history.

What happened to the abbey in its final years? The services of the medieval church came to an end in 1560, but the convent of canons continued as property owners for some time. The canons who remained were entitled to pensions and some of them lived at the abbey until around 1564. The last known document to bear the canons' signature is a charter of 1578 signed by John Brounhill and Andro Angus, the last-known canons of the abbey.

The fabric of the abbey had suffered in an English attack in 1542 and there is evidence that in 1581 the 'Commendator of Inchcolm', James Stewart Jr. of Beath, sold ashlar from the abbey to the town council in Edinburgh for the repair of the city tolbooth. After Stewart's death in 1590 the abbey and island were feued to the Earl of Moray; in the disposing Act of Parliament the island is termed a 'receptakle for Pirates'. Inchcolm also served as a quarantine station for plague-stricken vessels entering the Forth as late as the early 1600s. The abbey remained derelict and the island uncared for for many decades. In the 1790s a Russian hospital was set up in the abbey

Barrage balloon protects Forth Rail Bridge during the
Second World War. (Alex B. Paterson)

buildings to serve the Russian fleet anchored in the Forth during the Napoleonic Wars, and a military fort remained extant until the 1800s. During the First and Second World Wars, Inchcolm, together with Inchgarvie and Inchkeith, played an important role in the defence of the Forth Railway Bridge and the naval base at Rosyth. A number of wartime observation posts, searchlight and gun emplacements may still be seen on the island. In 1924 the Earl of Moray gave the island and abbey site to the nation.

There's still plenty to see at Inchcolm Abbey, recalling its turbulent history and legend. Examples of architecture on site range from the twelfth to the sixteenth centuries. Remains of the abbey church, the chapter house, the cloister and living quarters are still there to explore. Go to the old warming house and see the carved *sententiae* – thoughtful sayings for philosophical reflection – left by the canons, that still speak across the centuries:

STULTU[M] E[ST] Q[UO]D VITARI NO[N] P[OTEST]
['It is foolish to fear what cannot be avoided' – a proverb popular in medieval times].
TUTISSI[M]A [R]ES E[ST] NIL TIMERE P[RAE]TER DE[UM]
['The safest thing is to fear nothing but God'].
[SUPERAT CONSCIENTIA] QUI[CQUID] MALI FINXERIT L[INGUA]
['Conscience overcomes whatever evil the tongue has composed'].

Inchcolm's neighbours in the Forth are the Cow and Calves and Inchmickery. To the east, and also a part of Fife history, is the island of Inchkeith once called *L'île des chevaux* (Island of Horses) by the French troops garrisoned there in the mid-1500s. Almost a mile long and rising to 180 ft, Inchkeith enters history in the grant to Robert de Keith in 1010 by Malcolm II in return for assistance in battle against the Danes. Yet the island has a more curious entry in Fife legend.

Fife folk remembered James IV as a chivalrous, devout and pleasure-loving king, whose reign bridged the Middle Ages and the Renaissance. His enquiring mind was well known and, according to the antiquary Sir Robert Sibbald, led him to a curious experiment on Inchkeith. Interested in how spoken language develops, James placed two orphaned babies on Inchkeith, in the care of a deaf and dumb woman. His objective was to see what language the children would grow up speaking; the outcome of the experiment is not known but one chronicler fancifully averred that the children spoke Hebrew.

James IV put the island to a more practical use as a training ground for his hawks. Thereafter it had several grantees including Sir Alexander Wood of Largo. In the days of the 'Rough Wooing' between 1544–45 – Henry VIII attempts to have the infant Mary, Queen of Scots as a bride for his son Edward – Inchkeith developed as a military base. It was to have this rôle reinstated during the First and Second World Wars. By way of several owners, from the Strathmores of Glamis to the Campbells of Argyll, Inchkeith passed to the Dukes of Buccleuch, who sold it to the government in 1878. The first lighthouse was built on the island in 1803 on the site of one of the medieval forts.

The island remains privately owned, but has attracted the literary and romantic. In 1817 author Thomas Carlyle rowed to the island with fellow Dumfriesshire-born theologian and orator, Edward Irving. Carlyle immortalised the trip in his *Reminiscences* (1866).

The historical heyday for merchant shipping in the Forth was undoubtedly the fifteenth and sixteenth centuries, when influences such as James IV gave a boost to the pilgrimage trade. His own deep personal piety fired the king to make regular pilgrimages to shrines across Scotland, many as penitential remembrances of his father, James III, killed in 1488 during the skirmish at Bannockburn mill. One of James IV's favourite pilgrimage sites was the Priory of the Blessed Virgin and St Adrian on the Isle of May.

The Forth had witnessed the vessels of pilgrims since the seventh century, when its waterways ferried clerics bound to and from Iona to the holy site at Lindisfarne. It was because of the tomb of the holy man Ethernan (who died around 875) on the Isle of May that the location became an important place of worship. Recent excavations have now revealed what is likely to have been the ninth–tenth-century mortuary chapel of St Ethernan, better known to us as St Adrian.

In his *Oryginale Cronykil*, Andrew of Wyntoun, canon of St Andrews and prior of St Serf's, Lochleven, tells us that St Adrian settled on the Isle of May with brother missionaries in order to proselytise the Pictish province of Fife. Here legend tells us Adrian suffered martyrdom at the hands of Halfdane the Dane. Scholars generally agree that the priory of May was founded by David I around 1153, for the Benedictine house at Reading, Berkshire. The *Scotichronicon* recounts that in 1296 Alexander III became alarmed that the priory was a centre of English espionage and purchased the island for 700 merks, conferring it thereafter on the Augustinians of St Andrews.

By the early 1300s the convent of May was transferred to Pittenweem priory, with one cleric remaining on the island to tend the chapel of St Adrian. During the Wars of Independence much of the fabric of the priory on the Isle of May was destroyed, but the chapel of St Adrian was retained. It was to the good harbour on the island, where the vessels of pilgrims bound from the south to the shrine of St Andrew at St Andrews called regularly, that James IV came for his summer pilgrimage. In 1506 he travelled to Fife in his new 700-ton warship the *Margaret*, and in 1507 aboard the warship *Lion*; in his little argosy came the choir of the Chapel Royal at Stirling to intone the mass. After entertaining the nobility of Fife in one or other of the southern ports of the county, James IV repaired to a convenient quay to be transported the five and a half miles from Anstruther by a local crew to his devotions on the Isle of May.

Amongst James IV's Fife intimates was Admiral Sir Andrew Wood of Largo. To Wood, only two weeks before his death at the Battle of Flodden in 1513, James granted lands in return for which 'the grantee and his heirs should accompany the King and Queen on their pilgrimages to the May, whenever required'. The island itself was to have a number of owners; after the Reformation it passed to John Forret of Fingask, and in time was acquired by Allan Lamont, who sold it to the Cunninghams of Barnes. In 1635 Alexander Cunningham of Barnes built a lighthouse on the island. By 1766 the island was owned by General Scott of Balcomie, and his daughter, the Duchess of Portland, sold it to the Commissioners of Northern Lighthouses in 1816.

Today the only remaining part of any ecclesiastical building on the Isle of May is the thirteenth-century chapel at the south end of the island on its own plateau. Fife folklore remembers the Isle of May in one superstition. Barren women were often ferried across to the island to drink the waters of the holy wells of May and pray to St Adrian for a successful pregnancy. One holy well at Pilgrims' Haven survives.

7

KIRKCALDY AND SOUTH FIFE

Thomas Carlyle (1795–1881), the Scottish author and sage who came of peasant stock, lodged at 22 Kirk Wynd and knew Kirkcaldy well. He said of the burgh that it was 'a mile of smoothest sand, with one long wave coming on gently, steadily and breaking in gradual explosion into harmless white, the breaking of it melodiously rushing along like a mass of foam, beautifully sounding and advancing from the West Burn to Kirkcaldy harbour'. Much has changed in Kirkcaldy since Carlyle's time, but the shops and houses are still set along the deep rim of a shallow bay. Daniel Defoe observed but 'one street, one mile long' that was to give the town its nickname of 'The Lang Toun'. Kirkcaldy's main thoroughfare is still some four miles long, from seventeenth-century Linktown, through sixteenth-century Pathhead to seventeenth-century Sinclairtown and Gallatown.

Kirkcaldy's policies once formed one of the most ancient burghs in Scotland, when David II handed it over to the monks of Dunfermline in 1365, who in turn gave it over in 1450 to the baillies and community of Kirkcaldy. Charles I ratified all the privileges of the burgh in 1644 and in 1661 his son Charles II did the same, thus making Kirkcaldy a royal burgh.

The burgh developed from its main street and sixteenth-century harbour, and the Teil (West) Burn, noted by Carlyle. The harbour was repaired in 1663 and extended in 1843. In Carlyle's day too, the ruin of Seafield Tower, threatened by modern developments, would be a pastoral stroll away. The square tower built on igneous rock by the sea was the home of the Moutrays from the sixteenth century. The name Prime Gilt Box Street is a fascinating relic of days when the harbour was bustling with its 100 registered vessels. The derivation is from *prymgilt*, the first anchorage of a ship using a port. The Prime Gilt Box Society of Kirkcaldy was a charity for dependants of mariners lost at sea.

The invention of linoleum made Kirkcaldy the 'oil-cloth capital', despite such of the burgh's older trades as textiles (Kirkcaldy was the first town to have a powerloom in operation in 1821), early salt panning and various other industries. It was the linseed oil that gave Kirkcaldy its distinctive aroma, immortalised by Mrs George Smith of Kirkcudbrightshire, whose poem 'The Boy in the Train' contains the couplet:

> For I ken mysel' by the queer-like smell,
> That the next stop's Kirkcaldy.

Kirkcaldy's floorcloth industry was developed from 1847 by a weaver of canvas called Michael Nairn (1804–58), who had diversified from weaving ships' sails to manufacturing a backing for floorcloth. In 1849 Nairn was making his own floorcloth developed from the 1860 invention of lino by Frederick Walton. The Nairns became the town's main benefactors.

The early industries of Kirkcaldy, incidentally, are commented on in the introductory part of John Buchan's historical novel *The Free Fishers* (1934). Born in Perth, Buchan (1875–1940) spent part of his early youth in Kirkcaldy at Pathhead where his father was minister; his sister Anna (pen-name O. Douglas) was born in the town.

Kirkcaldy's inner dock was constructed in 1904 to expedite cargoes of coal and linoleum, and once the whalers of the North Atlantic fleet docked here to add to the town's seagoing lore. Opposite the harbour is Sailor's Walk. Built on a foundation of dwellings which date from around 1460 the seventeenth-century pair of houses was a lodging for Charles II in 1650 as he passed through the town after his coronation at Scone. This part of the town is a place of many wynds – the old Scots word for alley – and near to the harbour was the area of the old salt pans where Oswald of Dunnikier extracted salt from sea water.

When Thomas Carlyle was a teacher at the now-vanished Burgh School in Hill Street, he lodged in the shadow of Kirkcaldy's 'Old Kirk'. The original church was consecrated in 1244 and its Norman-style tower of around 1500 is all that remains of the pre-Reformation church, rebuilt 1806–08. At the top of Kirk Wynd is St Brycedale's Church (1877–78) with its distinctive 20-ft spire; it

Foreshore and dock, Kirkcaldy, at the turn of the
twentieth century. (STARALP)

took its name from the patron saint of Kirkcaldy and the nearby
estate on which it was built.

At No. 220 High Street (The Pend) lived the famous Scottish
economist Adam Smith (1723–90), whose *Inquiry into the nature
and causes of the Wealth of Nations* (1776) has never been out of
print. Tolbooth Street recalls the old town hall rebuilt in 1678; here
also was the town jail – a new tolbooth was built in 1826 and served
the community until 1953. It is interesting to note whenever a Fife
town jail is being researched that imprisonment was never in high
favour as a form of punishment for most offences; up to the living
memory of Victorians, hanging, scourging and banishment were
favoured penalties. Long-term imprisonment was not popular
amongst local baillies and many a Kirkcaldy miscreant would have
had his ears nailed to a post hereabouts . . . there he, or she, would
be left until courage was plucked up to tear the head away.
Opposite the site of the Tolbooth, and set in the street, is a large red
cross, said to have marked the site of the old Mercat Cross, removed
in 1782. (Local historians believe that the cross is more likely to
have marked the site of an earlier Tolbooth). At No. 132 High Street

the remarkable Marjorie Fleming was born in 1803. Although she died at the age of eight, her journal *Pet Marjorie* (1858) became cult reading. She is buried in Abbotshall churchyard.

Off High Street is Glassworks Street where Sir Sandford Fleming was born in 1827; he became chief engineer of the Canadian Pacific Railway and the inventor of Standard Time, accepted internationally from 1883.

Along Nicol Street is Bethelfield Church (1831); a story is told concerning the incumbent of an earlier building. One day in 1778 the Revd Robert Shirra assembled his parishioners on the beach and called upon the Almighty to stop the threatened pillage of the town by John Paul Jones; it is said a storm blew up and Jones had to abandon his plans.

Running almost parallel with High Street is Kirkcaldy's mile-long Esplanade (1922–23), beginning at its west end at Linktown, site of Gladney House, the home of the Adam family of architects; Robert Adam was born at Kirkcaldy in 1728. For a week in April the Esplanade is thronged with crowds who come to the Links Market; Kirkcaldy's Easter Chartered Fair was recognised as early as 1305. Today the event is a cacophonous gathering of colourful carousels and the cries of barkers.

Kirkcaldy's Balwearie Road remembers a famous name in the burgh's history whose legend became international. In the tower house of Balwearie Castle lived Sir Michael Scott, says the Fife legend; here history and legend diverge, for the castle dates from 1484 and Sir Michael lived *circa* 1172–*circa* 1235. Durham, Melrose and Kirkcaldy all claim to be his birthplace. A Scots scholar of great capability, he was educated at Oxford and Paris, where he studied mathematics and chemistry; at Padua he learned astrology and honed his supposed skills as a magician; in Toledo, Spain, he pored over books of the abstract sciences, medicine and necromancy, and learned Arabic to digest the volumes left by the Moorish invaders. In time he became Astronomer Royal to Frederick II, King of Sicily, at Palermo.

Eventually Sir Michael returned to the Scott family home of Balwearie Castle in the area long called 'Wizard's Gap'. Legends of his magical power led Sir Michael to be the theme for many writers. The Italian poet Dante (1265–1321) mentions him in his *Inferno*:

> That other there, whose ribs fill scanty space
> Was Michael Scott, who truly full well knew
> Of magical deceits the illusive grace.

Sir Walter Scott also gave him life in *The Lay of the Last Minstrel* (1805);

> In these far climes it was my lot
> To meet the wondrous Michael Scott;
> A wizard of such dreadful fame . . .

In his *Anster Fair*, William Tennant mentions the old Fife legend that Sir Michael wrote a *Book of Magic*:

> . . . in Satan's arts malignly bold,
> His book of dev'lish efficacy wrote . . .

Feasts held at Balwearie by Sir Michael became legendary for their magical food and entertainment, and Kirkcaldy children long had the 'ropes of sand' pointed out to them where the Teil Burn meets the Forth as being made by 'Fife witches at the instruction of Michael Scott'.

No one knows for sure where Sir Michael Scott is buried. On moonlight nights Sir Walter Scott used to take his house guests down to Melrose Abbey and show them the wizard's purported grave in the south transept. In *The Lay of the Last Minstrel* Scott has the old monk say this to Sir William of Deloraine:

> I swore to bury his Mighty Book,
> That never mortal might therein look;
> I buried him on St Michael's night,
> When the bell tolled one, and the moon was bright;
> And I dug his chamber among the dead,
> Where the floor of the chancel was stained red,
> That his patron's Cross might over him wave,
> And scare the fiends from the Wizard's grave.

At the east end of Kirkcaldy lies Ravenscraig Castle. James II began its building in 1460, and it was completed as a dower-house for his widow, Mary of Guelders. Ravenscraig was one of the earliest examples of a Scottish castle to provide defence from and by

Ravenscraig Castle. James II began the building of the castle in 1460 and it was completed as a dower-house for Queen Mary of Guelders. (Author's collection)

artillery. It was ultimately exchanged for other properties with Earl William St Clair. In 1547 the castle was put to the torch by English raiders, and Cromwell 'knocked it about a bit' in 1651, but it remained in the Sinclair family until 1896. It was taken into state care in 1955.

Sir Walter Scott immortalised Ravenscraig in *The Lay of the Last Minstrel* with the lines from the 'piteous lay' of Harold:

> O, listen, listen ladies gay!
> No haughty feat of arms I tell;
> Soft is the note, and sad the lay
> That mourns the lovely Rosabelle . . .
> Last night the gifted Seer did view
> A wet shroud round a layde gay;
> Then stay thee, Fair, in Ravensheuch:
> Why cross the gloomy firth today?

The lady Rosabelle St Clair of Rosslyn did attempt to cross the Firth of Forth and died for her pains. To either side of Ravenscraig Castle are flights of steps to the beach; both sets are claimed by locals to be 'the 39 steps' of John Buchan's novel (1914); the beach was supposedly played on by Buchan and his siblings during their

father's ministry at Kirkcaldy. Ravenscraig Park was formerly a part
of Dysart House (1755–56), once in an earlier form a hunting lodge
of the Earl of Rosslyn.

Within the burgh boundaries of Kirkcaldy since 1930, Dysart
retains its own historic identity. It was made a burgh of barony in
1510 and was famous long before this for its coal, nails, linen and
salt. Smugglers also thrived in the harbour. One piece of local
partisan doggerel remembers the old trades:

> Dysart for coal and saut,
> Pathhead for meal and maut,
> Kirkcaldy for lasses braw
> Kinghorn for breaking the law.

Street names too give clues as to Dysart's past, with sixteenth–
seventeenth-century Pan Ha' – the ancient name for this old part of
Dysart – and Hot Pot Wynd – which recalls the fiery pans for salt
evaporation – attracting attention. For decades Dysart's houses,
such as Bay House, with its lintel proclaiming 'My Hoip is in the
Lord 1583', have been inspiration for painters and renovators.
Writers too have woven these buildings into their stories: The
Anchorage of 1582 (reconstructed 1965), for instance, was the
'Harbour House' of Anna Buchan's (O. Douglas) novel *The Day of
Small Things* (1930). Rising above all is the tower of St Serf's church
of *circa* 1500, perhaps one of the finest examples in Scotland of a
battlemented church tower.

St Serf, or Servanus of Culross, is said to have dwelt in the
anchorite cave now in the garden of Dysart House. The present
church of Dysart was built in 1872–74, having been established as a
church in 1843. In the centre of Dysart the town hall and the much-
altered tolbooth (1567–1617) are of typically Scots design. It was
used as a prison up to the 1840s.

Perhaps Dysart's most famous son was John McDougall Stuart
(1815–66) who in 1861–62 was the first man to cross Australia, from the
southern coast to the north, through the central desert. The
seventeenth-century house in Rectory Lane where Stuart was born has
been restored.

An important historical neighbour of Dysart is the castle and
estate of Wemyss, belonging to the ancient Scottish family of the

St Serf's Tower and Pan Ha', Dysart. (STARALP)

same name. The family and three villages take their names from the numerous large *weems*, or caves, along the coastline; some of the caves still exhibit a variety of inscriptions from the prehistoric double disc symbols to the graffiti of unfolding ages. The caves were often used as hideaways for smugglers, outlaws and gypsies. Several of the names, like King's Cave and Court Cave, recall local legends. Writing in 1899 folklorist Robert Boucher Jr. recalled how James V visited the caves on one of his peregrinations of Fife. His party came across a group of gypsies in one cave and the king took a shine to one of the gypsy women, 'a favourite of the patriarch', wrote Boucher. To mollify the aggrieved gypsy leader one of the king's gentlemen offered a golden coin, whereupon the glint of gold stirred the gypsy band to thoughts of armed robbery. The king was safely extracted by his gentlemen.

The village of West Wemyss lies along the shore of the Forth, and although it offers a maritime appearance, its people long depended upon the coal industry. The village grew up as a consequence of Wemyss Castle. The local folk once referred to the sixteenth-century port village of West Wemyss as the 'Haven Town of Wemyss', and were proud of its status as a burgh of barony, granted by James IV in 1511. West Wemyss' Tolbooth is of the early eighteenth century, erected 'for the cribbing of vice and service to crown' by David, fourth Earl of Wemyss (1678–1720).

The earliest part of Wemyss Castle dates from the fifteenth century, but has been added to and altered many times. One of the oldest Fife families, the Wemysses, have been associated with the area since Anglo-Norman times, and Sir John Wemyss owned coal mines at Lochgelly in the thirteenth century. It was at the old castle of Wemyss in 1565 that Mary, Queen of Scots, met Henry Stewart, Lord Darnley, who became her second husband the following year. St Adrian's Church below the castle was built by the Wemyss family in 1895 and it contains a rare example of a modern altar mural (1979). To the west of the village lie the remains of St Mary's Chapel, a pre-Reformation church now the burial place of the Wemyss family.

East Wemyss was once called 'Castleton' because of the nearness to Macduff Castle. This was the original home of the Wemyss family before they built Wemyss Castle. Fife legend has it that Macduff Castle was the home of the legendary Macduff, from whom the Erskines of Wemyss claim descent.

There's a local tradition that the earliest inhabitants of Buckhaven were Dutch seagoing folk whose ship was stranded here in the sixteenth century. It is more likely, though, that a fishing community was present here from as early as the ninth century. The development of the coal industry swept away the last vestiges of the fishing port and small weaving industry which Daniel Defoe visited during his tour in 1723, and Buckhaven – pronounced 'Buckhyne' by the old folk – became (with Methil) the industrial core of Levenmouth. The town of Buckhaven is remembered in the old rhyme:

> The canty carles of Dysart,
> The merry lads of Buckhaven,
> The saucy limmers* o'Largo
> The bonnie lasses of Leven.
> *cheeky women

Methil, a free burgh of barony by 1665, became a seaport of the three sister towns, edging into prominence after land reclamation projects made Leven unsuitable for large vessels. Methil rose to prominence, too, through the enterprise of the Wemyss family, whose coal and salt interests led to dock development. Between Methil and Leven lay the once separate fishing and salt-panning community of Innerleven, which, like Kirkland, Aberhill, Denbeath and Methilhill had long enjoyed its own identity. Innerleven, from which fish was sent to the Priory of Markinch in medieval times, is perhaps the most 're-named' place in Fife, having variously been called Coldcoits, Dubbieside and Salt-grieve.

Set in Largo Bay, at the mouth of its eponymous river, Leven once formed the busy port of Levynsmouth which saw the unloading of meat carcasses bought for the royal court when based at Falkland Palace. In 1602 Leven was banned from importing and exporting goods, so great was the contraband trade in these parts.

Formerly the Durie family held sway here as landowners and their estates passed on to the famous Scottish judge, Sir Alexander Gibson of Libberton (c.1570–1644), raised to the judiciary as Lord Durie in 1646. He was kidnapped by a Borders freebooter called 'Christie's Will' acting albeit under his own auspices for the Earl of Traquair, whose case in Durie's court had gone against the earl. The incident won immortality in Sir Walter Scott's *Minstrelsy of the Scottish Border*. Durie House (1762) was bought by the Christies in 1785.

Scoonie parish on the edge of Leven remembers the grant of these lands by Tuathal, Celtic Bishop of St Andrews, to the Culdee clergy of Lochleven; this early Fife benefice was later transferred to the Priory of St Andrews, and on 30 May 1243 Bishop David de Bernham of St Andrews rededicated it to St Memma the Virgin. The church was swept into the Protestant maw in 1566 and lasted as a parish church until 1775, when the congregation decamped to Leven. The ruins of Scoonie became a burial vault for the families who dwelt in Durie House.

Another neighbour is Aithernie estate whose forlorn ruined castle gives no clue to its once important ecclesiastical and secular role in Fife's history and legend. It is another fine example of how Fife properties were subsumed by the crown to give to servants and toadies for services rendered. It was granted by the Earl of Fife to the nuns of North Berwick in 1160 and remained in their hands as late as 1587, when Prioress Margaret Home agreed to James VI's secularisation of the property for her kinsman ambassador to the English court, Sir Alexander Home; later it became a free barony of North Berwick, and the property was sold on Home's death in 1608. The list of subsequent owners of Aithernie reads as a rollcall of prominent Fife families from the Scots of Scotstarvit to the Wemysses of Wemyss.

The road from Windygates to Kennoway passes the Pictish motte of Maiden Castle, known locally as Dunipace Hill, which Fife legend assigns to the ownership of Macduff. Both Windygates and Kennoway prospered by being on the coach route from Pettycur to Tayport, but declined when the traffic was re-routed via New Inn.

The church lands of Kennoway, a village of weavers, belonged to the Priory of St Andrews from the middle of the twelfth century, and its secular policies to the earls of Rothes. The original village centred on the Causeway, which retains some eighteenth-century houses and memories of the malting, brewing and weaving days. A Fife weaver's house was usually a small one-storey dwelling roofed with red pantiles, and was the weaver's workshop as well as his living quarters; one small building had to house his loom, his wife and his family. The pre-Reformation church at Kennoway, dedicated to St Kenneth, a Columban preacher of St Andrews, was administered by the Augustinians of St Andrews; the present parish church was erected in 1850. Forbes House (*c.* 1800) and Seton House (eighteenth century) has predecessors which claim to have sheltered Archbishop James Sharp in the days before he met his murderers on Magus Muir. To the north of Kennoway is the estate of Montrave which in 1160 belonged to the nuns of North Berwick. The old mansion was built in 1810 and the estate was acquired by the Gilmour family in the late 1860s; the mansion house was reconstructed in 1887 and demolished in 1969.

Milton of Balgonie lies along the banks of the River Leven, and the village began as an agricultural community, but mining was carried on here from the thirteenth century until the pit closures of 1960. Its 'Milton' derived from the flax mills. Milton House dates from 1770 and the village church was built in 1836 by the Balfour family as a chapel of ease to its parent St Drostan's at Markinch.

The site of Balfour House lies across the River Leven and was the home of the Balfour family, who had owned the land here since around 1040. The estate fell to the Beaton (Bethune) family who were great royal favourites and influential at court; two scions of the family, who had close connections with Fife, were the uncle and nephew Archbishops of St Andrews, James (*c.* 1480–1539) and Cardinal David Beaton (*c.* 1495–1546). The house – claimed to be the first in Fife to have electricity fitted in 1882 – was dismantled in 1930, and the four trees planted in honour of her 'Maries' by Mary, Queen of Scots, during a visit to the house, were cut down in the mid-1980s. One of the 'Maries' was Mary Beaton of Criech and Balfour.

Balgonie Castle is situated on the south bank of the River Leven, across from Milton of Balgonie. It comprises an early fifteenth-century tower standing in the north-west corner of an enclosure made up of a late fifteenth-century north range and a much-altered seventeenth-century east range, with a west and south wall of the fifteenth and sixteenth centuries respectively. Few early references to Balgonie Castle exist, but by the late fourteenth century it was in the ownership of the Sibbalds, to whom the main tower can be ascribed. During the 1490s the castle was in the hands of Sir John Lundin who built the north range. The castle's most famous owner was General Sir Alexander Leslie (*c.* 1580–1661; first Earl of Leven, 1641) who became leader of the Protestant army of the Solemn League and Covenant during the civil wars of Charles I. By 1635 Leslie was granted the barony of Balgonie: he too added to the castle's fabric and it is said he set out a garden; of the policies Daniel Defoe wrote: 'the situation [is] very pleasant. The park is large, but not well planted; at least the trees do not thrive'. Sir Alexander died at Balgonie on 4 April 1661 and was interred 'in his own iyle' in Markinch Church.

The Jacobite Rebellion was launched by John Erskine, Earl of Mar, on 1 August 1715. On 20 January 1716 Rob Roy MacGregor marched 200 men from their temporary base at Falkland Palace and captured Balgonie Castle which the Hanoverian General William Cadogan had targeted as a headquarters for the quelling of Fife. The castle sustained some damage but remained habitable, and in 1755 David Leslie, later sixth Earl of Leven, modernised the living quarters. The castle was sold in 1823 by a later Earl of Leven to James Balfour of Whittingehame and the Balfours owned it until 1950 when it was purchased by the Balgonie Coal Company. Private restoration of the castle began on its resale in 1971 and excavations took place within the courtyard in 1978. Today it remains a family home. It would be unusual, to say the least, for Balgonie Castle not to be considered haunted, and it has been featured on US television as one of 'the scariest places on earth'. A whole range of historical characters can line up for the phantom cast from James IV to Mary, Queen of Scots, both erstwhile visitors in the flesh. Local legend also speaks of a phantom at Balgonie called 'Green Jean' – Fife ghosts seem to favour green, as a 'green lady' is said to walk at Wemyss Castle.

Once called Dalgynch, the Pictish capital of Fife, Markinch was long both an industrial centre and a watering hole for travellers, advertised as 'the garden of Scotland'. The town spread out from its parish church situated at Kirk Brae, high above Glass Street, but now it has been overtaken by its young neighbour, Glenrothes. The much-restored church is on the site of one dedicated to one of Scotland's apostles, St Drostan, a seventh-century Abbot of Deer, Aberdeenshire; the church was gifted by the Earl of Fife to the Priory of St Andrews around 1203. The Norman tower of the church remains, but the spire was altered in 1807 and the interior reconstructed in 1883. At the church gate is a session house into which is inserted a thirteenth-century foliaceous capital and a niche canopy of later date.

Chartered by Charles II in 1673, Markinch has hilly places steeped in legend; the sister hill to the one on which the parish church stands is Markinch Hill, with its interesting cultivation terraces suggesting medieval activity. Locals dub them 'Roman' and the area was presented to the town by Edward Balfour in 1919. Next to Markinch Hill, set on the banking to the left of Stobbcross Road, is Stobb Cross, which is thought to have stood at the entrance to St Drostan's early church. The monument is considered by historians to be a gyrth cross which marked the boundary of an early sanctuary area. In medieval times every consecrated church had the right of sanctuary, and often provided the only refuge from summary feudal justice until a just and proper trial could be arranged. A knoll around which Northall cemetery was set out in the 1840s is the last resting place of many of the Balfours.

To the north-west of Markinch lies Balbirnie Park, another Balfour family home. Balbirnie House is seventeenth century in origin with developments of 1777–82 and is now a hotel. Within the old Balbirnie estate is a Bronze Age stone circle. Of all Fife's villages, the name Star is one of the most pleasing, derived from 'starr', a swamp. The village lies north-east of Balbirnie and was a weaving community; the slightly elevated village has some fine views of the Lomond Hills and the historic routes across Fife. The old schoolhouse was the home of the Scottish novelist, Annie S. Swann (1859–1943); she lived in the house when her husband Dr James Burnett Smith was dominie.

Born out of the New Towns Act of 1946 the evolution of Glenrothes was conducted by the Glenrothes Development Corporation, starting in 1948–49. The town is set out on land from the old Rothes, Balfour, Balgonie and Aytoun estates; in history the area had two villages, Woodside and Cadham, which formed a focus for the scattering of farmhouses and cottages. This was once a heartland of industrial Fife with its mines at Cadham (1741), Thornton (1842) and Lochtyside (1845).

A close neighbour of Glenrothes, across the valley of the River Leven, is Leslie, once called Fythkill, or Fettykill. The name Leslie derives from a former landowner hereabouts, the descendant of Bartholomew the Fleming from Leslie in Aberdeenshire. Leslie was a spinning and weaving community and the symbols of the trade are still to be seen carved on door lintels; but paper and plastics have contributed to Leslie's more recent industrial life.

A burgh of barony in 1458, Leslie did not develop municipally until 1865 when it became a police burgh, but it was long thought to be the location of the popular Scottish poem *Christis Kirk on the Grene*, attributed by some to James I and by others to James V, although both monarchs are unlikely to have penned the verses. The poem refers to Leslie wappinshaw, or fair, for the town was once famous for its ebullient festivities:

> Was never in Scotland heard or seen
> Sic dancing and deray;

> Nowther at Falkland on the green,
> Nor Peblis at the play,
> As was of woers , as I ween,
> At Christ's Kirk on ane day . . .

The chapmen of Fife (see page 159) are said to have had a headquarters at Leslie where they met on the Green for sport and recreation; new members were initiated in a ducking ceremony. Martinmas Fair was also popular at Leslie, for this was the final fling for the villagers and their neighbours before the hardships of winter. Leslie was a place of combats and bull-baiting and its Bull Stone is still situated on the Green. To this granite boulder bulls were chained, to be baited by dogs. The stone is deeply grooved with chain and rope marks. Bull-baiting was popular from the twelfth to the nineteenth centuries; it was declared illegal in 1835.

Leslie House, 1667–74, the 'Villa de Rothes' from a title derived from estates around Elgin in Morayshire, was the centre of the burgh of barony by the fifteenth century. The house was built for John Leslie, Duke of Rothes, Charles II's Lord High Chancellor of Scotland; the house was visited by Daniel Defoe in 1707 and he declared it to be the 'Glory of Fife'. The house was the residence too of the earls of Rothes and was destroyed by fire in 1763; the west wing was reconstructed during 1765–67. The house long displayed a dagger with which it is said Norman Leslie, Master of Rothes, murdered Cardinal David Beaton at St Andrews Castle in 1546.

Leslie's post-Reformation church was founded in 1591 and dismantled in 1819; a new one was built in 1820, and his building forms the rear of the present church, extended in 1868–69 to include a steeple. The churchyard contains the twin-gabled burial vault of the Rothes family. To the west of Leslie is Strathendry House built by Robert Douglas in the early nineteenth century and nearby are the ruins of Strathendry Castle. Within the vicinity of Leslie too are the ruins of the seventeenth-century Pitcairn House.

Glenrothes' neighbour to the south is Thornton – Thorn Town – which sprang to fame as an important railway junction and was the centre of the East Fife coalfields. It was once an important staging village with famous hostelries such as the Beech Inn and Strephan's Inn.

One of the avenues in Thornton celebrates the new type of flute – the flutorum – invented by an eccentric Dunfermline weaver who opened a pub in Thornton. His name was David Hatton and he had tried to win fame with the invention of the 'mouse treadmill' for winding spools of thread – the industrialists of the day were unimpressed. For many years before he died in 1851 Hatton used to exhibit the coffin in which he was to be buried, and for a penny would lie in it to entertain his clientele. Another famous resident of Thornton was James Black, the government clerk who copied out the American Declaration of Independence (4 July 1776) from Thomas Jefferson's own copy.

The cadgers of Fife

Once packmen, pedlars, cadgers and chapmen were common sights on the roads and byways of Fife. Pedlars and cadgers in particular plied the Fife thoroughfares from Ascension Day (Holy Thursday, ten days before Whitsunday) to Lammas, and their stock-in-trade was the lifeblood of Fife's medieval fairs. A particular role in Fife was the supplying of food, goods and entertainment for the medieval pilgrims to the county's holy sites.

In Fife the word 'cadger' was a late fifteenth-century catch-all to describe an itinerant dealer or hawker, especially in fish; but by the seventeenth century it also came to mean a carrier of goods, or a carter. Fife packmen were travelling merchants, especially in soft goods, and were often called pedlars too. Although dealing in anything from bonnets to pepper, the chapman also sold printed materials called 'chapbooks'; this description covered goods from tracts and pamphlets to bound volumes. The most popular of these were almanacs, some of local knowledge. Several of Fife's chapmen specialised in specific goods: John Duncan (fl.1750s) of Colinsburgh, was known for his fine linen napkins.

Fife's chapmen, itinerant dealers, were a colourful bunch of rogues, not averse to a little illegal dealing. They became kenspeckle characters with their own language and folklore. One such was Robert Low of Flisk (fl.1590s) who was based at Glenduckie, in Flisk parish; he boasted tenant farmers and the 'lesser aristocracy' as his customers.

As time went bv foot-chapmen gave way to mounted chapmen, and by the eighteenth century they had formed themselves into Chapman Societies. Fife had its share of such incorporations from Cupar to the East Neuk, with branches acting almost as secret societies of mutual aid and local knowledge. These incorporations had a medieval root, for it is known that a group met and struck bargains before the altar of their patron, St Michael, set in St Andrews Holy Trinity Church. In St Andrews the chapmen and carters were known as the Whiplickers who established their society by 1872. These Whiplickers had their own annual race days. All these were forerunners of the modern haulage trade.

8
DUNFERMLINE AND WEST FIFE

North Queensferry

The landfall of the kingdom of Fife at North Queensferry has long
been a place of spectacular views. Medieval pilgrims crossing the
Forth, bound on their holy quest to Dunfermline Abbey and
St Andrews Cathedral, obtained their first glimpse of the heights of
the Ferry Hills looming out of the mist on many a morning sailing.
Now, where the tribesmen of the *Venicones* took up position to
watch the Roman fleet disgorge Gauls of the 5th Cohort bound for
Jupiter's own fort at Cramond, modern visitors speed across the
road bridge opened in 1964 and the railway bridge of 1890.

It was Margaret, Saxon wife of King Malcolm III, who first set
the fashion for crossing the watergang, or passage, over the Firth of
Forth. She regularly sailed aboard the royal ferry to and from her
chapel at Edinburgh Castle. When she died at the castle in 1093 her
remains were carried over the same route in solemn procession to
her last resting place at Dunfermline.

According to the *Register of Dunfermline*, King David I granted
to the abbot and convent of Dunfermline the 'passage and ship of
Enderkeithin' in 1129; thus it was he who instituted a regular ferry
service through his decree that all travellers should have free passage
over the Forth water to the court at Dunfermline. At first the
passage was called *passaqium de Inverkeithin*, but after the formal
grant of lands it was named for all time *ad portum reginae* after the
famous queen. The ferry rights were confirmed by subsequent
monarchs and popes, and Malcolm IV added the grant of hospital
lands to the monks at Ferry Fields. These lands were undoubtedly
those associated with the 'hospital' which Turgot, Bishop of St
Andrews in the early twelfth century, tells us was set up here by
Queen Margaret for pilgrims and the poor. When the ferrying of
passengers became too much for the monks at Dunfermline, the
franchise was given to 'substantial seamen'. Down the centuries the

ferry feus were granted to various people on both sides of the Forth, but they remained a point of contention, especially when the ferrymen (and women) began to charge clerics. A fixed charge of one penny per person and twopence per horse was fixed by Act of Parliament in 1474.

James VI gave governance of the ferry as a wedding gift to his new wife, Anne of Denmark, and it passed through various hands until in 1809 it was vested not in private operators but in trustees. New piers and shelters were erected and a steamboat, designed to suit the new piers, was put into service in 1821. Thus the ferry *Queen Margaret* began a long line of ferry boats which continued to ply until the new road bridge was opened in 1964.

North Queensferry was once a close-knit community, and only locals were allowed to act as boatmen and publicans. A few relics of the location's medieval past remain. In the heart of North Queensferry the burial ground is formed partly by the gable of the chapel founded by Robert the Bruce in the early fourteenth century and tended by the monks of Dunfermline Abbey. The church was dedicated to Our Lord's cousin, St James the Apostle, who was fittingly the patron saint of pilgrims. The chapel was extensively damaged by Cromwell's men in 1651. Over the Ferry Hills and on the way to the hamlet of Jamestown lay a lazaretto, dating from the Middle Ages when leprosy was the scourge of society.

Inverkeithing

Inverkeithing, with its eponymous bay, has a modern history of shipbreaking and papermaking, but High Street and Church Street form the heart of the medieval town. Situated astride the old north–south route and affording safe anchorage in the inner bay, Inverkeithing has a charter granted by William the Lion around 1165. Some historians aver that these shores sheltered the Roman fleet of Julius Agricola when in 82–83 he launched an attack on the Caledonians north of the Forth, and certainly there seems to have been a settlement at Inverkeithing long before William's charter. In the twelfth century Inverkeithing belonged to Gospatrick, Earl of Dunbar, but in time the land passed into the hands of the Moubrays of Barnbougle who held sway until the seventeenth century. Documents show that David I was a landowner here, and he set the fashion for Inverkeithing as a medieval watering place. Robert III's wife, Annabella Drummond, resided at Rotmills Inns in the town and died here in 1403. So important was the town that the Convention of Royal Burghs was held in it in 1487.

In Church Street stands the parish church of St Peter, which started as a wooden Celtic church and was developed into a Norman stone structure bequeathed to Dunfermline Abbey in 1139. All that remains of the pre-Reformation church is the fourteenth-century tower, for the church itself was destroyed by fire in 1825; rebuilt from 1826, the church had restoration work in 1900. One of its treasures is the font discovered during excavations in 1807; local legend has it that it was concealed from the despoilers of the Reformation and is thought to have been gifted by Queen Annabella Drummond and Robert III at the baptism of their son, David, Duke of Rothesay.

Opposite St Peter's is the distinctive, turreted L-shaped town house known as Fordell's Lodgings, built 1661–71 by Sir John Henderson of Fordell. Providence House of 1688 – so called because its lintel is carved with 'God's Providence is my Inheritance' – is worthy of note too. Rosebery House in King Street belonged to the Rosebery family and is a much altered sixteenth-century edifice. The house was once known as 'The Toofall' before it was purchased by the Earl of Rosebery, and was owned by John, Earl of Dunbar, in 1668; in 1672 the house was gifted by Charles II to the third Earl of Lauderdale. In the High Street is the house where one of Inverkeithing's famous sons was born in 1735: Sir Samuel Greig, the son of a shipowning baillie of the royal burgh, became a distinguished admiral in the Imperial Russian Navy. In Heriot Street stands Moffat Cottage, named after the famous Scottish divine and missionary, James Moffat, who explored the Cape and translated the Bible into modern English. Another celebrated missionary, David Livingstone, is also associated with the dwelling; Livingstone married Moffat's daughter and was a frequent visitor to Inverkeithing. At the rear of the cottage is the summerhouse he built during his stays.

The Hospitium of Greyfriars Monastery stands in Queen Street. Its history is largely unauthenticated, but some sources credit its foundation to Philip de Moubray, Lord of Barnbougle around 1268. The friary and its garden area were transferred to one John Swinton in July 1559. The friary was restored during 1932–34. It is believed that the Dominicans (the Blackfriars) also had a house in Inverkeithing, and mention is made in land transfers of a 'hospital' here which probably belonged to the foundation at North Queensferry founded by Malcolm IV.

Inverkeithing's Town House, with its pepperpot steeple, replaced an older tolbooth in 1770. Above the door of the Town House is the old burgh coat of arms; it shows St Peter, the first-century apostle and martyr with tiara, key and a church on the dexter side of the arms, and a ship on the sinister side.

The burgh's Mercat Cross has had a number of sites. Originally it stood at the north end of High Street and was moved to face the Town House in 1799 as it was impeding the passage of stage-coaches; today it is located in Bank Street, a few yards round the corner. One of the finest crosses remaining in Scotland, its core dates from 1398. Two of its shields bear the arms of Annabella Drummond and the Douglas family. Sundials have been ingeniously worked into intersecting octagonal prisms. The cross was possibly set up as a memorial of the marriage of the Duke of Rothesay with the daughter of the Earl of Douglas. The unicorn was added in 1688 and is the work of John Boyd, mason of South Queensferry. At the base of the cross is a plaque commemorating the Battle of Inverkeithing in 1651.

In common with most Scottish burghs Inverkeithing had four main fairs: at Candlemas (February), Beltane (May), Lammas (August) and Martinmas (November) – from the latter we get our word 'mart'. Today the Lammas Fair remains and was described in the burgh records of 1652 as a day of 'fun, frolic, fit races, ale and drunken folks'; it drew people from miles around and James IV bought his horses at Inverkeithing's Lammas Fair. The annual 'Hat and Ribbon' Race takes place at the Lammas Fair at Inverkeithing and dates back to the seventeenth century.

The hamlet of Hillend lies at the foot of Letham Hill Wood. To the right (down the B916) is Fordell Castle, which stands in a magnificent wooded parkland on the edge of a ravine above the Keithing Burn. Based on a thirteenth-century estate gifted to the monks of Inchcolm by Richard de Camera around 1220, Fordell Castle was the seat of the Henderson family from the sixteenth to the twentieth century; they consolidated the estate and invested heavily in mining operations. Across the estate once ran Scotland's first private railway to transport coal to St David's harbour. Fordell estate also sponsored salt panning.

These were the days when Fife miners were virtual slaves, to be bought and sold with the equipment of the collieries. Sir John Henderson, sometime MP for Fife, Dysart, Kirkcaldy Burghs and Stirling Burghs, granted the miners of Fordell and Dalgety their freedom, and for many decades this grant was celebrated in the Fordell Annual Parade. Fordell Castle today is a mid-sixteenth century fortalice of the Z-plan; that is, it is a version of the building design of two wings set at diagonally opposite corners of a main block allowing all-round flanking fire in time of siege. The castle was long maintained as a folly by the Henderson descendants after Sir John Henderson built a more modern mansion in 1721.

The battle of Inverkeithing

The Battle of Inverkeithing is perhaps Scotland's most forgotten engagement. The Scots army of Charles II was licking its wounds: at Dunbar on 3 September 1650, Cromwell had routed the Scots force under David Leslie. The Scots withdrew to the Stirling area, leaving Cromwell to dominate the territory south of the Forth. On Sunday, 20 July 1651, Cromwell sent a force of some 4,500 soldiers of his New Model Army across the Forth, under General John Lambert, commander of the army in the North. They landed at Port Laing, Inverkeithing Bay, and entrenched themselves on Cruicks to the west rim of Inverkeithing. To try to stop Cromwell opening a second front in his attempt to conquer Scotland, Charles II sent a counter force of 4,000 or so from his base at Torwood, Dunkeld, under Lieutenant-General Holburne, with Sir John Brown of Fordell as commander of cavalry. This force took up position on Selvage Hill, south-west of Inverkeithing. Among the Scots were 800 or so Maclean clansmen under Sir Hector Maclean of Duart.

Lambert launched his right wing up Selvage Hill and scattered the Scots' left; although Holburne's Scots' right wing were initially successful, they were driven back by Cromwell's cavalry hidden at Welldean. On the run, the Scots descended to the valley south of Pitreavie Castle. By this time Holburne had fled with his staff officers. The Macleans (and Loch Lomond Buchanans) fought a brave last stand; over 750 were slaughtered. Here a clan legend was forged on Fife land: seven brothers from the same Maclean family surrounded their stricken chief. As they fell to Cromwellian swords each brother cried out '*Fear eile airson Eachainn*' (Another for Hector). Sir Hector too fell in the battle.

Following the battle, General George Monk, first Duke of Albemarle, Cromwell's commander-in-chief in Scotland, occupied Inverkeithing, plundered Rosyth Castle and Spencerfield House and ravaged the vicinity. An authoritarian Cromwellian regime, backed by military force, was now welded on Scotland for nine years.

In July 2001, the 350th anniversary of the battle, a Glensanda Quarry granite cairn from Morvern, Argyllshire, was erected to commemorate the Maclean clansmen who died in the Inverkeithing campaign; it lies on a grass verge a few hundred yards from Pitreavie Castle where they are buried.

Dalgety

Dalgety has developed from a nineteenth-century village into a new town. Construction began in the early 1960s and the location was to see Scotland's first privately built new town. Tradition has it that the village dates back to the thirteenth century and that Dalgety's first inhabitants were fisherfolk, possibly with Norse connections. Once Dalgety's superior coal, a part of the Fordell mining enterprise, was a must for the steam navigation companies. Despite Admiral Sir Philip Calderwood Durham of Fordell's investment of £2,000 in a new harbour for Dalgety the coal trade declined, as the salt panning had done, and the village reached a new low point. Buildings were demolished and people scattered; the hamlet that once supported St David's harbour became a lost village too.

The historical star attraction at Dalgety is St Bridget's Church, reached past Old Dalgety parish church down the narrow Four

Lums Road. Built by the monks of Inchcolm, the church of St Bridget is made up of a later two-storey building comprising a burial vault on the ground floor and a 'laird's loft' above, from which access was gained to a western gallery within the church. The edifice was dedicated to the Ulster-born fifth-century saint, the Abbess Bridget, in 1244. It was used as a residence in the house of 1610 added to the western elevation by the Covenanting pastor Andrew Donaldson who was ejected at the restoration of episcopacy in 1661. Just, outside the walls is a small stone building which acted as a watch-house against the resurrectionists (body-snatchers), whose activities kept the anatomy tables of Edinburgh well filled. The church was deroofed in 1830.

Although service wings (*c.* 1720), a chapel (1729–30) and stables of vanished Donibristle House remain, the historic estate of Donibristle is remembered in mining lore and legend. This was the location of the mining disaster at Donibristle colliery, sited a few miles to the north of Dalgety, on Monday, 26 August 1901. Eight miners perished. Many poems and songs were written about the underground tragedy; this excerpt of one recalls the grief:

> Between Donibristle and Cowdenbeath,
> Moss Morran's desolate plain does lie,
> And here the poor miners met their death
> Beneath an autumn's dismal sky.

Murder at Donibristle

Donibristle estate stretched from St David's harbour to Aberdour and was the seat of the Earl of Moray. The lands once belonged to the monks of Inchcolm, and the first castle on the site belonged to James Stewart, Lord of Doune, Commendator of Inchcolm. It became the principal residence of his son who entered immortality as 'the Bonny Earl of Moray' famed in ballad:

> Ye Highlands and ye Lowlands,
> O where have ye been?
> They ha'e slain the Earl of Moray
> And laid him on the green.

The 'green' was the shoreline in front of Donibristle House. James Stewart, second Earl of Moray – 'The Bonny Earl' – was born here, and after his marriage to Elizabeth Stewart in 1580, became the son-in-law of James Stewart, illegitimate half-brother of Mary, Queen of Scots. The Bonny Earl was the darling of the Protestant cause and found enemies at court because he was a friend and cousin-german of the fifth Earl of Bothwell, then a hunted man. The Bonny Earl had further earned the jealousy of King James VI, for the balladmongers linked the handsome Moray with his queen, Anne of Denmark:

> He was a brave gallant
> And he played at the gluve,
> And the Bonny Earl of Moray,
> Oh, he was the Queen's luve.

The king gave the Bonny Earl's mortal enemy, George Gordon, sixth Earl of Huntly and leader of the Roman Catholic Party at court, a warrant for Moray's arrest. Huntly followed the Bonny Earl to Donibristle and set fire to the family home. Moray escaped, was caught on the seashore and murdered on 7 February 1592.

Although the house was replaced, it burned down again in 1858. The Moray estates were sold to the property developers who built the new town of Dalgety Bay in the 1960s.

Aberdour

Modern Aberdour is made up of Easter Aberdour, which was made into a burgh of regality in 1638, and Wester Aberdour which was a burgh of barony from 1501. As a burgh of regality, Easter Aberdour owned title to the Douglas earls of Morton, while its western counterpart was a barony under the Abbey of Inchcolm and the Stewart earls of Moray. The town has seen a great deal of expansion since the Second World War, but still sports some fine eighteenth-century buildings and nineteenth-century houses. Among the showpieces of Aberdour is its church, a gem of Scottish ecclesiastical architecture. St Fillan's Church stands by the road leading to the Silver Sands beach and dates from the twelfth century; it was used continuously for worship until 1796. It was derelict until 1925 when it was restored and re-dedicated. Today it is a church showing many phases of architecture, from its late fifteenth-century entrance porch to its Gothic windows. Local legend has it that Robert the Bruce, thought to be a leper, worshipped at the now-sealed leper's squint at St Fillan's after the Battle of Bannockburn in 1314.

Nearby is the castle of Aberdour, the oldest part of which is the rhomboidal tower of the fourteenth century; the other buildings were added during the sixteenth and seventeenth centuries. In the grounds a fine dovecote or doocot remains in good repair. The house was once owned by the Mortimers, who inherited it from the Norman barons the Viponts, then the Mortons who held the castle until the middle of the eighteenth century. One famous Morton owner was James Douglas, fourth Earl of Morton, who was the regent of Scotland from November 1572 until the *coup d'état* of March 1578. Morton looked upon the castle as a place of leisure and spent time developing the gardens. His residency made the castle a temporary cockpit of political intrigue and Morton entertained guests such as Sir Henry Killigrew, the English ambassador. Morton

Aberdour Castle. Its rhomboidal tower dates from the fourteenth century with other buildings added during the sixteenth–seventeenth centuries. The castle was the home of the Regent, James Douglas, 4th Earl of Morton. (Author's collection)

was executed in 1581, having been denounced by his enemies as an accessory to the murder of Henry Stewart, Lord Darnley. The last long-term occupant of the castle was Robert Watson of Muirhouse, who died there in 1791. In 1924 the castle and grounds passed into the care of the state.

More and more castles and tower houses in Fife are being brought back to life and modernised to preserve their role in Fife's history and legend. One example is Couston Castle by Otterstone Loch, a mile and a half west of Aberdour. It seems that the original land grant of Couston was rendered around 1199 to Robert de London, an illegitimate son of William I, the Lion. What kind of original building was sited here is difficult to say, but records show 'a castle' of the fourteenth century, while most of today's edifice is of the sixteenth century. The Logans of Couston lived here in the seventeenth century and by the nineteenth it was in the hands of the Earl of Moray, who leased it. By the 1850s the castle was derelict, but was renovated in the late 1980s. In the pages of history Couston Castle was the home of the Covenanting clergyman, Professor Robert Blair, famous for his verbal tennis with Oliver Cromwell during the Protector's visit to Edinburgh in 1648. Blair was an 'outspoken Presbyterian opponent' of Archbishop James Sharp, who forbade Blair to travel within twenty miles of his archiepiscopal city of St Andrews. In Blair's day Couston Castle became a focus for dissenting opinion and visitors. The divine died here in 1666, aged seventy-two.

Fifers have often added idiosyncrasy to their homes. From Aberdour the A82 leads directly to Burntisland; just before dropping down into the town the road passes very close to the curious 'fantasy castle' at Easterheughs – this was built 1946–59 by William Thomas, a retired works manager. He based his plans on seventeenth-century Scottish architectural styles and used stone from High Birn village.

Burntisland

Once the docks at Burntisland hummed with exports of coal and imports of bauxite; James V used it as a naval base and the town saw the first railway ferry in the world opened in 1850 between

Burntisland and Granton. The ferries ceased in 1952. The verifiable history of Burntisland begins in the twelfth century when the harbour and lands around it belonged to Dunfermline Abbey. The abbey built the original Burntisland Castle (Rossend Castle), it is said in 1119, and the old church of Kirkton; round these two sites the town evolved. Burntisland was chartered in 1541 and in 1586 it was proclaimed a royal burgh, with John Clephane as its first provost. Cromwell captured the burgh in 1651 and Samuel Pepys noted that Burntisland was bombarded by the Dutch in 1667. In medieval times Burntisland had two weekly markets and a 'common fair' dedicated conjointly to the apostles Peter and Paul. Burntisland's present fair began, tradition has it, as a horse race between cavalrymen from Cromwell's New Model Army in 1654.

The little church of Burntisland at Kirkton was re-dedicated to St Serf by Bishop de Bernham in 1243 and was sited in modern Church Street. The predominating church today is St Columba's, which boasts of being the first church built after the Reformation, 1592–95. It retains many interesting features, including panels of the mariners' loft and signs of the various long-defunct trade guilds; a forestair of 1679 is still to be seen which was used by sailors making a quick exit from the church to 'catch the tide'. The church contains an unusual canopied pew built for Sir Robert Melville – latterly known as the Magistrates' Pew – which was used for 'The Kirkin' o' the Coonsel', this being a Scottish traditional municipal rite in which the local town council processed gowned to the church for a civic service. Like other parts of Fife Burntisland's individual civic authority ceased in 1975. It was at a meeting at Burntisland in 1601 that the General Assembly proposed the Authorised Version of the Bible.

It was not often in history that a Scotswoman defied social convention. One such was Mary Somerville, the daughter of Vice-Admiral Sir William Fairfax, one of Nelson's captains. Born at Jedburgh in 1780 and brought up at Burntisland, she struggled all her life for her own education – 'Latin's no for lassies', her Burntisland dominie had told her – and for the education of women in general. She went on to become a distinguished mathematician and her fame is remembered in the Oxford college of 1879 which bears her name. The house where she lived (nos.

30–31) is in the now renamed Somerville Square. The painted ceilings which were once in the house are now preserved in Edinburgh Castle where they were moved in 1957.

Overlooking Burntisland harbour, the Rossend Castle we see today began as an L-shaped tower house and was constructed around 1554. The tower was extended in the early seventeenth century and again in the nineteenth to provide additional accommodation at its lower levels. This replaced an earlier structure, possibly of the twelfth century, built by the clergy of Dunfermline Abbey. Certainly it was still in the ownership of the Abbot of Dunfermline, one George Durie, in the early sixteenth century, and was later confirmed by Mary, Queen of Scots for Sir Robert Melville of Murdocairnie. The queen's visits added to the lore of the castle as did those of Rob Roy McGregor and James Francis Edward Stewart, the Jacobite James VIII and III, the Old Pretender.

Rossend Castle continued to be owned by the Melville family for many years, but in the eighteenth century it passed to the

Rossend Castle, Burntisland. The old keep replaced a fourteenth-century structure. Mary, Queen of Scots visited the castle in 1563. (Author's collection)

Campbells and then to the Wemyss family. In the 1930s it was taken over by Burntisland Town Council; it fell steadily into disrepair and was severely vandalised. Plans to demolish it were stoutly resisted and eventually the building was restored by a firm of architects.

The road east out of Burntisland follows an old track over the Links ceded by James V in exchange for harbouring rights and on to Pettycur. This was formerly the northern terminal of a Forth ferry. There are still milestones in Fife which bear the name Pettycur, relics of the period when travellers might calculate their distance from the ferry. To the north of Pettycur stands Witch Hill, where local legend recounts witches were executed. Halfway to Kinghorn stands the Celtic cross in memory of King Alexander III, who was killed here in 1286.

Sudden death at Pettycur: a king's fate

Alexander III, nicknamed 'The Glorious', was born at Roxburgh Castle on 4 September 1241, the son of Alexander II and Queen Marie de Courcy. The last of Scotland's Celtic kings, he was seven when he succeeded his father and ten when he married his first wife, Margaret, daughter of Henry III of England; she died in 1275 and ten years later he married Yolande de Dreux. After a period of predictably fraught regencies Alexander assumed power personally in 1262 and pursued his late father's policy of trying to recover the Hebrides from Norway. Haakon IV of Norway proved obdurate in surrendering the islands and foolishly brought an invasion force to Scotland in 1263 to secure the whole of the Hebrides and the Isle of Man. Alexander trounced the aged Haakon's forces at Largs and the whole of the Western Isles were ceded to Alexander, plus 4,000 merks.

Alexander's reign was generally peaceful and prosperous, but Fife was to see the nadir of his final years. In 1284 his male heir, Alexander, died; he had been preceded by his brother David, aged eight, in 1280; and the king's daughter Margaret, married to Erik II of Norway, died in childbirth in 1283, leaving Alexander an infant granddaughter, Margaret, the Maid of Norway, as heir to the Scottish throne.

On 19 March 1286 Alexander attended a council at Edinburgh. It

Memorial to Alexander III, Kinghorn. The king was
killed in a riding accident nearby in 1286. (STARALP)

was a dark and stormy night as he crossed the Forth and rode into
Burntisland, but the king wanted to press on, as he was anxious to join
his wife Yolande at the Tower of Kinghorn. In the dark he became
separated from his aides on the road which then led across the cliffs,
and on the 150-ft precipice of Kinghorn Ness his horse stumbled and
Alexander was thrown down the escarpment. Today the 1886 memorial
of Peterhead granite at Pettycur is near to the spot where Alexander was
found dead. The event plunged Scotland into a protracted period of
calamity.

Fife's own chronicler, the Augustinian canon, Andrew Wyntoun,
summed up the horror of the king's death in his *Chronicle*: 'Quen
Alysandyr oure kyng was dede, that Scotland led in luive and le,
away we sonce of ale and brede, of wyne and wax, of gamyn and
gle; our golde wes changed into lede. Cryst! Born into virgynyte,

succour Scotland and remede that stad is in perplexyte.'

Alexander's heir, Margaret, died on board ship in a storm off the Orkneys in 1290. Scotland then entered a period of interregnum marked by the interference of Edward I of England.

Kinghorn

Kinghorn was once a prosperous spinning and shipbuilding centre, described as a 'douce, well-aired town'. It was an ancient settlement when David I created it a royal burgh in the twelfth century. Kinghorn Castle, once Glamis Tower because of its ownership by the Lyons of Glamis, has now vanished, but it was a favourite haven for both monarchs and nobility alike. In the old regal hierarchy of Scotland the name of Kinghorn appears for the offices of Constable of Kinghorn and Keeper of the King's Door, which were important court positions. Today too, the town's name appears in a Scottish earldom, that of Strathmore and Kinghorn.

Before Kinghorn received its Town House in 1822 the site was occupied by a medieval edifice, St Leonard's Tower, a chapel which fell to secular use. The 1774 parish church stands by the sea, down the Nethergate, and is on the site of several churches. The present one was rebuilt in 1894 and internally reconstructed in 1930; outside is the ruined choir of an earlier edifice. In medieval times Kinghorn had a hospital for the poor which was founded around 1478; this was set in the grounds of a chapel dedicated to St James.

Several estates to the north of Kinghorn have featured prominently in Fife history. Abden, for instance, was once the land of the bishops of St Andrews. The castle of Piteadie once belonged to the Earl of Rosslyn and is interesting for its gunports and two wings bearing the initials of Sir Henry Wardlaw (d.1631), chamberlain to Queen Anne of Denmark. The much reconstructed Balmutto House was the seat of the Boswell family for 500 years; it was built around a fifteenth-century keep.

The tale of Sir Patrick Spens

> The king sits in Dunfermline towne
> Drinking the blude red wine.

Thus begins one of the most famous quotes relating to Fife. It comes from the early Scots ballad, *Sir Patrick Spens*, and was given prominence in *Reliques of Ancient English Poetry* (1765) by the antiquarian, Thomas Percy (1729–1811).

The ballad tells how Sir Patrick is sent from his home at Aberdour on a mission by King Alexander III. In his version of the ballad Sir Walter Scott makes the object of the expedition the task of bringing to Scotland Princess Margaret, the Maid of Norway, Alexander's granddaughter and heir. Alexander's daughter had married King Erik of Norway, and the Scots king was anxious to see his little granddaughter. As a matter of historical record, Margaret died with the ship's company in a storm when she was being taken to Scotland after Alexander's untimely accident at Kinghorn.

It is 1280, recounts the ballad, and Alexander sits in Malcolm Canmore's tower at Dunfermline drinking and feasting with his nobles. The mission is on his mind. He tells the assembled company that he needs a 'skeely skipper' to sail his royal barque to fetch his granddaughter. Who could undertake such a task? A courtier answers:

> Sir Patrick Spens is the best sailor
> That ever sailed the sea.

Thus Sir Patrick sets off in winter across the sea to Norway with a company of Scots lords. The ballad is laden with forebodings of disaster.

> I saw the new moon late yestreen
> Wi the auld moon in her arm;
> And if we gang to sea, master,
> I fear we'll come to harm.

On the return journey the barque hits a storm; the anchor ropes snap, the topmasts lap, and the sea gushes through holes made in the hull. The entire company are drowned.

> Half ower, half ower to Aberdour
> Full fifty fathoms deep
> There lies the gude Sir Patrick Spens
> Wi' the Scots lords at his feet.

Did Sir Patrick ever exist? It is unlikely, although the Spens family were prominent in East Fife. The Spens of Wormiston were hereditary constables of Crail, and although records of them here are of a much later date than Alexander III's time, there was one William Spens who played a heroic role at the Siege of Dunbar in 1338.

Dunfermline

'Fortunate indeed the child who first sees the light of day in that romatic town'. This is how philanthropist and steel magnate Andrew Carnegie remembered his birthplace. Today Carnegie's name and legend loom large in Dunfermline, his story being told at his birthplace museum in Moodie Street. Born in 1835, the son of a handloom weaver, Carnegie and his family emigrated to America in 1848; he graduated from bobbin boy to telegraphic messenger, and thence to railroadman and entrepreneur in the iron and steel industry, becoming the world's richest man. He sold the Carnegie Steel Company in 1901, and his personal share of the proceeds was £60 million. He set about spending his fortune on various public benefactions. His many gifts to Dunfermline included the Carnegie Baths (1877), the library (1881) and scores of grants and donations. He died in 1919.

Known locally as 'The Glen', Pittencrieff Park is the real heart of Dunfermline. Local legend has it that as a boy Andrew Carnegie used to look with envy at the private policies of Pittencrieff House and swore that one day he would be laird of Pittencrieff. He did just that and gifted the land and the house to his native burgh in 1903. The park extends to 76 acres, and Pittencrieff House itself was built around 1610 by Alexander Clerk; it was renovated in 1911 under the eye of Sir Robert Lorimer and now houses museum and art displays. Malcolm Canmore's Tower, within the park, and nearby St Margaret's Cave, recall Dunfermline's legendary and historic foundations.

More than a thousand years ago a handful of monks sought rest in what is now Pittencrieff Park. They were clergy of the Culdee church, who had taken their name from *céli dé*, 'companions of God', and were a class of ascetic clerics who are recorded as being in

Andrew Carnegie. Born at Dunfermline, Carnegie's
fortune helped found trusts and libraries in his native
county. (Author's collection)

existence in the first half of the ninth century (see page 112). They
liked the place and founded a little church in the glen which was to
give modern Dunfermline its name, signifying 'the hill by the
winding stream'. On this peninsulated hill, at Pittencreiff, King
Malcolm Canmore built a fortress tower around 1065, probably on
the site of a Pictish habitation. Malcolm's patronage brought much
needed work and succour to the starved and ragged people in the
hamlet of wattle huts that had sprung up near to the chapel of the
Culdees.

When Malcolm, son of the King Duncan who was murdered by
Macbeth, moved his court here from Forteviot, Perthshire, he set in
motion a series of events which were to make Dunfermline an
important Scottish capital; a role it kept until after the assassination
of James I at Perth in 1437. To Malcolm's castle, the remains of
which can still be seen in Pittencrieff Park, there came the Saxon
Princess Margaret, granddaughter of Edmund Ironside. In 1069 she

married Malcolm as his second wife and she began a further series of events, cultural and ecclesiastical, in her own right that were to transform Malcolm's old Celtic kingdom into a new Anglo-Saxon realm.

Soon after her marriage, Queen Margaret, who had been educated by the Benedictines, persuaded Malcolm to enlarge the little Culdee chapel into a fine church for Benedictine monks. Dedicated to the Holy Trinity, the new church was formed, around 1072, into the priory peopled by Benedictines sent at Margaret's request by Lanfranc, Archbishop of Canterbury.

Queen Margaret died at Edinburgh Castle on 16 November 1093 after hearing of Malcolm's death at the battle of Alnwick. Her body was brought to Dunfermline for burial. Two of Margaret's sons, succeeding monarchs, carried on her work. In 1128 David I had the priory elevated into the Abbey of Christ Church, with Prior Geoffrey as its first abbot.

In 1250 an event occurred that was to make Dunfermline famous throughout Christendom: Queen Margaret was canonised and her body transferred to a sumptuous shrine decorated with gold and precious stones. The cult of St Margaret grew: her oratory, which was a cave in the side of Pittencrieff Glen, became a focus for pilgrims, as was St Margaret's Well (now Headwell) and St Margaret's Hope, a sheltered bay on the Forth where she first landed in Scotland, and St Margaret's Stone, between Rosyth and Dunfermline (near the gates of Pitreavie Castle) where she is supposed to have rested on her journey through west Fife.

In Margaret's time she sanctified the priory with the 'Crucifix of the Holy Saviour', an artefact made of ebony, gold and silver, and studded with gems; she had brought it with her when she fled from the Normans and it enters Scottish legend as the Holy Black Rood, fashioned to hold a reputed portion of the True Cross from Calvary. This became one of the most venerated relics in Scotland, and so powerful was its religious mystique that it was carried off to England by Edward I. Somehow the Scots regained possession of the cross and it was in David II's entourage at the Battle of Neville's Cross in 1346. Thereafter it was displayed at the shrine of St Cuthbert at Durham, but disappeared in 1546.

Margaret was the founder of a great library at Dunfermline and her devotional books became legendary. One such was called the *Evangelistarium*, or 'Queen Margert's Gospel Book'. Of it her biographer Turgot, Bishop of St Andrews, says: 'She had a book of the Gospels beautifully adorned with gold and precious stones, and ornamented with the figures of the four Evangelists painted and gilt. All the capital letters throughout the volume were radiant with gold'. The book disappeared for centuries, but in 1887 it was discovered in a parish library at Brent Ely, Suffolk; it was sold at Sotheby's for £6 to the Bodleian Library, Oxford. Margaret's legends also include mention of the *Camisa Beate Margarete Regine*, the tunic in which she died; this was kept beside her shrine and the queens of Scotland up to the Reformation had it by them when they went into labour. We are told of its removal to the bedside of Mary of Guelders, when she was about to bear the future James V, in an entry to the *Accounts of the Lord High Treasurer*.

Dunfermline Abbey was to have five main periods of development. Between 1128–1450 Queen Margaret's church grew and its fine nave was laid out around 1140; its consecration cross can still be seen. Around 1240 the choir of the monastic church was extended and the shrine was built; considerable rebuilding took place in 1329, and in 1450 the west gable was rebuilt by Abbot Richard de Bothwell. From 1594–99 the north-west tower of the nave was reconstructed by William Shaw. During the seventeenth century buttresses were erected to support the walls of the nave, and inside the splendour was continually enriched as seven kings, four queens, two princesses and five princes were laid to rest.

The abbey grew in power and wealth over centuries. Some twenty-six altars were endowed by individuals and guilds of the burgh. The Abbot of Dunfermline, who was a mitred abbot – making him second only to a diocesan bishop – ruled lands from Urquhart in Moray to Berwickshire in sight of the English border. The abbot was overlord of four burghs and administered three courts of regality; he supervised the abbey's fishing, salt panning, mining and grain-milling rights.

In Dunfermline's Maygate stands the Abbot's House, but this was not the home of a true abbot. The house was built after the Reformation in the late sixteenth century and is a fortalice in style which became the mansion of Robert Pitcairn, Commendator and

Reconstruction of Dunfermline Abbey as it might have appeared
1226–1560. From Ebenezer Henderson's composite drawing of 1879.
(Author's collection)

View of the west elevation of the frater, gate house and pend of
Dunfermline Abbey, 1817. (Author's collection)

titular Abbot of Dunfermline to 1584. Above the lintel of the door is the couplet:

SEN VORD IS THRALL AND THOCT IS FRE
REEP VEILL THY TONGUE I COINSELL THE

Sir Walter Scott quoted this in Chapter 25 of his *Fair Maid of Perth*, where he comments that it was the belief that it alluded to Commendator Robert Pitcairn's mistress. The house is now a treasury of Dunfermline artefacts as the Abbot House Heritage Centre.

The abbey's power added to the influence of the town which Alexander I had made a burgh of regality around 1124–27. The abbey had its ups and downs: it was largely destroyed by Edward I's forces in 1303 and its buildings were partly demolished by the reforming Protestant lords in 1560. The choir of the medieval church has completely disappeared, but the nave remains in state care. The eastern part of the abbey had a new choir and transepts grafted on to it in 1812–21, and that part belongs to the Church of Scotland. This area of the church plays a role in the history and legend of Robert the Bruce.

Bruce was buried with great pomp in the abbey in 1329, but his tomb of white French marble was destroyed by the Reformers. On King Robert's early tomb this epitaph was displayed:

HIC JACET INVICTUS ROBERTUS, REX BENEDICTUS
QUI SUA GESTA LEGIT REPETAT QUOT BELLA PEREGIT
AD LIBERTATEM PERDUXIT PER PROBITATEM
REGNUM SCOTORUM: NUNC VIVAT IN ARCE
POLORUM

This might be rendered thus: 'Here lies the unconquered and blessed King Robert. Whosoever collects together [the records of] his warlike deeds, may recount what wars he prosecuted. He has led the kingdom of the Scots through uprightness to liberty; now he lives in the Citadel of Heaven'. For 500 years his tomb was lost, but when the ground was being cleared in 1818 for the new parish church, the site was rediscovered. A skeleton, presumed to be that of Bruce, was discovered wrapped in cloth of gold; its breastbone was split and this was deemed proof that it was Bruce's cadaver, as it was known that his heart had been removed at death, at his own request, so that it might be transported to the Holy Land on

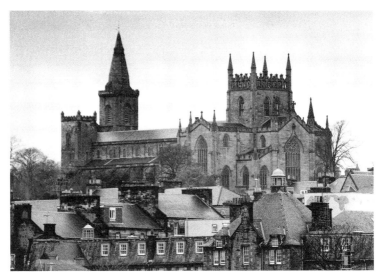

Dunfermline Abbey from the south-east. (STARALP)

Dunfermline Abbey; site of St Margaret's Shrine, left. (STARALP)

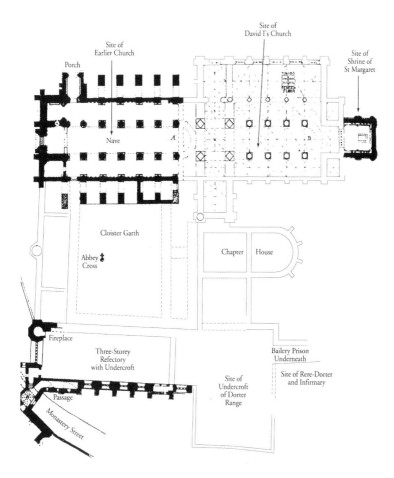

Ground plan of Dunfermline Abbey.

crusade. Bruce's heart was taken to Spain by Sir James Douglas, who commanded a division of the Christian army aiding King Alfonso XI of Castile and Leon in the Holy Crusade against the Moors of Granada. Carrying Bruce's heart into battle Douglas was killed, but his body and Bruce's heart were brought back to Scotland by Sir William Keith of Galston. Legend has it that Bruce's heart now rests in its cone-shaped lead container in the floor of the chapter-house of the Cistercian Abbey at Melrose.

A modern brass plate covers the last resting place of Bruce's bones at Dunfermline and reads:

ROBERTIS DE BRUS SCOTORUM REGIS SEPULCHRUM
AD MDCCCXVIII INTER RUINAS PAVSTE RETECTUM
HOC AERE DENVO CONSIGNATUM EST ANNO POST
PSIVS OBITUM DLX

The tomb of Robert Bruce, King of Scots, fortunately discovered among the ruins in 1818, has been marked anew by this brass in the 560th year after his death.

Perhaps the worst desecration carried out by the Protestant Reformers at Dunfermline was that of the magnificent shrine of St Margaret, a Scottish national treasure, the site of which can still be seen behind the east gable of the modern church. Abbot George Durie, no doubt apprised of the Reformers' approach, removed Margaret's bones and carried them off to Edinburgh. Venerated by Mary, Queen of Scots, the relics were taken to Abbot Durie's castle at Rossend (Burntisland) when Queen Mary fled to England in 1567. Legend has it that the relics remained at the castle until 1597, when they were handed to the Jesuits, one of whose number, John Robie, took them to Antwerp; by 1620 they were in the care of John Malderus, Bishop of Antwerp. In 1627 the relics were transferred to the Scots College at Douai, France and it is said that Philip II of Spain ultimately acquired a few and built a special chapel for them in the Church of St Lawrence at the Escurial palace. A portion of the relics was brought home to Scotland in 1862 by Bishop James Gillies to St Margaret's Convent of the Ursulines of Jesus, Edinburgh; this relic, a piece of St Margaret's shoulder bone, was a gift of Francis, titular King of Spain, and Queen Isabella II.

Dunfermline Abbey was presented to Anne of Denmark by

James VI as a wedding present in 1589 and in 1593 the buildings were annexed to the crown in perpetuity. From the monastic gatehouse, refurbished by James V for his queen, there evolved the royal palace, and the unfortunate Charles I was born in the upper storey of the west wing.

It was James VI who gave Dunfermline its royal, and confirming, charter in 1588; in 1624, however, the burgh was almost totally destroyed by fire. This contributed to the coming decline. As with St Andrews, the Reformation stripped Dunfermline of its importance as an ecclesiastical centre, and prosperity was not regained until weaving was introduced. The coming of the linen trade to Dunfermline was an interesting piece of industrial espionage. It seems that in the early eighteenth century a small damask-weaving manufacture was set up in Edinburgh by continental craftsmen. The damask process was secret, but in 1709 a Dunfermline weaver called James Blake absorbed its mysteries; he did this by impersonating an imbecile who hung around the looms of the immigrant weavers to amuse them. Blake was allowed to enter their workshops and as he capered for their pleasure he took note of both machines and processes. On returning to Dunfermline he was able to build his own industry. So weaving was established in the town by 1718 and the trade was revolutionised by the introduction of steam power in 1849. By 1852 Dunfermline folk had developed as individualistic Fifers; as the *Third Statistical Account of Fife* noted, they were 'a rather isolated, settled, self-centred community, composed predominantly of church-going, politically minded handloom weavers, with coal-mining taking place on the northern and western outskirts of the burgh'.

Of Dunfermline's famous citizens, one Robert Henryson may be mentioned. He was a poet, born in 1430, who came to the burgh to take up employment as a schoolmaster. His writings include the humorous version he compiled of *Aesop's Fables*.

One of the distinctive features of Dunfermline is the City Chambers of 1876–79; the 117-ft clock tower dominates the High Street. This was the successor of probably some four town houses, the first being destroyed in the fire of 1624; a later one stood on the present City Chambers' site from 1771 to 1876. The burgh's Market Cross, with a shaft of 1695, survives near the west gable of Abbot's

House. Dunfermline's Guildhall was built in 1807 by the Fraternity of Guildry, but was converted ino a courthouse in 1848.

Fife's mining heritage

Of all Fife's industries coal mining is the most ancient. As far back as 1291 the monastery at Dunfermline was granted a lease to exploit 'black stanes digged from the ground'; coal mining gave whole communities regular work and helped make the character of the people of west Fife. Indeed Fife was once the largest coal-producing centre in Scotland; still today where the mining communities flourished there is a doggedness of spirit, a ruggedness of independence, a toughness of character and a political loyalty which was forged for decades at the coalface. West Fife's mining areas had less landowner influence than the east – despite men such as the earls of Minto and Zetland being superiors to Lochgelly and Ballingry respectively – social philanthropy coming from the efforts of local working people through such bodies as the miners' welfare groups. Women were given a prominent role too, as around a third of those employed, say, at Dunfermline's Baldridge colliery in the early 1800s were women. Their jobs included the heaving of the coal from the pit bottom to the surface, and women often worked underground with babies strapped to their backs.

Rising to the east of Dunfermline is the Hill of Beath, once clad with a birchwood forest, from which it takes its Gaelic name. The hollow of the hill's summit is the crater of a volcano, and from this vantage point the lookouts could warn the local Covenanters at their secret services of the approach of soldiers.

When Queen Victoria passed through Cowdenbeath in 1842, on her first trip to Scotland, her entourage changed horses here. In those days the village was the centre of an agricultural region, with Cowdenbeath Inn an important coaching halt on the road north. Cowdenbeath, which became a burgh in 1890, began as a scattered agricultural community within a medieval barony. It was long considered the 'capital' of the west Fife mining area and its prosperity was closely linked with the vagaries of the coal industry. Iron ore first attracted miners here, but this was soon overhauled by the more profitable coal. There are still bitter memories of the Coal

Strike of 1921 and of the General Strike of 1926, out of which the loyalty and solidarity of the miners forged its own tradition.

The kirk of Beath at Kirkton was built in its present style in 1835–36 and added to in 1886, although there was a church here in the twelfth century, and probably a Culdee chapel before that. The church lands hereabouts were conjointly held by the abbeys of Dunfermline and Inchcolm. Its graveyard contains an interesting collection of headstone inscriptions and table tombs. The church also owned at least two mortsafes – heavy coffin-shaped gratings used to guard the dead from the bodysnatchers; the most immortal gruesome twosome, William Burke and William Hare, local legend has it, carried out a reconnoitre in the graveyard of Beath. The parish even got up a guard of farm workers to stand watch over the dead at the height of the grave-robbing scare.

The records of Lochgelly, formerly a portion of the barony of Glassmount, go back to 1485 and it was once a market town for the local agricultural area, with a noted weaving centre. There was mining here from the thirteenth century by such as Sir John Wemyss; but even by the sixteenth century Lochgelly was still only a hamlet of thatched huts. Lochgelly was built up to house the workforce of the Lochgelly Iron and Coal Company, and ironstone was used in four great blast furnaces once sited near the railway station. The town became a burgh in 1876, and its pits are now closed. In the old days there was some rivalry between the weavers and the miners, the former thinking themselves of a 'better class'. Lochgelly's name derived from the nearby eponymous loch, once known for the efficacy of its leeches used in medicine. Children once had reasons to dislike the name Lochgelly, as it was the commercial name of a locally made hard leather belt used in school for discipline. Children of eight years of age worked in the pits in early Victorian Lochgelly. Standing at 600 ft, Lochgelly is the highest township in Fife, and Wilson Street is probably one of the shortest streets anywhere. Local tradition has it that when the sale of liquor was restricted by the Forbes Mackenzie Act, crossed pipes in a Lochgelly shop meant that the shopkeeper was willing to slake the thirst of passers by. Up until the time of the First World War at least Lochgelly offered the miners a darker diversion from greyhound racing and pigeon fancying, for cockfighting proliferated – a sport illegal since 1849.

The modern layout of Cardenden takes in Auchterderran, Bowhill and Dundonald; the latter mining areas, with Powguild, Balgreggie and Glenniston all lay within important medieval estates. This is the cultural area of the Miners' Welfare system, and Bowhill Miners' Welfare Institute (1934) is a good example of its philosophy, housing a public library. The miners were great readers and many of them tried their hands at writing. One well-remembered local writer was the poet, Joe Corrie (1894–1968), who was generously described by T.S. Eliot as 'the greatest Scots poet since Burns'. The Communist Party once had great influence over this part of the mining community and local party members were sponsors of a Burns Club; Bowhill People's Burns Club was established in 1940, and their meetings are held in the Gothenburg Suite of the Bowhill Public House Society, which itself marks a Swedish public-house system long associated with miners in west Fife. The profits of the pubs in the scheme were used for the benefit of the local community. Long-vanished Carden Tower, a mid-sixteenth-century building, stood above the Carden burn within the Raith estate, and was owned by the family of Mertyne of Medhope. The wild desolate area around Cardenden was once the haunt of gypsies, who became a recognised group in Fife by the 1450s. Gypsy lore asserts that they came to Fife from Ireland, and that they chose boggy, barren wastes so that pursuers might be thwarted.

A centrepiece of Auchterderran is its church, dating from 1789, and it remains a typical example of Presbyterian austerity. Set in its choir is a sixteenth-century window from an earlier church, abutting the remnants of which is a memorial (1935) to the poet John Pindar (1837–1905). Pindar began work at ten years of age as a pony-and-cart driver at a pit in Lochgelly. He became a soldier, and latterly served with the Highland Light Infantry and fought on the north-west frontier. Pindar's *Random Rhymes* were published in 1894. The poet's memorial stands near a fine doorway, with 1676 on its lintel. It is recorded that the land upon which the outbuildings of the church stand has a social history going back to the eleventh century when Fothad, Bishop of St Andrews, gave it to the monks of St Serf at Lochleven, when Auchterderran was called Kirkindorath.

Local legend has it that the very last duel in Scotland was fought on 2 August 1826 in a field at Cardenbarns, Auchterderran. It took place between David Landale, a Kirkcaldy bleacher and merchant, and George Morgan, agent of the Bank of Scotland. Apparently Morgan had slandered Landale, who hit Morgan over the head with his umbrella. They decided to settle their differences through duelling with pistols, a pursuit that had been illegal since 1818. Morgan fired first, before time, and missed. Landale did not miss; he was arrested and sent for trial at Perth, but was acquitted. He lived in Kirkcaldy for many years after that and was a respected businessman.

The centre of an old hilly parish, Kinglassie was a weaving village before the exploitation of coal. At nearby Whinnyhall is the site of a fort which local tradition avers was used by the Romans; a Roman sword was found nearby in a marsh in 1830. Once called Goatmilk, Kinglassie was given by Alexander I to the monks of Dunfermline; the old name is still retained by two farms and the hills abutting the golf course. To the north of the village, on Redwell's Hill, stands the tower – visible for miles – known as Blythe's Folly; the 52-ft high tower was set up in 1812 by an eccentric Leith shipowner. Two ancient estates are sited nearby. Inchdarvie had an early fifteenth-century mansion with fifty-four rooms owned by the Aytoun family; it was destroyed by fire in 1930. Kinninmonth, once owned by a family of the same name, subsequently passed to the Earl of Minto. Just south of the B921 lies the Dogton Stone, an ancient Celtic cross with traces of animal and figure sculpture.

The old village of Ballingry, dubbed the Village of the Cross, has a church remodelled in 1831 which is said to have been founded by missionaries sent from Lochleven by St Serf in the sixth century. It retains a two-tier square bellcote with knob finial, and Sir Walter Scott mentions the church in his novel *The Abbot* (1820); he was a frequent visitor to the area from Blairadam, and his elder son, also Walter, married the heiress Jane Jobson of Lochore House. The mining pollution which wasted this area was reversed in the 1980s to form the Lochore Meadows Country Park, with Loch Ore as its centrepiece.

Once in its own island of Inchgall, 'the Isle of Strangers', Lochore Castle was built in 1160 by the Norman Duncan de Lochore. This remained the home of succeeding families like the de Valences whose scions were earls of Pembroke; Aymer de Valence was appointed Lieutenant of Scotland by Edward I and harried Robert I, the Bruce, in various campaigns; he was present at Bannockburn. The de Valences held Lochore until John Malcolm of Balbedie purchased it and in the seventeenth century the Malcolm family abandoned the castle and built Lochore House.

To the west of Kelty, a small town skirted by the old Fife county boundary, lies Blairadam Forest, of which over two-thirds lie in Fife. The setting up of forestry in this area dates back to 1733 when the famous Scottish architect, William Adam, purchased the estate of The Blair and built Blairadam House (over the border in Perthshire). During 1739–47 neighbouring estates were added and the Adams began a pioneer afforestation on treeless country for commercial purposes; most of it was felled in the two world wars.

William Adam's grandson, William, was Lord Chief Commissioner of the Jury Court, and in 1818 he and his friend, Sir Walter Scott, founded the Blairadam Club, whose purpose was from time to time to visit local sites of historical or literary interest. From Blairadam Scott set out on his expeditions into Fife. Here it was too that Sir Walter had his anonymity unmasked as the author of the Waverley Novels; the knoll in the park over which the Blairadam Club members often walked was called Kiery Crags by Scott in *The Abbot*.

The township of Saline was long a 'royal gift' apportioned to that member of the royal family who held the title of the Earl of Mar. In spite of ironstone and coal-mining activities Saline does retain some old-fashioned charm, with its eighteenth- and nineteenth-century dwellings, and is known for its heavily ornamented cottages with their castellated gateways. The present church was built in 1810 on a pre-Reformation site; many of the stones of the old church were built into the house of Devonview. Sir Walter Scott was a frequent visitor to Saline, staying at eighteenth-century Nether Kinneddar with William Erskine, Lord Kinneddar of Session. Scott dedicated the third canto of *Marmion* (1808) to Erskine, who is credited with the preface to *The Bridal of Triermain* (1813).

Blairhall is one of Fife's youngest villages, developing to house the miners of the colliery founded in 1911. Oakley once had six blast furnaces for its Oakley Iron Works, founded in 1846. This community grew in the 1930s and 1940s after the sinking of the Comrie mine (1936) and developed following the arrival of many Roman Catholic miners from the ailing Lanarkshire coalfields. The village has a white harled Roman Catholic church of interest; the Church of the Most Holy Name (1956–58) has notable stained-glass windows from France, and the woodblock Stations of the Cross are worthy of mention.

Carnock sports the ruins of a twelfth-century church from which the village is said to derive its name – St Cearnock was one of the disciples of St Ninian who brought Christianity to Scotland in the fourth century. It is possible that this church belonged to the Trinitarians, the Red Friars of Scotlandwell, Kinross. In the seventeenth century Sir George Bruce was one of the foremost of Fife's salt manufacturers and he had mining interests in these parts. The old church of Carnock was erected by Sir George in 1602 to replace earlier edifices. The manse of Carnock was built and repaired 1742–81. The present church was erected in 1840 and 'improved' in 1894. At the east end of the old churchyard can be found the grave of the Revd John Row (d.1646), a prominent Presbyterian who organised Communion Services; while at Carnock he wrote his *History of the Kirk*.

Kincardine

The kingdom of Fife may be entered from the west via the A977 for Alloa, or on the A876 which crosses the Forth just south of Airth. With its former two thriving shipbuilding yards, Kincardine-on-Forth was once one of the most important harbours on the upper Forth. Founded as a burgh of barony on reclaimed land in 1663, Kincardine once had nearly 100 ocean-going vessels registered to ply. Up to 1906, when the Dunfermline–Alloa branch railway line was opened, Kincardine was something of a backwater, difficult to get to despite the ferries, for its roads were narrow and twisting and the bridal paths inconvenient.

A focal point of modern Kincardine still remains the swing bridge, opened in 1936, and deemed 'one of the wonders of the twentieth century'; the bridge carries the A876 into the heart of the town. At 2,696 ft long, the bridge's central swing span was powered by two 50-h.p. electric motors, which moved it through a full ninety-degree swing. In 1988 the swing bridge was permanently fixed.

There are still some interesting examples of Scottish domestic architecture in Kincardine and the impressive seventeenth-century Mercat Cross is worth a look. Of Kincardine's famous sons, Sir James Dewar (1842–1923) may be remembered: he invented the vacuum flask.

Tulliallan is Kincardine's neighbour on the edge of the curiously named Devilla Forest, with its Moor Loch and Peppermill Dam. Once, with Culross Moor, it was a wild place, the sanctuary of outlaws and ne'er-do-wells. There are the remains of a hillfort at Castle Hill, south of the A907 by Bogside, and stone coffins and urns of prehistoric date were located at Tulliallan Nursery in 1856 and 1934. Near to Peppermill Dam is the Landsdowne family mausoleum. They were descendants of the Keiths who came to own Tulliallan, and the site of the mausoleum was formerly a pre-Reformation parish church.

It is said that the Forth almost washed the walls of the ruined Old Tulliallan Castle at Hawkhill, once the home of the Blackadders of the Merse, Berwickshire. The castle seems to have been a strong fortress when Edward I invaded Scotland in the thirteenth century. Perhaps the most famous of the Blackadders was Robert, Bishop of Glasgow in 1482, whose See was raised to an archiepiscopate in 1491. Blackadder was one of the commissioners appointed to negotiate the marriage of James IV with Princess Margaret, sister of Henry VIII, in 1501. The Tulliallan estate was bought by Admiral Viscount Reith in 1798; the castle had probably been abandoned as a home in the early seventeenth century and a modern mansion was built 1817–20 by Admiral George Reith Elphinstone, a one-time serving officer with Lord Nelson. Today the Gothic-Italian mansion is the heart of the Scottish Police College; the property was bought in 1950 and the first courses started in 1954. It has been much modernised and renovated; the mansion's stables and garages at Blackhall were converted for driver training in 1964, while the most recent extension was the classroom, library and study bedroom complex in 1978.

The old parish church of Tulliallan abutting the estate was unroofed when replaced by the present church of 1833, but the belltower dates from 1675. The old graveyard reflects the seafaring nature of the ancient community with its symbols of death interspersed with ships in sail above the lairs of those who served in the merchantmen which plied to the West Indies and the whalers to Greenland. Kilbaigie Street recalls the Kilbaigie whisky distillery (which became a paper-mill), an enterprise mentioned by Robert Burns in *The Jolly Beggars* where he comments on 'that dear Kilbaigie'. From the days when the Boundary Commissioners included Kincardine in Fife in 1889, from its status once in Perthshire, there was a keen rivalry between those who looked upon themselves as Fifers and not Perthshire-born.

Culross

Before arriving at Culross the B9037 from Kincardine passes the castles of Blair and Dunimarle. Blair enters Fife mining history as the centre of the Charles Carlow (1848–1923) Memorial Home for Miners founded by the Fife Coal Company and named after their erstwhile chairman and managing director. Dunimarle dates from 1840 on an eighteenth-century two-storey house site.

A programme of imaginative restoration by the National Trust for Scotland and various government departments has assured the preservation of Culross' essential charm. Here, conserved for all time, is an attractive small Scottish burgh of the seventeenth and eighteenth centuries with a wealth of Scottish vernacular architecture.

The royal burgh of Culross owes its early history to the legends of three popular Fife saints, St Kentigern (St Mungo to Glaswegians), St Thenew and St Serf. At the place we now call Culross, says St Kentigern's biographer, the monk Jocelyn of Furness Abbey in Cumbria, Palladius, first bishop of the Irish, ordained St Serf, or Servanus, as suffragan Bishop of Caledonia within the realm of Eugenius II, king of the dual kingdom of Strathclyde–Cumbria. Thus St Serf is said to have been working within a primitive religious community at Culross in the fifth century.

St Serf's most famous protégé was St Kentigern, Bishop of Glasgow. A medieval monkish hand has Kentigern as the son of Eugenius II and Thenew, daughter of Loth, King of Lothian, who either fled, or was expelled from her father's court and gave birth in 518 to her child Mungo where Culross was to evolve. There Mungo was baptised by St Serf with the new name of Kentigern, meaning 'chief of chiefs'. Today St Mungo's Chapel, built around 1503 by Robert Blackadder, Archbishop of Glasgow (1484–1508), near to the site of Mungo's purported birth, lies alongside the Culross–Low Valleyfield road.

St Serf was said to have been buried at Culross and his bones, said Bishop Forbes of Brechin in his *Kalendars of Scottish Saints* (1872) were still hallowed in the burgh in 1530. Up to the 1860s a procession in honour of St Serf took place in Culross on his feast day of 1 July every year, and local burgesses marched bearing eleven green branches.

Culross' importance was assured on 23 February 1217, when the abbey of Culross was founded by Malcolm, Earl of Fife, for the Cistercian monks of Kinloss. The extant parts of the monastic house today include the eastern elevation of the abbey, which still serves as a parish church of the Church of Scotland. In 1640 the north transept of the abbey was reconstructed by George Bruce of Carnock for the use of the salt panners and miners on his estate. The church was reconstructed in 1824, and again during 1905–06.

Monks of Culross Abbey produced many important illustrated books, of which the most important is the *Culross Psalter*, now in the National Library of Scotland. Up to the Reformation Culross Abbey was in the diocese of Dunblane, and remained so until the parish was united with Dunfermline Presbytery in 1595. At the Reformation nine monks are known to have been resident at Culross, by then somewhat dilapidated in its living area. Of these, five espoused the new faith and accepted pensions, while the other four adhered to the Roman rites and were expelled to their own devices. By 1589 a grammar school was located within the abbey carrying on a tradition of teaching in this place.

All visitors to the abbey site would be rewarded for their efforts by making time to look at the unusual (to survive) 1642 tomb of Sir George Bruce within the parish church; it has alabaster effigies of

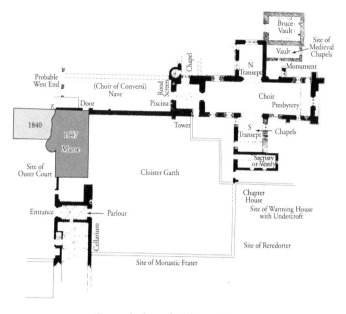

Ground plan of Culross Abbey.

himself, his wife Margaret and their eight children. Culross Abbey House was begun by Sir Edward Bruce in 1608; it was remodelled in 1830 and reconstructed by the Earl of Elgin in 1955.

During the sixteenth century salt panning, coal mining and trade with the Low Countries were the burgh's principal activities, and the foreshore port of Sandhaven ensured prosperity. One of Culross' famous products was the now rare iron baking girdle. James VI re-established the town hammermen's monopoly of its manufacture in 1599. Decline set in at Culross when political and economic influence moved to central and western Scotland, and the burgh was almost forgotten until the 1930s, when the restoration programme was begun.

Today Culross is an architectural feast of dormer windows, skewputts, decorative lintels and crow-stepping. A couple of hours' wander around Culross is richly rewarding, but it is a place to visit more than once. Along the Sandhaven, which flanks the Forth and forms the site of the old shore port, is the Town House built in 1626; its steeple was added in 1783 and the lower floor was a prison called the Laigh Tolbooth; in front of this is the Tron, the site of the public weigh beam. Incidentally a Culross chalder was the standard Scottish measure for weighing coal.

Along from the Tolbooth is the palace, built by the merchant and entrepreneur Sir George Bruce between 1597 and 1611. Its name derives from the Latin *palatium* – or hall – and does not signify any royal connections, although James VI did stay at Culross Palace in 1617. Sir George's name is featured a great deal in the history of west Fife, for his mining activities were famous; he installed an ingenious apparatus to drain his mines and is credited with sinking the first mine under the sea.

Near the palace is Bessie Bar Hall and Well. Bessie Bar was a sixteenth-century personage who sold malt; the well was constructed by the council in 1598. Local legend has it that the waters from Bessie's Spring had medicinal uses. From Sandhaven the Back Causeway leads to Tanhouse Brae and the 'House with the Evil Eyes' (so called from the shape of its windows in the Dutch gable) west of the parish church. In Tanhouse Brae are the former sea-captain's dwelling, the House of the Greek Inscription, which spells out 'God provides and will provide' and the Snuff-Maker's House of 1673. Round the window of Snuff Cottage is the inscription 'Wha wad ha' thocht it'; the second line of this old jingle, 'Noses wad' ha' bought it', was on another snuff-maker's house in Edinburgh. In the Back Causeway is 'The Study' of 1610 with its oak panelling dating from 1633. This is said to have been used by Bishop Leighton of Dunblane on his visitations. Immediately below the outlook tower of the bishop's study is The Haggs, or Stinking Wynd, whose camber recalls an interesting social custom of past days. The centre of the cobbled way is several inches higher that its edges; this was the – 'croon o' the causie' (causeway) where local fine folk walked – the poor gave way in the gutters.

Parallel with Back Causeway is Mid Causeway with Bishop Leighton's Lodgings, his refuge in troubled ecclesiastical times. Wee Causeway contains the Nunnery, which takes its name from the veiled head of a woman carved on the lower end of the crow-stepped gable. All the causeways lead to the Mercat Cross which originates from 1588 and was restored in 1910. Above Culross the Moor Road leads to Bordie Tower where the army of King Duncan encamped before the Battle of Culross, marked by the Standard Stone.

The next community encountered after Culross is Valleyfield, which developed into the mining settlement of High Valleyfield and sits on the hill above the older Low Valleyfield. The estate of Valleyfield belonged to Sir Robert Preston, who employed Humphry Repton (1752–1818), one of the great English landscape gardeners, to improve his parkland. Preston's house was demolished in 1918 and much of Repton's landscaping is irredeemably lost, destroyed by its later owner, the East Fife Coal Company, who bought the estate in 1907 for its mineral rights. Valleyfield is still remembered in mining lore for the pit disaster of 1939 when thirty-five miners lost their lives. Look for the restored 'Endowment', built by Sir Robert Preston in 1830 for a dozen pensioners.

The Bluther Burn runs under the B9037 at Newmills, which gets its name from the mill which once stood here. Formerly a part of Perthshire, this was the site of the monkish *Novum Molendinium* which had the monopoly of the grinding of corn in the vicinity.

Witch mania was once rife in Torryburn and many an unfortunate demented soul was consigned to the flames along these shores; on the foreshore by the railway bridge stands a rock with the remains of an iron ring associated with Lilias Adie, who in 1704 was the last Torryburn witch to die; she was buried here by the high watermark. Standing above a fast-moving burn, Torryburn and Newmills parish church was built in 1800 and reconstructed in 1928. Its hexagonal bellcote stands above an outside stairway leading to the choir loft, and at its gate is an interesting watch-house. The table tombs in the graveyard are worthy of note for their symbols. From the time of the Reformation the churches of Torryburn and Crombie were associated and in 1622 the parishes were united; the present church of Crombie was built in 1800 on the site of older foundations. The small oblong ruin in the churchyard is probably thirteenth century and has long been used as a vault for the Colville family. Alison Cunningham, a native of Torryburn, born here in 1822, became nanny to Robert Louis Stevenson and is immortalised in the dedication of *A Child's Garden of Verses* (1885); she died at Edinburgh in 1910 aged ninety-two.

East of Culross

If you take the road east towards Dunfermline, you come to Cairneyhill. This is an old weavers' village, now a dormitory town for Dunfermline. To the west lies Conscience Brig, so called in local lore because a murderer is said to have confessed his crime here.

Next comes Crossford. The ford crossed by the monks on their way between the abbeys of Dunfermline and Culross is long gone, but Crossford retains its main street of old houses. Once a busy weaving and market garden community thrived here on land distributed by the drawing of lots. This was called *cavelling* the land, and it probably gives a derivation to nearby Keavil House, a medieval mansion now converted into a modern hotel, with large housing developments on its estates.

Just before the A994 leads to Crossford, on the right is the golf course and Pitfirrane estate. For centuries Pitfirrane was the mansion of the Halkett family, but when Miss Madeline Halkett died in 1951 the house and grounds were purchased by the Carnegie Trust and now form the clubhouse and course of Dunfermline Golf Club. The buildings seen today are largely of the late sixteenth century, but the core of Pitfirrane is the fifteenth-century L-plan tower. The south wing was added in the seventeenth century and the castle yett now forms the gate leading to the gardens. The house retains fine armorial bearings in two public rooms.

If the A985 is taken towards Rosyth, the visitor comes to Crombie and the second part of west Fife's shoreline. The warships from Rosyth dock long received their ordnance here, where once passenger ships called on their way up and down the river from Leith to Stirling.

It is not often that someone perpetuates his name in the layout of a village. In 1756 Charles Bruce, fifth Earl of Elgin and ninth of Kincardine, opened a limestone quarry in seeking to expand his business interests; he built kilns and laid out a harbour and a model self-sufficient village. The village of Charlestown, which lies to the south of the modern A985, was set out in the shape of its founder's initials, C.E. Still along the shore at Charlestown is the largest group of limekilns in Scotland – fourteen in all – which processed the lime exported all over Scotland. It was used to sweeten soil and add flux in the iron- and glass-making process. Limestone mortar from here built the docks at Dundee and Leith and Perth Town House. Elgin created this 'total environment' for his workers and their families some sixteen years before Robert Owen set up New Lanark; much of his creation still survives. The school built in 1780 once catered for some 240 pupils and the harbour was once used by the shipbreakers who worked on the scuttled imperial German High Seas Fleet of the First World War. The whole is preserved by the Charlestown Lime Heritage Trust.

Between Charlestown and Limekilns lies Broomhall House, the seat of the earls of Elgin and Kincardine, and it is set out on lands once owned by the monastery of Dunfermline. In the middle ages the estate was known as Gedeleth and was acquired in 1562 by Robert Richardson, treasurer to Mary, Queen of Scots. The property was purchased in 1600 by Sir George Bruce, who changed the name to Broomhall. It was Thomas, seventh Earl of Elgin (1766–1841), who secured the marbles from the Parthenon when he was Ambassador-Extraordinary in Turkey; as 'the Elgin Marbles' they were placed in the British Museum in 1816. Today the Earl of Elgin remains the nearest male relative to the line of Robert the Bruce, and at Broomhall are retained relics of the famous king; a large two-handed sword and a helmet are displayed, both said to have been borne by Bruce at Bannockburn in 1314. Broomhall was built in its present form during 1796–97 and is not open to the public.

Once press-gangs roamed the ancient thoroughfares of the seaport of Limekilns on the lookout for likely seamen to serve on the grain, wood and lime ships of the Limekilns fleet, but nowadays piers like Capernaum serve as moorings for the sailing club; here was situated the medieval port for Dunfermline. Limekilns formerly had a soap and rope works, saltpans and a brewery, and in Academy Square the sixteenth-century King's Cellar stored provisions for the palace of Dunfermline. Its 1581 doorway bears the arms of the Commendator of Dunfermline, Robert Pitcairn. In his novel *Kidnapped* (1886) Robert Louis Stevenson has his characters David Balfour and Alan Breck stop at the Ship Inn to beg for food and a passage across the Forth; this was not the present inn on the Promenade but another, now a private house, some hundreds of yards to the east.

Amongst the handful of buildings at the mini-hamlet of Pattiesmuir there is to be found a 'college', the social meeting place for weavers, once chaired by Andrew Carnegie's grandfather as 'professor', but nothing remains of the palace of the king of the Gypsies who sojourned here.

The A985 leads on to the town of Rosyth, created in 1903 when the admiralty bought land here for a naval base. Historically the foreshore has long been known as St Margaret's Hope, the place where Queen Margaret landed in 1069. On this peninsula is set the late fifteenth-century Rosyth Castle, once on its own island but now surrounded by the off-limits paraphernalia of the dock. The castle was used as a seaside resort by Mary, Queen of Scots, who later embarked from Rosyth Castle after her escape from Lochleven Castle in 1568. Its chief feature today is the massive tower house, which was both fortress and home; it fell to Cromwell's soldiers in 1651. Local legend has it that Oliver Cromwell's mother was born in the castle built here by Sir James Stewart. Queen Victoria remarked on the tradition in her *Leaves from the Journal of Our Life in the Highlands* (1868), when she remembered embarking on the little steamer for North Queensferry during her first visit to Scotland in September 1842. It is a legend that is easily exploded: Cromwell's mother was Elizabeth Lyon, daughter of William Steward (from Steywood, not the royal Stewarts) of Ely, Cambridgeshire, whose family had founded their wealth on the fall of the Roman church.

A.J. Balfour's Conservative government finally decided to build a dockyard at Rosyth in 1903; it was to be a complete repair establishment capable of taking the *Dreadnought* class of battleship. The dockyard stands on reclaimed land and construction began in 1909; the first vessel to be repaired in the graving docks was HMS *Zealandia* which entered no. 1 Dock in March 1916. Submarines, then known as R-craft, first came to Rosyth in 1917.

The naval base at Rosyth was reactivated in 1939 and developed steadily following the Second World War to undertake important refitting and repair work on a wide range of vessels. Until the Royal Navy base closed in 1995, and until the yards were bought by the engineers Babcock in 1996, the complex also housed HMS *Cochrane* (1968) as fleet accommodation centre and HMS *Caledonia* (1979) as an apprentice training establishment. The

Royal Navy Flag Officer Scotland and Northern Ireland was located at the Maritime HQ at Pitreavie Castle, once the home of the Wardlaw family; the castle dates from around 1615. A prominent owner of the castle was .Sir Henry Wardlaw (d.1638), chamberlain to James VI's consort, Anne of Denmark. Pitreavie Castle was sold in 2001 for private development.

Cromwellian Fife

From Scotland's position as an ally of the English parliament in the 1640s, Fife, like the rest of the country, remained under Cromwellian military occupation until 1660. When Oliver Cromwell's army defeated the Royalist force at Dunbar on 3 September 1650, he was master of south-east Scotland and occupied Edinburgh. Fife was now vulnerable, with the Royalist army at Stirling, so on 17 July 1651 part of the Cromwellian army crossed the Firth of Forth and defeated a Royalist contingent at Inverkeithing on 20 July. Fife was overrun; Burntisland fell by 29 July and a programme of repair and strengthening was carried out to the harbour; part of the sea-wall was long known as 'Cromwell's Dyke' and the Cromwellian quays were in use well into the twentieth century. Cromwell took up residence at Dunfermline Palace, and Fife's Tay shores were secured with General George Monck's capture of Dundee. With a portion of the Cromwellian garrison from Burntisland, Colonel Commissary General Edward Whalley marched along Fife's southern coast, while shadowed by Cromwellian men-of-war. Harbours and quays were secured and the likes of Anstruther plundered. Back at Burntisland, which, wrote Cromwell 'it hath pleased God to give us', garrison commander Colonel Robert Lilburne taxed and harried the inhabitants. Apart from Burntisland there were Cromwellian garrisons of cavalry and infantry at various times at such places as Dysart (Tolbooth), Falkland (Palace), and Struthers (Castle), Ceres. During April 1652 the parliamentary union of England and Scotland was proclaimed at Edinburgh, involving the loss of national independence.

   Throughout the occupation, a programme of harassment was carried out in Fife to thwart and seek out Royalist 'rebels'. On 12

September 1653, for instance, four Fife ministers were arrested for praying for the exiled Charles II. Both gentry and people were divided in their loyalties between king and Cromwell; the latter found willing collaborators in men such as Colonel James Hay, Sir Andrew Bruce of Earlshall, Sir John Wemyss of Bogie and Sir Alexander Gibson of Durie. Royalist families included the Earl of Rothes, Sir John Henderson of Fordell, James Stewart of Rosyth, the Earl of Lindsay and Sir Arthur Erskine of Scotscraig.

A legend of Cromwellian times was long preserved at Strathmiglo. For centuries the locals had honoured the 'Rocking Stone of Balvaird' for its supposed supernatural powers of protection for the locality. Poised one above another the upper stone could be rocked with the touch of a finger. Cromwellian soldiers destroyed it because of its superstitious associations, and locals blamed the bad luck surrounding the Cromwellian occupation as a consequence of the stones' destruction.

CHRONOLOGY

*c.*7500 BC	Bands of hunter-gatherers present at Fife Ness.
	Mesolithic activity at such places as Strathmiglo and Kemback.
*c.*300 BC	Farming introduced to Fife.
	Neolithic activity in such areas as Balfarg and Balbirnie.
*c.*2000	Copper and bronze artefacts made in Fife; finds at Dalgety Bay and the Lomond Hills.
*c.*1500 BC	Bronze Age developments in fishing, agriculture and brewing; sites at Leuchars and Drumoig.
*c.*500 BC	Iron Age activity in Fife from Clatchard Craig, Newburgh, to Down Law, Howe of Fife.
1st century	Agricola temporary camp at Bonnytown, by Boarhills. *Venicones* tribe have heartland in Fife.
	Roman activity in the roads of the *Tina* (River Eden), the *Bodotria Aest* (Forth) and the *Tava* (Tay).
3rd century	Septimus Severus, temporary camps at Edenswood, by Cupar, and Auchtermuchty; Waulkmill, east of Dunfermline.
8th century	Pictish powerbase at Kilrymont (St Andrews). The Pictish tribes of the *Decalyclones* and the *Verluriones* establish a powerbase at *Fortriu* (or *Fortrean*, Strathearn); associate name *Fibh* (Fife) develops, with overtones of 'Kingdom'.

	Appearance of the relics of St Andrew at Kilrymont.
10th century	Christian symbolism appears in Fife artefacts and carved stones. Cf: examples at Mugdrum, Nr Newburgh. Many fragments built into walls of later churches.
c.1070	Dunfermline Benedictine Priory founded by Queen Margaret.
1093	13 November: Malcolm III, Canmore, buried at Dunfermline Abbey (his body is later moved to the Escorial, Madrid).
1094	12 November: Duncan II buried at Dunfermline Abbey.
	Anglo-Norman influence dominant in Scotland.
c.1123	Augustinian Priory of Inchcolm founded by Alexander I.
c.1124	April: Alexander I, the Fierce, buried at Dunfermline Abbey.
	Dunfermline made royal burgh.
1127	Augustinian Order established in St Andrews.
c.1115–1120	Title 'Earl of Fife' evolves, becoming hereditary in 1129.
c.1127	Leper Hospital of St Nicholas founded at St Andrews for Friars Preachers.
c.1140	St Andrews achieves burgh status. By 1144 first Provost identified as Maynard the Fleming.
	April: Senzie Fair established; attracts international custom.
1143	Augustinian priory founded at St Andrews.
c.1144	Leper Hospital of St Andrews founded by Robert of Nostell, Bishop of St Andrews.

1150	Crail made royal burgh.
c.1153	Benedictine Priory of May founded by David I. 24 May: David I buried at Dunfermline Abbey.
c.1154	Hospital founded at Ardross by Duncan, fourth Earl of Fife, run by the nuns of North Berwick.
c.1160	Inverkeithing made royal burgh.
	Founding of cathedral church of St Andrew.
c.1165	Hospital founded at North Queensferry by Malcolm IV.
	Kinghorn made royal burgh.
	9 December: Malcolm IV: buried at Dunfermline Abbey.
c.1184	Hospital of St Leonard founded at Dunfermline.
1191	Tironesian Abbey of Lindores founded by David, Earl of Huntingdon.
c.1196	Hospital founded at Inverkeithing, dependent on Dryburgh Abbey.
c.1200	Location focal points established at St Andrews and Dunfermline.
	Bishop's castle and palace established at St Andrews by Bishop Roger.
c.1217	Cistercian Abbey of Culross founded by Malcolm, Earl of Fife.
c.1227	Cistercian abbey of Balmerino founded by Queen Ermengarde, widow of William the Lion and Alexander II.
1235	Inchcolm priory elevated to abbey.
1240	David de Bernham, Bishop of St Andrews (1239–53), begins his massive dedication and consecration programme of churches; the first in Fife was Abdie.

*c.*1268	Franciscan Friary of Inverkeithing founded by Philip de Moubray.
c. 1270	Collegiate Church of St Mary of the Rock founded at St Andrews.
1274	Dominican friary of the Assumption and Coronation of the Blessed Virgin Mary founded by William Wishart, Bishop of St Andrews, at St Andrews.
1275	Alexander II's wife, Margaret of the House of Anjou and Henry III's daughter, dies at Cupar Castle.
1276	Alexander III holds an assembly at Cupar to discuss affairs of state.
1286	Alexander III's horse plunges over cliff at Pettycur Bay taking the monarch to his death.

19 March: Alexander III buried at Dunfermline Abbey. |
1291	Charter for coal mining at Pittencrieff granted to Abbot Randulphus de Greenlaw of Dunfermline.
1296	Edward I captures Cupar Castle.
1303–04	Edward I, his second wife Margaret of France and Edward, Prince of Wales, reside at St Andrews Castle. Causes lead to be stripped from the cathedral roof to be used in the siege of Stirling; he later pays for the lead and gifts jewels to adorn the relics of St Andrew. Holds a parliament of England and Scotland at the cathedral.
1310	Robert I, the Bruce, confers a charter of privileges on Crail.
1314	Sir William Keith of Struthers Castle raises and trains a band of Fife fighting men to support Robert I at Bannockburn.
*c.*1318	Augustinian Priory of Pittenweem founded.

1324   5 March: David II born at Dunfermline Palace.

1327   Cupar made royal burgh.

1329   June: Robert I, the Bruce, buried at Dunfermline
             Abbey (his heart is buried at Melrose Abbey).

1335   Randolph, Earl of Moray, prorogues a parliament of
             nobles at Dairsie Castle, to assess plans to liberate
             David II from English captivity.

1337   Estimates of 33,000 pilgrims per year visiting the
             shrine of St Andrew at St Andrews.

1348   Dominican Friary of St Katherine founded at Cupar
             by Duncan, Earl of Fife.

1378   St Andrews Cathedral burned down.

1381   28 June: Robert III grants to the burgesses of Cupar
             the right to have their own 'port' on the Water of
             Motray (modern Guardbridge).

1394   25 July: James I born at Dunfermline Palace.

1402   Prince James, later James I, spends time at St
             Andrews under the tutorship of Bishop Wardlaw at
             the castle.

1403   Queen Annabella Drummond dies at Rotmills Inns,
             Inverkeithing.

1410   By this time teaching of a university standard had
             evolved within the cathedral precincts of St Andrews.

1412   Academics at St Andrews obtained a charter of
             incorporation and privileges from Bishop Henry
             Wardlaw.

1414   February: Academics' charter confirmed and
             amplified by a series of papal bulls issued by Pope
             Benedict XIII to fully and formally found the
             University of St Andrews.

             Fife thus hosts the first university in Scotland.

1428	James II confirms 'Waters of Eden' as free port area for Cupar.
1430	Pedagogy founded at St Andrews.
1450	Collegiate Church of St Salvator founded by James Kennedy, Bishop of St Andrews.
1452	May: James III born at St Andrews Castle.
1458	Franciscan Friary of St Andrews founded by Bishop James Kennedy.
	Falkland made royal burgh by James II; prior to this it was the capital of the Stewartry of Fife.
1471	Dominican Friary of St Monan founded at St Monans by James III.
1472	17 April: Pope Sixtus IV erects the See of St Andrews into an archiepiscopal and metropolitan see, at Rome. Patrick Graham (d.1478) the new archbishop.
c.1478	Hospital of St James founded at Kinghorn.
c.1486	Cistercian preceptory of Gadvan, Dunbog, founded by Balmerino Abbey.
	Franciscan nuns' priory founded at Aberdour by James, Earl of Morton.
1487	Convention of royal burghs held at Inverkeithing.
1490	Culross becomes burgh of barony.
1496	Perkin Warbeck, pretender to the throne of Henry VII, a guest at Falkland Palace. Fife royal court involved in his future plans.
1501	Wester Aberdour becomes burgh of barony.
1512	St Leonard's College, St Andrews, founded by Alexander Stewart, Archbishop of St Andrews and John Hepburn, Prior of St Andrews.

1517	Collegiate church of Crail founded by William Myrton, Vicar of Lathrisk.
	Auchtermuchty elevated to royal burgh.
c.1527	Collegiate church of Strathmiglo founded by Sir William Scott of Balweary.
1537	St Mary's College, St Andrews, founded by James Beaton, Archbishop of St Andrews.
1540	24 February: James V makes Pittenweem and Anstruther burghs of barony.
	7 June: Sir David Lindsay's play *Ane Satyre of the Thrie Estates* first performed at Cupar.
1542	First instances of witch trials in Fife at St Andrews.
	14 December: James V dies at Falkland Palace.
1546	1 March: Martyrdom of George Wishart, St Andrews.
	29 May: Cardinal David Beaton, Archbishop of St Andrews, murdered at St Andrews Castle.
1558	The Bloodless Battle of Cupar-Muir; the Protestant forces of the Prior of St Andrews (later the Regent Moray) and the Earl of Argyll face the Catholic army of Marie de Guise-Lorraine, Queen Regent.
1559	Treaty between Marie de Guise-Lorraine and the Protestant Lords of the Congregation at Tarvit Hill, Cupar.
	15 June: St Andrews Cathedral severely damaged by retainers of the Protestant Lords and the mob inspired by the sermon of John Knox in the Church of the Holy Trinity.
	Fife's focal points of Dunfermline and St Andrews lose their economic and political influence because of Reformation.

1567	Anstruther becomes royal burgh and capital of the herring fishery.
1570	Growth of the Fife salt trade.
1578	Kilrenny given charter to erect a market cross and hold a weekly fair.
1583	Anstruther Easter granted royal burgh status.
1586	Burntisland's charter of 1541 advanced to royal burgh status.
1588	Culross created royal burgh.
	Dunfermline confirmed as royal burgh.
1589	Elie confirmed as burgh of barony.
1594	Dysart confirmed as burgh of barony.
1600	Fife predominantly an agricultural society.
	19 November: Charles I born at Dunfermline Palace.
1614	St Andrews made a burgh of regality under the Archbishop of St Andrews.
1620	James VI and I advances St Andrews to royal burgh status.
1621	St Monans a burgh of barony.
1624	Dunfermline burgh severely damaged by fire.
1633	Charles I living at Falkland Palace.
1635	Ceres erected into a burgh of barony by Sir Thomas Hope of Craighall, King's Advocate.
1638	Easter Aberdour made burgh of regality.
1644	Charles I ratifies privileges making Kirkcaldy a royal burgh.
1645	Meeting of the Scottish Estates in Parliament Hall, St Andrews.

1646	Sir Robert Spottiswoode, Lord President of the Council of Session, executed at the Market Cross, St Andrews, for treasonable support of Montrose's rising.
1650	Charles II tries to make Falkland Palace a rallying place for Fife and other Royalists; he fails and the troops of Oliver Cromwell occupy the palace.
1651	20 July: Battle of Inverkeithing. Harassment of Fife Royalists and supporters by Cromwellian troops.
1663	Kincardine-on-Forth founded as burgh of barony.
1673	Markinch chartered by Charles II.
1679	3 May: James Sharp, Archbishop of St Andrews, murdered at Magus Muir.
1715	Rob Roy McGregor occupies Falkland Palace on behalf of the Jacobite Pretender Prince James Francis Edward Stuart. John Erskine, Earl of Mar, rallies Fife Jacobites. Jacobite activity at Elie, Pittenweem and Crail led by Brigadier William Mackintosh.
1718	Weaving of linen-damask introduced by James Blake, Dunfermline.
1771	Lady Anne Lindsay immortalises legend of 'Auld Robin Gray'.
1788	Vincente Lunardi makes balloon trip from Edinburgh to Coaltown of Callinge, by Ceres.
1812	William Tennant's comic poem celebrates 'Anster Fair'.
1821	First power-loom (linen manufacture) established in Kirkcaldy.
1826	Last duel fought in Fife at Auchterderran.
1834	King William IV becomes patron of the Society of St Andrews Golfers and thereafter the club becomes the Royal and Ancient Golf Club.

1842	Queen Victoria makes her first visit to Scotland. On Tuesday, 6 September, she crossed the Forth to North Queensferry. Then by Inverkeithing the royal party, escorted by Captain Wemyss, changed horses at Cowdenbeath and continued to Kinross.
1847	Factory to manufacture floorcloth opened by Michael Nairn, Kirkcaldy. Fife now known for mining, shipbuilding, weaving and lino manufacture. Railway from Burntisland to Perth (via Ladybank spur to Tayport), opened by Edinburgh and Northern Railway Company. Railway network in Fife developed.
1852	Last public hanging at Cupar.
1868	John Key constructs first iron steam-vessel, the whaler *The River Tay* at his Abden Yard.
1878	Roads and Bridges (Scotland) Act extends Fife routes. Ladybank becomes a burgh. Tay Rail Bridge opened to link Fife with the north.
1879	28 December: Tay Rail Bridge collapses during gale at a cost of seventy-five lives.
1883	East Coast railway line extended from Anstruther to St Andrews, via Crail.
1887	New Tay Rail Bridge opened.
1889	Kincardine-on-Forth becomes a part of Fife.
1890	Forth railway bridge opened to link Fife with the south. Cowdenbeath becomes a burgh.
1897	Queen Victoria's Diamond Jubilee; several memorials set up in Fife; Cupar Market Cross renovated as celebratory project.

1901	Donibristle pit disaster.
1903	Construction of Rosyth dockyard begins.
1909	Rosyth laid out as garden city for military and civilian workers.
1939	Valleyfield pit disaster.
1948	Glenrothes established as new town. First post-war building phase to alter the structure of population, making new generations of Fifers. Biggest character change since the development of the Fife coal fields.
1962	Development of Dalgety Bay as first private village in Fife. Influx of new Fifers.
1964	Road bridge (A90) opened linking Fife (North Queensferry) with Edinburgh and the south at South Queensferry.
1966	Road bridge (A92) opened linking Fife (Newport-on-Tay) with Dundee, Angus and the north.
1995	Closure of Royal Navy base, Rosyth.

HISTORY AND LEGEND-HUNTER'S GUIDE

Library sources

Fife Council Libraries   Central Area
East Fergus Place
Kirkcaldy KY1 1XT
Tel: 01592 412930

East Area
Library HQ, County Buildings
Cupar KY15 4TA
Tel: 01334 412737

West Area
Central Library, Abbot Street
Dunfermline KY12 7NL
Tel: 01383 312908

Museums

Andrew Carnegie Birthplace Museum, Moodie St, Dunfermline
  KY12 7PL
Buckhaven Museum, College St, Buckhaven KY8 1AB
Fife Folk Museum, High St, Ceres, By Cupar KY15 5NF
John McDouall Stuart Museum, Rectory Lane, Dysart KY1 2TP
Kirkcaldy Museum and Art Gallery, War Memorial Gardens,
  Kirkcaldy KY1 1YG
Laing Museum, High St, Newburgh KY14 6DZ
Pittencrieff House Museum, Pittencrieff Park, Dunfermline KY12
  8AP

St Andrews Museum, Kinburn Park, St Andrews KY16 9DP
St Andrews Preservation Trust Museum, 12 North St, St Andrews KY16 9PW
Scottish Fisheries Museum, St Ayles, Harbourhead, Anstruther KY10 3AB

Heritage centres

Abbot House, Dunfermline Heritage Centre, Maygate, Dunfermline KY12 7NE
Crail Museum and Heritage Centre, Marketgate, Crail KY10 3TL
Isle of May, c/o Scottish Natural Heritage, 48 Crossgate, Cupar KY15 5HS
Methil Heritage Centre, 272 High St, Lower Methil

Monuments, houses, castles, caves, windmills

Aberdour Castle, Aberdour KY12 7NE
Balmerino Abbey, Balmerino
Culross Palace, West Green House, Culross KY12 8JH
Dunfermline Abbey and Palace Visitor Centre, St Margaret St, Dunfermline KY12 7PE
Falkland Palace, Falkland, by Cupar KY15 7BU
Hill of Tarvit Mansionhouse and Garden, Ceres, by Cupar KY15 5PB
Inchcolm Island and Abbey
Kellie Castle and Garden, nr Pittenweem KY10 2RF
Ravenscraig Castle, Kirkcaldy
St Andrews Castle and Visitor Centre, The Scores, St Andrews KY16 9AR
St Andrews Cathedral and St Rule's Tower, The Pends, St Andrews KY16 9AR
St Fillan's Cave, Pittenweem
St Margaret's Cave, Chalmers St Car Park, Dunfermline KY12 8DF
St Monans Windmill, St Monans
Scotstarvit Tower, Ceres

SELECTED READING

Aitken, John. *Above the Tay Bridges*, 1986.
Bennett, G.P. *The Great Road between Forth and Tay*, n.d.
Boucher, Robert Jr. *The Kingdom of Fife*, 1899.
Campbell, J. *Balmerino and its Abbey*, 1867.
Campbell, Revd John *et al*. *Kirkcaldy Burgh and Schyre: Landmarks of Local History*, 1924.
Cunningham, A.A. *Inverkeithing, North Queensferry, Rosyth and Naval Base*, 1903.
Cunningham, A.S. *Rambles in the Parishes of Scoonie and Wemyss*, 1905.
Ferguson, K.A. *A History of Glenrothes*, 1982.
Findlay, A.M. *Kennoway, its History and Legends*, 1946.
Geddie, John. *The Fringes of Fife*, 1928.
Gifford, John. *The Buildings of Scotland: Fife*, 1988.
Hendrie, William F. *The Firth of Forth*, 1998.
Holman, R. *The History of Cowdenbeath*, 1941.
Houston, A.McN. *Auchterderran*, 1924.
Laing, A. *Lindores Abbey and the Burgh of Newburgh*, 1876.
Lamont-Brown, R. *Discovering Fife*, 1988.
Lamont-Brown, R. *The Life and Times of St Andrews*, 1989.
Lang, Theo. *The Kingdom of Fife*, 1951.
Marshall, D. *L'île des Chevaux: The Story of Inchkeith*, 1983.
Miller, A.H. *Fife: Pictorial and Historical*, 1895.
Pride, Glen L. *The Kingdom of Fife: An Illustrated Architectural Guide*, 1999.
Rankin, F. *Auld Buckhyne*, 1986.
Reid, A. *Kinghorn*, 1906.
Robertson, M. *Old Dunfermline*, 1979.
Ross, Revd William. *Aberdour and Inchcolm*, 1885.
Scott, Sir James. *History of Tayport*, 1927.

Seed, N. *Strathkinness*, 1986.

Sibbald, Sir Robert. *The History, Ancient and Modern of the Sheriffdoms of Fife*, 1710.

Snoddy, T.G. *Afoot in Fife*, 1950.

Stephen, Revd W. *History of Inverkeithing and Rosyth*, 1921.

Stuart, John. *Records of the Priory of the Isle of May*, 1868.

Walker, B. and Ritchie, G. *Exploring Scotland's Heritage: Fife and Tayside*, 1987.

Watson, Harry D. *Kilrenny and Cellardyke*, 1986.

Webster, J.M. *History of Carnock*, 1938.

Wilkie, James. *The Benedictine Monasteries of Northern Fife*, 1927.

Wilkie, J. *Bygone Fife North of the Lomonds*, 1938.

Withrington, Donald J. and Grant, Ian R. *Fife*, The Statistical Account of Scotland, vol. X, 1978.

Young, W. *Cardenden*. n.d.

INDEX